THE ANNALS OF A
COUNTRY DOCTOR

Carl Matlock, MD

THE ANNALS OF A
COUNTRY DOCTOR

credo
house publishers

Published in the United States by Credo House Publishers, a division of Credo Communications, LLC, Grand Rapids, Michigan credohousepublishers.com

ISBN: 978-1-625860-89-7

Cover and interior design by Frank Gutbrod
Editing by Donna Huisjen
Cover image by Ryan McGuire, Gratisopraphy

Printed in the United States of America
First Edition

This work is dedicated first to my brother, Joseph Matlock, who served as my office manager and lab director during the first nine years of my medical practice. Although in order to simplify the manuscript I didn't include him in the narrative, he was very much a part of my story. He also made vital contributions in writing two of the chapters. He was with me in the attempted infant resuscitation I recount in the book, and we stood together watching the tornado that appeared to be headed our way. He remains my best friend.

In addition, I want to dedicate this book to my three children and their families. They are a continuous source of inspiration to me. All three are working full time in the field of medicine. Their names are Mrs. Cynthia Rundell, Mrs. Diane Survance, and Dr. David Matlock.

CONTENTS

PREFACE

A s a young doctor in 1973 I set up practice in a small rural town in Indiana. I later moved my office across from the hospital where I practiced. Although I loved the rural practice, the sixty- to eighty-hour workweeks began to wear me down physically.

Solo private medical practitioners, once common, are an endangered species today. After nine years I found my second love in medicine as an emergency physician, a role in which I could function as part of a larger group and finally be able to spend more time with my family. My journey in medicine has been somewhat different in that it has encompassed multiple disciplines. Along the way I became board certified by both the American Board of Family Medicine and the American Board of Emergency Medicine. Both organizations made vital contributions to my career. I am also a member of the Indiana State Medical Association and serve as a part of IU Health Bedford Hospital's medical staff.

I had the joy and privilege of helping my son establish a practice in Mitchell, Indiana, when he chose to follow in my footsteps. Fortunately, he is part of a large group practice, Southern Indiana Physicians of IU Health in Indiana. Altogether, I served as a family physician for fifteen years and as an emergency physician for twenty-three years. After taking an eighteen-month sabbatical I returned to medicine with IU Health, Southern Indiana Physicians, as a geriatric practitioner serving local long-term care facilities in Bedford, Indiana.

The changes in medicine since 1971, when I graduated from Indiana University Medical School, have been profound—and in large part positive. One thing is missing, however: the ability to interact with patients without a computer barrier between doctor and patient. Even today I try to leave the technology out of the patient encounter, but the electronic medical record still awaits my attention. As a result, I am no longer able to comfortably visit with fifty or more patients per day. Doctors still work long hours, much of that time devoted to the electronic record. This has become a time-consuming focus, replacing as it has the brief penned notes accompanied by quality, face-to-face dialogue with those who rely on physicians for life and death decisions.

I wrote about my life in medicine because I love medicine and don't want my family, friends, patients, and readers to forget about what life was like before the computer barrier was erected.

The following chapters are based largely on my first two years of solo family medical practice. The names, ages, locations, and sometimes the genders of the patients have been changed in accordance with the medical community's respect for patient privacy. The patients in my story are sometimes composites of two or more people, many of them have since passed away, and there are no stories involving my later years of practice. I have taken the writer's privilege of embellishing the story, but all recounted events represent the delightful, amazing people who honored me in those early years by calling me their doctor. I won't forget them as long as I live in this temporary house of clay we call the body.

Thank you for reading my story.

Carl Matlock, MD

ULCER ATTACK

Soft snowflakes swirled through the frosty December air as late afternoon gave way to evening. A radiant full moon had illuminated the snow-covered landscape in my backyard but was now being blotted out by the increasing fury of the storm. The last cardinals had just departed from the birdfeeder, and shrubs were white and sagging under the weight of the wet snow. As I sat before the sliding glass doors leading to my patio sipping a scalding cup of coffee, I sank back into the welcoming arms of the Lazy Boy recliner.

The logs in the fireplace crackled, giving off a comforting warmth, casting weird shadows that danced merrily about the room. Bookcases lining the walls contained myriads of my favorite books—not to mention, of course, my medical library. Their presence infused me with a sense of comfort as I sought peace of mind and rest for my body. It looked as though I really might have a night off. I could travel to far-off lands and earlier times by losing myself in books that never grew old for me.

Gusts of wind fiercely shrieked down the chimney, intermittently sending sparks aloft, riding the updraft into the gathering darkness. Somewhere nearby a great horned owl hooted its displeasure; the hunting must be bad on a night like this.

After five months of rural family practice I was already feeling the need for a break. The small town of about twenty-five hundred souls was certainly keeping me busy. I had made up my mind, however, that this night would be different. My wife and I, along with our two-year-old daughter, had just enjoyed an uninterrupted late afternoon visit to our favorite steakhouse at the nearby county seat; the two of us had feasted on sizzling steaks cooked to perfection, delicious salads, baked potatoes, and corn on the cob, while our daughter had worked on chicken nuggets.

Now, while I waited for the two of them to join me in the study, I was determined to let nothing interfere with our family night. My wife and I wanted to think about baby names, as we were expecting a set of twins in late January or early February. Our two-year-old with her strawberry blond curls bobbing up and down already kept our home alive with laughter and joy, yet we could hardly wait for the new arrivals.

We enjoyed putting name combinations together, trying to guess whether it would be two boys, two girls, or one of each. This was before the days of ultrasound analysis, and the obstetrician hadn't initially believed me when I'd informed him there were two.

I can still remember the shocked look on my wife's face when I announced to her the presence of two distinct heartbeats, one approximately 120 and the other 160. Having stopped by the office one day to ask me to listen to make sure everything was all right, she thought I was joking at first—but joking hadn't entered my mind.

Our obstetrician had confirmed the diagnosis with an X-ray. No room for further doubting. Now we were joyfully anticipating their arrival.

As I heard the soft rustle of her skirt, my wife entered the room, leading Cindy by the hand. Janet was wearing her blue velvet dress that I liked so much, as it enhanced the blueness of her eyes. The song "She Wore Blue Velvet" had recently been popular. I still love it, that blue velvet dress, but most of all the wife who graced it and still, forty-seven years later, makes our home a welcoming place of refuge from the storms of life.

Janet and Cindy had just settled down in a chair when we were startled from our brief reverie by a loud, continuous pounding at the door, accompanied by the intermittent frantic ringing of the doorbell.

Hurrying through the darkened living room, I stumbled over a magazine rack and nearly fell. When I finally reached the entryway, flipped on the outdoor light, and jerked the door open, I was met by Molly, an eighteen-year-old patient, standing in the dim porch light with snow whirling about her. She and her entire extended family had recently adopted me as their doctor.

Hesitating only briefly, I began, "Hello, Molly—what seems to be the trouble?"

"It's Billy, Doc; he's having a very bad attack."

I began my usual line of questioning, only to be interrupted by Molly.

"Never mind the questions, Doc; we ain't got time for that. Grab your hat n' coat and your medical bag. Follow me. It's a life an' death emergency."

I tried to think of an intelligent response but saw that she was already disappearing into the darkness. Her beat up Ford pickup was parked in the driveway behind my vehicle, and she was making a beeline for it.

"Just a minute, Molly. You haven't really told me anything. I don't even know where you live."

Impatiently whirling about, she motioned for me to follow her, but her voice was lost in the wind. With a sigh of resignation I began gathering my things, briefly advising my wife of what little I knew of the situation. As always, she was the calm one, assuring me that it would be all right.

Tugging on my boots and grabbing my London Fog coat and black fedora hat, I picked up my bag and hurried, albeit reluctantly, out into the fury of the winter snowstorm. Visibility was down to one hundred yards or less. As I opened my car door I tried shouting at Molly once again to ask whether she could describe her brother's symptoms. I wanted to have some idea of what I would be walking into.

She impatiently ran forward to my side, cupped her hands, and shouted in my ear, "I told you: it's his ulcers."

She had told me no such thing, but before I could utter a word she ran back to her old truck, slipping and sliding on the driveway though somehow remaining erect and once again motioning me to follow. Jumping into the cab she fired it up, and it came to life with an unseemly roar and a great cloud of black smoke, momentarily blotting out the wind-driven snow behind it.

Struck suddenly by the ludicrous nature of the drama, I couldn't help but chuckle. By now I just wanted to see what was going on. My curiosity had been piqued, and I wouldn't be able to let it rest until I found out what was truly happening.

I was driving a five-year-old Ford station wagon, a fairly decent car I had bought on the cheap. It started up smoothly, and I slowly backed into the street as I look about rather wildly, trying to locate Molly and her pickup. In the dim illumination of the streetlight I saw her about fifty feet ahead, impatiently idling her truck. She apparently saw me too, for she immediately jammed on the accelerator, sending the truck sashaying all over the road as the wheels spun over the ice and snow-encrusted pavement.

I had to move fast to keep up, and my heart clenched as I headed straight toward my nearest neighbor's mailbox. By some miracle I slipped within inches of it and somehow lined up behind the truck that was still careening wildly. We were certainly off to an inauspicious start.

It was a short drive of about nine blocks, and the wind was dying down enough that I could see better where I was going. Christmas was only three weeks away, and houses lining the road were aglow with decorative lights on porches, rooftops, and fir trees, the magical effect serving to improve my mood.

During the brief trip I rehearsed the little I knew about Molly's family, a sizable clan with mom, dad, several adult children, and two or three teenagers I hadn't yet quite sorted out.

○

I had met Billy early on in my practice and remembered the day I made his acquaintance when he came in for a physical. Billy was clearly not the brightest young man, though he was certainly sincere. He asked whether I could do a physical, to which I responded in the affirmative. When I asked whether anything was wrong, he informed me that he was going to race stock cars over the weekend and wanted to be sure that if something happened he would be all right.

In disbelief I started to explain that my exam wouldn't protect him in the event of an accident, but he waved me away dismissively: "It's all right, Doc; this'll take care of everything." And so I had conducted my first pre-daredevil physical exam, at the end he of which my patient pronounced, "I know this'll do me some good in case of a pileup."

○

I was so engrossed in my thoughts that I almost ran into the back of Molly's pickup as she jammed on the brakes and slithered to a stop, sliding sideways. She had overshot the drive and was frantically rolling down the window, motioning me to back up so she could do the same before turning into the driveway.

Finally both vehicles were safely parked in the drive. As I got out I had to lean into the gale and grab the brim of my hat to keep it from blowing away. The wind had indeed picked up again as the winter storm continued to barrel out of the northwest. Brushing snow from my eyes and face, I noticed the vacated town marshal's vehicle parked idling at the curb in front of the house.

What in the world could be going on? Were they doing CPR inside? I realized with increasing trepidation that I had brought no true emergency drugs with me.

Just then Molly rushed up and grabbed me by the arm, pulling me up the steps. "Come on, Doc! You don't have time to stand here. We need you inside."

By the time I arrived at the front door my glasses were so fogged over that I couldn't see into the living room as one of the teenage boys held the door open for me. I immediately sensed his heightened state of alarm. He grabbed my hat and held my bag as I removed my overcoat.

As my glasses began to clear I took in a scene of pandemonium and was alarmed by the agitated screams from those engaged in physical combat on the floor. The room was warm and stuffy, smelling of wood smoke and body sweat. Nothing in my training had prepared me for this moment, and I stood in stunned silence.

I finally glanced to my left and noticed Tom, our town marshal, standing in the corner, well out of the way, observing the fray with what appeared to be objective interest. Casting a glance in my direction, he nodded and announced nonchalantly, "Evenin', Doc. Bad night to be out, ain't it?"

I had still not found my voice and could only nod at him. It was then that I noticed Molly tugging on my sleeve, great tears welling up in her eyes.

"Please, Doc! Please do somethin'! He's dyin', ain't he?"

I mumbled something incoherent before turning to Tom and imploring, "Can't you do something to stop this?"

Tom remained rooted to the spot, seemingly oblivious to the chaos around him. I know police officers are supposed to maintain calm, but this was ridiculous. He actually seemed to be enjoying this whole charade. Glancing at me once again, he briefly put up his hand to cover his face, hiding an unbidden smirk.

He continued to stand there authoritatively, revolver fastened down in its holster, hands on hips, feet spread well apart, short leather jacket open to reveal his badge and carefully pressed tie. As though this were an everyday occurrence, he finally remarked casually, "Didn't expect to see you here tonight."

I stood totally mesmerized by the drama unfolding before me, uncertain whether I was witness to an ensuing comedy or a tragedy. I could barely hear myself speak above the combatants wildly rolling about on the floor. I tried counting the participants but found this impossible, what with the flailing arms and legs, the occasional head popping up out of the revolving mass of struggling humanity, and the loud grunts and groans punctuated by occasional screams of genuine agony.

No artist could ever have depicted the kaleidoscopic gladiatorial contest I witnessed that night. The combat appeared to be taking an ugly turn as the volume of the shouts and curses increased and someone yelled "He bit me!" This multi-headed monster before me looked like something out of Grimm's Fairy Tales as it seethed across the floor, kicking, biting, hitting, scratching, and screeching in rage.

After several moments it became apparent that five or six people were engaged in the fight of the century. As I recognized first one and then another face flashing by in that writhing conglomerate of humanity, I finally discerned that Billy was the center of the attention. It appeared that the Jackson clan was trying to subdue Billy, who was at least for the time being endued with superhuman strength as he threw off first one and then another tormentor. That he was fighting a losing battle was readily apparent, because his collective family had no intention of giving up. No sooner would one be thrown off than with a shout of triumph he would reenter the fray.

This thing was getting out of hand, so much so that the marshal and I began to move out of the way as the fight gathered steam, moving inexorably in our direction. It was only then that I noticed Molly still jerking on my sleeve, still crying hysterically.

I turned back to Tom, who stood planted in place with an angelic smile, arms now folded across his chest. I had some uncharitable thoughts about the degree to which he seemed to be enjoying this cheap entertainment. He must be one of those sadists who enjoys Saturday night wrestling mayhem.

Raising my voice above the din, I shouted at Tom, "Can't you put handcuffs on him?"

Tom cupped his hand over his ear as he looked toward me. "Say what?"

I tried again: "Put handcuffs on him."

"Nah. You give him something, Doc. He's sick, you know."

"Someone's going to get hurt, Tom."

I could see at once that he was unmoved by my logic. This was, I decided, one wily old marshal; he simply shrugged and resumed his spectator mode. He wasn't about to get mixed up in this. "Give 'im a shot, Doc," he repeated.

Tom could be exasperatingly calm, but in the given situation his demeanor, far from de-escalating the fever pitch of excitement, wasn't helping at all. Unfortunately, Molly heard him say something about a shot. Digging her fingernails into my arm, she wailed in a rising crescendo, "Give 'im a shot, Doc!"

The pandemonium appeared to have reached peak intensity; someone was going to have a heart attack if no one intervened. But someone in the room recognized the wisdom of Molly's shout. It might've been Mrs. Jackson; I couldn't tell for sure. She was standing out of harm's way in the hallway leading to the kitchen, observing the entire proceedings while wringing her hands with a look of resigned apprehension. I never did determine who screamed next, but suddenly cries of desperation rang out from every quarter: "Give 'im a shot, Doc; give 'im a shot!"

As though on signal the entire clan took up the battle cry: "Give 'im a shot. Give 'im a shot. Give 'im a shot!" In an apparent attempt to preclude my doing anything, Molly began jumping up and down like a cheerleader at a championship

Super Bowl football game. She led the cheer from then on: "Give 'im a shot, Doc!"

The thunderous chorus nearly drowned out the non-choreographed shouts of the combatants. I didn't like the silly grin the marshal had on his face one bit, but now I found that I had become the center of attention. Everyone able to do so simply stared at me, a look of synchronized expectancy on the faces of the spectators.

If I hadn't been so frustrated I have no doubt I could've enjoyed, or at least appreciated, the whole incongruous scene. Why, the rhythmic chanting and shouting were nearly enough to induce a man to tap his feet and clap his hands.

Frantically, I searched through my supplies, feeling as though the entire world—or at least its representatives in the room—were shouting with one pitched voice for me to do something. This is what I had been trained for—or was it? Was this even real? Was I even playing a role in this fiasco?

I had no time for philosophical meanderings, however, though I've had my share of them through the luxury of hindsight since. I still have no words of wisdom to rationalize what I did next. Though I frequently made house calls, I carried relatively little for such an emergency as this. Aside from a few packs of antibiotics and mild oral analgesics, I had only a vial of Demerol—no Thorazine or Haldol or any other major tranquilizer.

Demerol is a narcotic injectable for acute pain, and back in those days we used quite a bit of it. From what little I could see, Billy was not so much in pain as in acute emotional distress. But I had no other recourse.

It was my turn to sweat. My training had been inadequate for a situation like this; I had no idea what to do other than to try the shot. Besides, everyone present expected it, thanks to our marshal.

Trembling with apprehension, I opened my black bag wide enough to spot the vial of Demerol and some carefully packaged sterile syringes. I grabbed an alcohol wipe, a syringe, and a needle. Unfortunately, I had only a large, eighteen-gauge needle, one I wouldn't normally have used for such a procedure. However, if anyone deserved a painful jab at this moment, it had to be Billy.

Having little faith in what I was doing, and hoping no one would notice my extreme nervousness, I carefully sterilized the top of the vial with the alcohol wipe, placed the needle on the syringe, and plunged it into the vial, drawing out fifty milligrams as I carefully noted the two-milliliter mark on the vial and expelled the air bubbles. Prepared for action, I gathered my wits about me and noted my next problem. How in the world was I to identify Billy in that brawling mass of humanity? I was getting uncomfortably hot; my face felt flushed; and I saw that Tom was still relishing the entertainment far too much.

"I can't do it," I yelled. "I don't even know which one is which."

It was then that I made a remarkable discovery: this was one resourceful family. From somewhere in the center of the fray, a commanding voice shouted, "Get his pants down."

Now the family took up a new chant: "Get his pants down. Pants down. Pants down."

The final act began to play out as several hands appeared to be working in a concerted effort to expose Billy's derrière. I could hardly believe my eyes; this family was so efficient that it almost appeared they had been through this with Billy before.

Hoping against hope that the mob had the right person, I quickly made my move. There were no other recognizable— that is to say, visible—features of my writhing patient. Holding the syringe in a death grip, I prepared to administer the fateful injection.

Too frenzied to worry that anyone might notice my nervousness, I chose what appeared to be the outer quadrant of the buttock on the upper right side, or at least what I took to be the right side, and plunged in the needle with more relish than I perhaps should have. I quickly aspirated to make sure I wasn't in a blood vessel and then delivered the narcotic deep into the muscle.

I stood back in utter amazement as bodies slowly and methodically separated from the pile, resolving themselves into individuals I had known and treated over the past few months. As for Billy, he lay calmly on the floor, stretched out, eyes closed, totally at peace with the world.

I looked at my syringe in amazement, quickly grabbed up the vial to verify that it was indeed Demerol, and turned back to take in the remarkably transformed scene. I was totally bewildered by this sudden response. Demerol can't possibly take effect that immediately, not even when administered via IV, and I hadn't administered nearly enough to knock him out. Something else must have been amiss here—or at least those were my thoughts.

I pulled out my stethoscope to check Billy's heart and lungs, but when I neared his face I drew back in inadvertent disgust. The malodorous reek of alcohol nearly overwhelmed me as I turned away to suck in a breath of fresh air.

I glanced up at Molly, who stood by still wringing her hands, while unchecked tears rolled down her cheeks. I managed to ask, "What about his ulcer?"

"I'm sorry, Doc. I forgot to tell you—there really wasn't time. He always has the Friday night ulcer attack after he drinks Jack Daniels."

I glanced around the room at the various other combatants, all of whom were now sprawled in chairs or otherwise lying indisposed on the floor, most gasping for breath and sweating profusely, but with the look of champions on their faces. For the first time it occurred to me that I had been seriously over-trained for certain aspects of my job.

Billy's father, a heavy smoker, was struggling for breath, his face flushed and his dirty T-shirt sweat-drenched. The others were in little better condition, though they all looked smugly satisfied following the success of their conquest. Once again Billy had been saved from himself.

Shaking Billy gently, I noticed that he was very much awake as he looked up at me with his big brown, bloodshot eyes, smiled crookedly, and uttered, "Tanks, Doc. You saved my life. I won't forget it."

I hurriedly prepared to leave, accompanied by the marshal, who was humming softly to himself and appeared to have thoroughly enjoyed the show.

It was only then that I indulged in the luxury of feeling a little angry. Why, that little faker! There was no way my injection could have affected him so quickly. He must have tired of the whole sham and pretended to be knocked out— and he must be laughing at everybody now.

Mrs. Jackson stood at the door waving at us, profusely expressing her thanks. Molly came out on the porch and announced, "Thanks for coming, Doc and Marshal. When Billy has these ulcer attacks they're really bad."

As we made our way toward the vehicles, I narrowed my eyes as I stood glaring at the marshal. "Yeah! Sure. Ulcer attack, indeed. You knew what was wrong with him, didn't you, Tom?"

With an impish grin he nodded and winked at me. "Sure, Doc. Bad ulcers," he said with emphasis while started toward his car, chuckling unabashedly to himself.

I decided I wanted to learn a little more about our marshal and followed him to his car after first placing my medical bag in the Ford. "Wait up, Tom. I want to ask you something. You've been in on this before, obviously. Why do you let this go on until that young man loses his dignity?"

Tom turned toward me with a blank look on his face that was slowly replaced by a beatific smile. The storm was abating somewhat, but the wind still howled. "Get in, Doc, and I'll tell you a story." I slid into the passenger side of his car, enjoying the warmth of the heater, and waited expectantly.

"Last summer," he began, "the Jackson's had a big wiener roast out back there. While it was going on, Billy was in those woods to the right over there, working up an ulcer attack. Everybody knew it was coming. Just didn't know how or when.

"Well, along close to ten o'clock, when the eating was about over but with the fire built up for storytelling, the most awful screech came from the woods. A wild thrashing in the brush was followed by Billy hollering, "Jack be nimble. Jack be quick. Jack jump over the candlestick." He came charging out of the woods, clad only in white tennis shoes and red socks, and jumped over the bonfire. He was so loaded it was a wonder he didn't fall into the fire. But he fled back into the woods.

"Some of the men were going to thrash him for appearing in front of their women and children disrobed. But he was clothed and sleeping peacefully in the woods when they found him. Claimed he couldn't remember ever doing it. His ulcers leave him in that condition. Anyway, Doc, don't waste any sympathy on him or his dignity—he's never had any.

"And look at it this way, Doc. Most people have to pay for such entertainment. You got to see it and charge for it, too. I'll get paid for just standing there watching along with you."

I shook my head before smiling at Tom. I could see his point of view, but I can't say I agreed. As I got out of the car he was still chuckling.

"Billy's not a bad fella, Doc. He's just ate up with those ulcers."

THE BOUNCER

Before the days of board-certified emergency physicians, it was common practice in small county hospitals to staff their emergency rooms with family or general practitioners on a rotating schedule. Thus I spent many a long weekend at our county hospital, located about twenty miles from my home in Glen Oaks. The only redeeming feature of those lengthy shifts was the extra pay that helped provide for my young family.

Beginning one Friday at 6:00 p.m., I entered the hospital fortified with snacks, novels, my stethoscope, and paperwork to catch up on, determined to avoid boredom. In those days county emergency rooms served as resources for true emergencies and semi-emergencies; the attending physician was less likely in the seventies than today to see simple sore throats and colds. It was usually possible, in fact, to enjoy several hours of down time before my shift ended at 6:00 a.m. Monday morning.

Donning a green scrub suit and a white lab coat, I checked in to the hospital room reserved for my rest. Usually this was simply a vacant one-person private-occupancy room on the second floor, equipped with the typical plain furnishings of bed, hospital tray, bed stand, television, and one or two chairs normally reserved for visitors. A painting of a pastoral scene typically completed the décor.

Stowing my belongings in the closet and bed stand, I strolled down to the ER to check in with the nurses and give them my pager number. Finding no one waiting for examination, I wandered to the other end of the hospital to our cafeteria to check out the menu. The dietitian excelled in roast turkey, mashed potatoes and gravy, and assorted vegetables, so I settled down to enjoy my meal while perusing the evening newspaper of Glen Falls, the town of twenty-thousand in which our county hospital was located.

One bad habit many young doctors develop is that of rapidly devouring their meals. So many interrupted meals go unfinished that one develops a sense of urgency to eat as quickly as possible in order to prevent hunger pangs during the ensuing long hours of work. It isn't uncommon to finish a meal when on call and barely taste the food. This common affliction equally affects physicians of both genders. It takes a concerted effort to break this habit once it has been ingrained in the psyche by the frenetic pace of work. Fortune smiled on me that particular night, however, as I finished my meal before the first call to evaluate a patient.

Beginning at about 7:30 p.m. the usual flurry of strains and sprains filtered in; weekend warriors had started early that Friday. Working my way through the stack of charts until there was again time for a break at about 10:00 p.m., I returned to the cafeteria and checked the refrigerator in the kitchen. The dietitian always made sure to leave some treats for the night workers.

Sitting down in the cafeteria to savor a piece of pie and while away some time, I was jarred by my beeper's high-pitched squawk calling me back to the ER. Dialing the ER nurse from the cafeteria wall phone, I found to my relief that I could finish my lemon pie since the patient was in no actual physical distress. Still, since it was no longer possible to relish every bite, I bolted my food and headed back to see the patient.

Our emergency room was rather small, with three good-sized rooms for trauma and major medical emergencies, along with one larger room in which two patients could be provided a little privacy by pulling a curtain between them. For the most part that room was reserved for minor or low acuity problems. There were also a couple of minor treatment rooms.

Once arriving back in the ER, I was handed a chart by the nurse, an enigmatic smile on her face. "Mr. and Mrs. Paul are in the minor treatment area; you should see them right away. She's the patient tonight."

Scratching my head, I wondered about that strange look on the nurse's face as I made my way into the room, chart in hand, stethoscope in my white coat pocket. I noticed a nervous Mr. Paul hovering over his young wife in a most solicitous manner, stroking her hair, patting her dainty hands, holding one up and kissing it every so often, and whispering words of love and devotion in her ears.

"Hello. My name is Dr. Matlock. I believe you are Mr. and Mrs. Paul. Is that correct?"

"Hello, Doctor; that's right. I'm Henry Paul, and this is my wife, Laura."

Laura Paul was a very petite young woman, quite attractive with her brunette hair and brown eyes but with mascara smeared over her cheeks due to tears overflowing from her eyes, which she mostly kept closed, except when occasionally fluttering them open as she answered questions; for the most part she allowed Henry to fill in her medical history.

"Doc, it's like this. Laura is having chest pain again. That happens a lot; then she loses her breath and cries because she feels like she's dying. Isn't that right, Laura?"

Nodding her head yes, she dabbed at the smeared mascara and freely flowing tears, while a visible shudder ran over her body.

Bending still lower over the cart, Henry finally had his head down even with hers as he continued his soothing ministrations, patting her hands, stroking her hair, and sighing audibly. I noticed that he sat where he could watch the doorway leading out of the examining room into the waiting area. He kept turning his head back and forth, as though it were on a swivel, gazing first at his weeping wife and then at the door as though he expected someone important to arrive at any moment.

Somewhat puzzled by this unusual behavior, I began my usual examination. One of the first things a physician learns is that a great deal of the time a good medical history alone will establish either a diagnosis or a short list of probable diagnoses.

"When did you first notice the pain, Mrs. Paul?"

Sniffing and continuing to blot tears, she finally managed to say, "After we ate out tonight."

"Did you notice the time when your pain started?"

Shaking her head no, she opted to remain silent, glancing up at Henry and nodding for him to continue the narrative.

"It was about an hour ago, Doc. She has this problem every so often. I'm really worried about her heart."

In an attempt to get her to describe her pain, I continued, "Can you tell me what it feels like?"

Sighing impatiently, signaling her desire to remain silent, and shrugging her shoulders, she only replied, "It's just bad."

"What do you mean by bad?"

"That's what I mean. It's bad. I don't know any other way to tell you. Henry, you tell him."

"That's right, Doc. It's just very, very bad."

"On a scale of one to ten, with ten being the worst, how bad would you say it is?"

That question she gladly answered: "It's a twenty! It's bad."

Henry interrupted, "Doc, I don't see what this has to do with anything. I just want her fixed. That's all she wants too. Who cares if it's a ten or a fifty? Just fix her. Please!"

It was plain that Henry was about to lose control as he fixed his gaze once again on the doorway to the waiting room.

Tiring of his bent-over position, he straightened a little but never shifted his gaze from the door.

In exasperation, I decided to skip further questions, since they were both visibly agitated. Taking a light from the wall mount, I looked in her throat, which was entirely normal. Next, I listened to her heart and lungs with my stethoscope, palpated her abdomen for tenderness, and checked her legs for blood clots. Finding no abnormalities, I jotted down an order for a chest X-ray and an EKG, returned to the nurses' station, and handed the charge nurse the chart.

The charge nurse was a gray-haired, steel blue-eyed, no-nonsense woman of fifty-five or so who reminded me of a Marine drill sergeant. She went by the name of Sam; her middle name was actually Sammy, but apparently her father had been set on her being born a boy. Sam just looked at me, rolled her eyes, and pronounced, "You don't know them yet, do you?"

Young doctors are often second-guessed and questioned by the seasoned nurses; being somewhat accustomed to such a response, I tried to answer without appearing too defensive: "No, I don't know them. She isn't likely having a heart attack, but she does take birth control pills, which I see by your record. I just want to be sure she doesn't have a pulmonary embolus or perhaps some other condition, such as pericarditis, as the etiology of her pain."

With a knowing look of condescension, she sighed and declared resignedly, "Okay, you're the doctor."

With a shrug, I started to take a seat as Sam suggested, "Why don't you go see the family now? The rest of them are out in the waiting room, as usual. Fred, our janitor, is here to back you up if you need any help."

Knowing that Fred was also our security officer for the night, I noticed him sitting in a corner smiling at me as though in anticipation.

"Do you want me to come with you, Doc?"

"That won't be necessary right now, Fred. Thanks anyway. I'll call if I need you."

Assuming an aura of bravado I wasn't really feeling, I made my way into the waiting room. I couldn't help but wonder at the enigmatic behavior of everyone involved with this case. I had no idea what awaited me there.

The waiting room was amply large for several families to gather in; however, except for four tall men at the far end of the room I didn't see anyone else. They stood clustered in a tight circle and didn't present a threatening attitude; in fact, the two facing me looked rather apathetic.

Approaching them expectantly, I asked, "Are you folks with the Paul family?"

At that the circle parted to reveal a short, stout woman in its center. The shortest of the men was about six-feet two inches in height; the other three were a good three to five inches taller. All four stood around the short woman in the center, who was now prancing up and down, fists doubled up, specks of foam flying from her lips as she swore under her breath.

As I involuntarily backed up a couple of feet, I noticed that all four men stood silently, heads slightly bowed and shoulders sagging in complete submission to this apparition in their midst. None of them looked particularly dangerous or threatening, and they were otherwise fine physical specimens, muscular, tall, . . . and silent.

The woman at the center of attention clearly wielded full authority in that room. She had on tight, calf-length sweat pants that displayed bulging muscles in her thighs and calves as she danced up and down in place, and she wore a tank top with the cartoon caricature of a bulldog wrestler on the front. Her arms were bare from the shoulders down, revealing massive deltoid and biceps muscles that would have made Pop-Eye the Sailor Man proud. She began weaving, throwing punches like a shadow boxer and then flailing at the air. A tattoo of what looked to be one of the notorious Beagle Boys of cartoon fame adorned her right biceps, while the left was adorned with a large heart inscribed with the—in this case incongruous—word "Mother."

She was beside herself with rage, none of which, I gratefully realized, was as yet directed at me. Briefly speechless, I struggled momentarily to understand what she was saying. Finally I was able to discern her rough, infuriated speech, spewed from between gritted teeth:

"Where is he? That lowdown skunk, that snake, that human garbage, that piece of worthless debris! If he laid a hand on my baby girl, I'll personally rip his lungs out; I'll tear him in half. I'll kill him dead—here, now. Right, boys?"

The "boys" either answered softly, "Right, Ma," or simply nodded in tacit agreement.

Still speechless, I studied her face, realizing in shock that it was wrinkled and flabby like a bulldog's. It made me wonder whether she owned just such a pet and was through some strange osmosis taking on its facial features; however, she also had little, blood-shot, pig-like eyes from which hatred emanated with unabated fury. Finally, I gazed in wonder at her black, greasy hair pulled back tightly and ending at the back of her scalp as a four-inch pigtail. When her anger actually started to escalate, due evidently to my continued silence, the four-letter words began to fly; the boys stirred restlessly and moved a little closer to me as she danced up within inches of my face. Although I'm six feet tall, her eyes seemed only inches away, boring into me whenever she leaped high enough for her spittle to give me a facial shower.

Realizing that I was about to lose whatever control of the situation I might have presumed to have, I took a deep breath and began to placate her with what I hoped would be a calming speech: "Now, now, everything is alright. I examined your daughter, and she has no injuries that I can see. She's having chest pain, and I'm running some tests to make sure her heart and lungs are okay. When the tests are completed you can go back and see her. Give me about ten minutes, and everything should be ready for you to visit."

Without waiting for a response, I negotiated an about-face and exited the room, fleeing to the relative sanctuary of the nurses' station. I have no doubt I was a little flushed at the adrenaline surge I had experienced in the waiting room, for Sam and two younger nurses, along with Fred, rose as one to their feet, laughing and congratulating me on my escape from the notorious but highly concerned family.

When I caught my breath I finally asked, "Do we see them here often?"

Sam handed me the normal EKG and hung the perfectly normal chest X-ray on the view box before answering, "They provide our entertainment once or twice a week. They're the Malones. Don't worry—two of Glen Fall's biggest, toughest police officers are here with the canine unit. They're just outside the ER door, so everything will be A-okay."

Fred chimed in, "The boys won't be any trouble—they're all on probation—and the two officers have a big German shepherd and plenty of pepper spray to handle Muscles."

"I assume Muscles is that belligerent female Harpies in the waiting room."

Fred smiled his confirmation: "Right; Doc. She prefers to go by Muscles Malone. No one even knows her first name; the boys won't tell because she threatens to thrash all four of them if they ever do."

Still in somewhat of a daze, I went back to advise Henry and Laura Paul that her tests were all normal. On entering the room I noticed that Laura was no longer tearful; in fact, she had taken the time to rearrange her makeup. She and Henry were on the best of terms as she reassured him that she would smooth everything over with her family.

I dismissed them in bewilderment with a limited prescription for Valium, hoping it would keep everyone calm for the weekend and wondering what had precipitated the row in the first place. I noticed that Henry went out to stand with the police officers as his mother-in-law conversed with her daughter across the parking lot, all the while glaring in Henry's direction.

The boys stood silently by until Muscles barked, "Into the truck, boys." I watched as they all piled into the ancient, battered truck and drove off in a cloud of smoke with Muscles at the wheel.

Then, arm in arm, Henry and Laura strolled to their vehicle and drove off sedately.

I joined the officers just outside the ambulance entrance to gaze in amazement at the departing vehicles.

The officers waited until the family had all driven off, then nodded cheerfully at me as they led their dog back to the police car. The younger one turned and assured me, "All in a day's work, Doc. You'll get used to them. They're regulars. Muscles'll also send you customers; she's the bouncer at one of the bars in the worst section of town. You'll have a lot of opportunities to see and repair the guys who run afoul of her."

He paused before getting into his patrol vehicle, adding with a knowing smile, "She's also a female wrestler, Doc, so don't let her get you in a wrestling hold. She's been known to break a man's back."

Smiling amiably at me from the comfort of their black-and-white patrol car, the officers drove off to continue with their duties.

Shaking my head in amazement, I couldn't help but wonder what kind of man the father of those four young giants might be. How had he ever summoned the nerve to marry Muscles? Was he still alive, or had he died from a broken back?

MARY EVANGELINA

For the first nine years of my practice I delivered babies—several hundred of them. The largest number I ever delivered in one month was sixty-one; however, a more typical tally was three to nine per month. In our small county hospital there were for several years no obstetricians in residence. All of the family doctors delivered newborns, with surgical back-up support consisting of two surgeons who had both been missionaries and performed numerous Caesarean sections.

I encouraged my patients to start prenatal care early in their pregnancies in order to detect complications and provide optimal care from the start. One unforgettable couple was Gladys and Bobby. Gladys was eighteen and Bobby nineteen. They appeared to be happily in love and committed to one another. Unfortunately, neither one of them possessed a towering intellect or practiced particularly exemplary personal hygiene.

During the early pregnancy Gladys had no unforeseen problems and visited me at monthly intervals in the office. For the last six weeks she came weekly to have her blood pressure taken, her weight monitored, and urine and other routine tests done. She never did catch on to my delicate hints that cleanliness was of utmost importance.

Her pregnancy extended beyond the normal forty weeks—first to forty-one weeks and then to forty-two. In the seventies there was no availability of ultrasound technology to evaluate pregnancies. I was quite certain of the EDC—expected day of "confinement" or delivery—so I was concerned, aware as I was that excessively late deliveries, as much as premature deliveries, can be fraught with problems, including fetal mortality.

During her final office visit prior to hospitalization, I discussed at some length with Gladys the risks and my concerns. "According to our calculations, you're just now at forty-two weeks' gestation."

"That's right, Doc, and I sure am tired of this. I feel like I'm going to pop like a balloon."

"Indeed, Gladys. You're certainly far enough along; the baby is between seven and eight pounds now. Since you only weighed 105 pounds and are five-feet three inches tall, this is a good-sized baby to deliver."

Beaming at me as she responded, Gladys nodded her affirmation: "You're tellin' me, Doc. I ain't never been this miserable before. Can you do somethin' to make it get here?"

"That's why I wanted to have this discussion with you today. I think it's time to intervene and start your labor. I did want to talk with your husband also, before admitting you to the hospital. Is he in the waiting room?"

"No, Doc. He's at work, but he won't care. In fact, he told me today to see if you would do somethin' so we can stop drivin' over rough roads to start my labor; it don't seem to be doin' any good to hit all those bumps cause nothin's happenin' anyways. Besides, he tore our old truck's muffler off last night in a chuck hole on a county road, and it didn't do a thing." Shaking her head sadly, she continued, "Still no contractions."

I initially felt remorse over the fine dinner I would likely miss at home while supervising an IV drip of Pitocin, a drug to initiate uterine contractions, so this young woman could give birth to her first child. I couldn't help but notice the cheap fabric of her clothes, the old shoes she wore, and the inexpensive wedding ring that adorned her finger. Her hair was black, straight, and shoulder length, and her face was plain but honest appearing, her otherwise colorless expression now etched in hope. As I considered the implicit trust being placed in me by this unsophisticated couple, I suddenly surrendered my urge toward self-pity in favor of fulfilling my duty.

"Gladys, I'll tell you what: I'll meet you and your husband at the hospital as soon as I finish here. It'll take me about one hour to see my last few patients and get over there. Just in case, I want you to skip your evening meal. It's almost four p.m. now: I'll see you in an hour on the OB floor."

A beatific smile lit up her countenance as she jumped up, thanking me repeatedly before hurrying out the door to go home for her suitcase.

Upon my arrival at the hospital the OB nurse, Mrs. Jarret, accompanied me to the labor room, where she assisted in performing one final examination before starting the IV medication.

"Gladys, one more exam to be sure everything's okay. Then we start."

"Sounds good to me, Doc. I'm ready."

While Mrs. Jarret stood by I conducted an internal exam; after scrubbing and donning sterile gloves I palpated the cervix, determining that it was ripe—thinned out enough to allow the medication to work. As with many primagravidas—first-time pregnancy patients—her cervix had not only thinned out but had also dilated to three centimeters already. The baby's head was well down into the ample pelvis, so I anticipated no problems.

Mrs. Jarret handed me special forceps, with which I grasped and ruptured the amniotic membrane sac, allowing the baby to settle down even further into the pelvic canal as fluid escaped around its head. Sometimes this alone will stimulate labor.

Next she handed me the electrodes on the end of a long wire; these I attached to the baby's scalp to monitor the heartbeat more accurately during labor. Once the nurse had the other end of the wire attached to the fetal monitor, we were relieved to hear the reassuring sound of a strong and regular rhythm of 140 beats per minute.

Stepping to the sink and washing yet again after removing my sterile gloves, I returned to the bed, patted

Gladys reassuringly on the shoulder, and told her, "We're going to start the medication now; I'll be right here in the hospital if you need anything. Just tell Mrs. Jarret, and she'll give me a call."

"That's great, Doc. I can hardly wait for the baby to get here."

"By the way, Gladys, is your husband here yet?"

"He's on his way—and happy as can be. He should be here right away."

With one further glance at the monitor I left to find a magazine to occupy my mind during the expected hours of waiting. In those days there was no intern, resident, or OB doctor to take over and monitor the patient, usually resulting in a long wait during which the attending doctor couldn't leave the hospital as long as the patient required an infusion of uterine stimulating medication.

I initially sat down near the nurses' station in the main OB hall to read and monitor Gladys's progress. While Mrs. Jarret was busy in the back, where the labor and delivery rooms were in use, I greeted Bobby as he arrived from work at his construction job. I paid little attention to his attire, being used to his appearance from the office. I advised him of what had transpired and assured him that all was well.

A few moments later, however, I glanced up from my Field and Stream magazine to see Mrs. Jarret hurrying back toward the main nurses' station with a shocked expression on her face.

"Is something wrong, Mrs. Jarret?" I asked in alarm.

Mrs. Jarret was a tall, thin, stately woman who took pride in carrying out perfectly her nursing procedures, in being up-to-date in her methods and knowledge, and in proper decorum and dress by all under her supervision. Noticing that the small white cap she habitually wore sat askew on her head, I became concerned. Something must be very wrong.

"The patient is fine, if that's what you mean, Doctor. However, I believe that a young colt just galloped down the hallway into the labor room, pony tail flying, leaving dirt and havoc behind him."

Standing up so I could peer over the counter, I took in the large patches of yellow-brown mud that had flown from his boot heels during Bobby's grand entrance. It had been a warm and humid, though rainy, day in Glen Falls, but the construction crew had still put in a full day of labor, sheltering under the eaves of the house they were building during the intermittent downpours. His path to the labor and delivery area served, in fact, as mute testimony to his hard work that day.

I sensed Mrs. Jarret's increasing frustration as she strode to her desk, where she called for housekeeping to come and clean the floors, looking at me with mixed agitation, frustration, and—to her credit—a hint of mirth. I decided that perhaps I should intervene.

"I'll see what I can do, Mrs. Jarret." I hurriedly made my way back to the room, where I first checked the fetal monitor to make sure there were no signs of distress. Once satisfied that the baby was stable, I turned to Bobby.

I had never noticed the likeness before, but the description given by Mrs. Jarret of a spirited young horse was apropos. Bobby, easily six feet three inches tall, stood proudly at the bedside. His long blond hair was combed straight back and tied in a ponytail that extended to his waist. His face was rugged and weathered for one so young, and he presented with a strong, dimpled chin and a large hooked nose. Yellowed, carious teeth appeared prominently whenever he flashed his open-mouthed smile. He sported dark, blue-bibbed overalls with a brown flannel shirt that was soaked by the rains he had endured all day long.

I regularly encouraged young fathers in those days to gown and attend the delivery as observers, so, I hoped my suggestion now would resolve Mrs. Jarret's anxiety: "Bobby, I don't know how long this will take, but you might want to go ahead and get ready in case we have to rush into the delivery room. You don't want to miss the birth, do you?"

"Shoot no, Doc. I sure don't want to miss it. Can I wear some fancy duds like you have on?"

"You sure can. Let me show you where you can change."

With that I led Bobby to the dressing room, noticing with some dismay that he was now tracking mud all over the locker room used by the doctors.

After housekeeping had done a thorough cleaning, mollifying Nurse Jarret yet again, I settled back down to wait, trying to read my magazine.

It was near midnight when Mrs. Jarret left for the night, turning over her work to the night nurse, Mrs. Long, another extremely competent and experienced OB nurse—in her case short, obese, and jolly. The patients invariably loved her, as she made them feel at home and important.

As I was trying to decide whether to settle in for a nap, I heard Mrs. Long hurrying from the back, calling my name: "Doctor Matlock, you'd better come here and look at the monitor. The baby appears to be in distress. The heartbeat is dropping into the sixties, with and without contractions. That just started."

Mildly alarmed, I hurried back to the bedside. Brief decelerations of the heart rate aren't unusual with contractions, but irregular slowing, particularly after contractions, constitutes an ominous sign of fetal distress.

Staring first at the fetal monitor in time to witness the heart rate dropping into the forties with no contraction occurring, I felt my own heart begin palpitating. Reaching over to the IV drip, I quickly shut it off. Mrs. Long was already at my side, gloves and lubricant in hand in preparation for my examination.

After a brief scrub I noted that the cervix was now completely dilated but that the baby was still too high in the pelvis; not only that, but the head was positioned occiput posterior—what we referred to as "sunny-side-up"—meaning that the baby could be born looking up at the ceiling instead of in the usual facedown position. I didn't feel any cord prolapse or other problems but I couldn't ignore the monitor or the positioning of the fetus. This could turn out to be a difficult brow presentation.

Turning to Mrs. Long, I quickly instructed, "Call in the surgery crew stat. I'll get Dr. Hendrick on the line."

Rushing to a desk reserved for the doctors to write on their charts, I picked up the phone, dialed the operator, and asked that Dr. Hendrick, our on-call surgeon, be summoned at once. I had no sooner hung up the phone when it began ringing. Picking it up quickly, I responded, "Hello. OB floor, Dr. Matlock speaking."

A sleepy voice on the other end responded, "Hi, Carl. What's going on? This is Bill Johnson; I'm covering anesthesia tonight."

Filling in our anesthetist briefly, he replied, "I'll be right there. It'll take me ten minutes to dress and get to the OR. Take the patient on over."

Since both of our doctors lived within minutes of the hospital, it would require only a few minutes to prepare. Already the night supervisor of nursing was on the floor, marshaling her staff to help Mrs. Long meet the crisis.

In the midst of the chaos I had briefly forgotten Bobby. Getting up from my chair now, I noticed him standing just outside the labor room with a worried expression. "Is everything okay, Doc?"

In a few words I outlined my concerns about the baby. Gladys, who had been making an effort to remain as still as possible during the contractions, began to wail loudly, exclaiming over and over, "My baby, my baby. What's wrong with my baby?"

Grabbing a mask and head cover from the wall in preparation for the OR, I entered the labor area and tried to soothe Gladys's worries while advising her at the same time of the necessity for haste. Bobby stood in the corner of the room, pale, sweating and looking as though he could faint.

Firmly taking Gladys by the hand, I assured her, "Gladys, you're doing fine yourself. The baby is experiencing some type of distress and will have to be taken by Caesarean section. Do you understand me?"

"Yes, Doc. Only please, don't let anything happen to my baby."

"We'll do our best. Right now I see that some of the OR nurses have arrived, and we'll be taking you immediately to surgery. Dr. Hendrick is on his way, I'm told, and he's a very good surgeon."

Nodding toward Mrs. Long, I advised Bobby that she would show him where to wait. With the two OR nurses and the night supervisor assisting, we rolled the hospital cart to the OR, where I was grateful to see Dr. Hendrick already at the sink scrubbing for surgery. The nurses took over while I scrubbed alongside my friend, discussing the details of the case with him while preparing to enter the surgical suite.

It gave me a good feeling to have the backup of a competent practitioner like Rob Hendrick, a man who would respond to any emergency when he was on call, night and day, without uttering a complaint. Once in the OR Rob stepped to the right side of the patient, while I positioned myself on the left. As soon as Bill indicated that the patient was under anesthesia and the surgical nurses were fully prepared, Rob made the incision to expose the uterus, then rapidly but carefully dissected into the lower uterine segment. Grabbing a special forceps blade, he placed it beneath the baby's head to gently leverage it out of the pelvic canal. I stood by with the bulb syringe to suction the infant and begin resuscitation.

Within mere seconds Rob had delivered the head, quickly followed by the rest of the blue and struggling infant. We noted immediately the cause of the distress: the cord was wrapped tightly around the neck four times, compromising the blood flow to the baby during the later stages of labor.

Rob handed off the infant to me after cutting and clamping the cord, and I quickly moved her to our overhead radiant warmer used for infant resuscitation. After suctioning and stimulating the seven-and one-half pound girl, I was rewarded with a loud and lusty cry of indignation from the town's newest citizen. She was definitely opinionated about having been disturbed by this unceremonious extraction from her warm, dark sanctuary just below her mother's heart.

Thanking Rob profusely for his help, I hurried with him to the waiting area to relieve Bobby's anxiety. The lobby, where Bobby had now been joined by several members of his family, was itself quite spacious. Bobby saw us approaching, jumped up from his chair, and ran to meet us. Seeing the smiles on our faces, he visibly relaxed and asked, "What do we have, a boy or a girl?"

He began pumping my hand in a hearty handshake as I answered, "A very pretty little girl with a full head of dark hair."

Sighing in relief, he asked, "What did you name her?"

Dr. Rob chuckled as he answered, "You have to name her; she's your baby."

With a flush of embarrassment Bobby quickly responded: "Oh Yeah. I forgot. Her name is Mary Evangelina; but I don't know how to spell it."

"You mean Evangelina?" I questioned.

"No—Mary," he responded without embarrassment.

And so ended another long and exciting day in my practice.

About two weeks later Bobby and Gladys brought Mary Evangelina to the office for a checkup. I noted with chagrin that she was covered in a fine and obviously pruritic rash, causing her to appear very uncomfortable. The etiology of the rash appeared to be a simple lack of hygiene, as the infant was coated with a fine covering of grime.

As gently as I could I suggested that a mild soap be applied twice a day, with a little antibiotic ointment to be used on the obvious areas of irritation. These simple souls appeared to take no offense at my suggested treatment and left satisfied with the visit.

That was the last time I saw Mary Evangelina, as her parents apparently moved on to another town. As I've observed of so many young people, their roots evidently didn't go very deep.

PARASITES AND TWINS

It was a glorious fall day in Glen Oaks, with maples, elms, and oaks dressed in brilliant reds, yellows, and browns offset by an azure sky bedecked with fluffy cumulus clouds above the neat rows of early- and mid-twentieth century homes lining tree-shaded streets. Taking a quick break from the office for lunch, I walked briskly across Main Street to the Glen Oak Drug Store, independently owned by my friend Barry House, our town pharmacist.

Just beginning my fourth month in practice on that invigorating October day, I was suffused with hope and happiness about the future. Already I had seen two patients in the Glen Falls hospital and nine others in my office, and I had nine more scheduled for the afternoon. If I had chosen a larger city, such as my hometown of Indianapolis, I would no doubt have been much busier by this point; however, I would have missed the contentment of living in this small town with its friendly citizens, farmers from the surrounding county, and small-business owners.

I loved my twenty-mile morning commute to the county hospital through rolling farmland dotted with cattle, crops, and woodlands. Since Main Street was only one and one-half miles long, one quickly left the town behind. Each early morning commute offered the gift of meditating upon my good fortune at being alive, serving the people in the town, and life with the wife and daughter I adored.

As I opened the door to our drugstore, the wooden frame protested with a loud squeak of the spring before slamming behind me with a familiar bang. Looking up from the counter, Barry's wife, Ethel, smiled as I made my way to one of the barstools to place my lunch order. The couple was always happy to see me.

As I seated myself at the counter, I relished the scent of hamburger sizzling on the grill, bacon frying for the BLT sandwiches, and fresh-baked bread and donuts. "What's the special, Ethel?"

Pointing to the chalkboard where she had just updated the day's menu, Ethel beamed her response: "Good to see you today, Doc. Our special was chicken and dumplings, but I just sold out. We've got a great burger, fries, and slaw combo I'm sure you'll like."

"I'm sure you're right about that, Ethel. I'll take the special and add a Diet Coke. How's business today?" Glancing down the counter, I noticed that every booth was occupied, along with half the bar stools.

"It's been a good morning, Doc. We certainly appreciate all the business you send our way. Before you came to town Barry wasn't sure we'd be able to keep the store open. There's no worry about that now. Just be sure and say hello to him back in the pharmacy before you return to the office. He has a couple questions for you about patients requesting refills."

Smiling my pleasure, I answered, "I'll be sure to do that; I'm glad things are working out so well for you now."

As I sat savoring my hamburger with pickle and mustard, Harold, one of my patients, settled down on a stool beside me. "Howdy, Doc. H-h-h-how are you t-t-today?"

"I'm doing very well, Harold. How about you?"

"Okay, I g-guess. I n-n-need to m-m-m-m-ake an appointment t-t-to see you again soon. I th-th-th-think I may need some s-s-tronger pills for my n-nerves."

Nodding in response as I finished my lunch, I continued, "Stop by this afternoon if you'd like. I'm sure we can work you in."

I headed back through the long aisles of general merchandise, including blue jeans, perfume, lotion, farm implements, horse halters, small gift items, and everything else imaginable an agricultural community might need. I stopped by to consult briefly with Barry before going back to work, my shoes echoing loudly on the wood-paneled floors that squeaked and sagged a little beneath me.

"Business looks great, Barry. You seem busier every time I come in."

"Everything's good, Doc. By the way, are your hedges recovering around your office yet?" With a friendly smile and wink, he asked, "Are you going to let Harold do any more work for you?"

Flushing just a little, I answered, "They were pretty bad, weren't they? I thought Harold would do a better job than that. In the future I'll try to give him something else to do."

"Folks around here appreciate that you gave him a chance, Doc. He does have a push mower that he can use fairly well if you want to have him do something else."

"I'll keep that in mind, Barry. Thanks for the suggestion."

On my way back across the street I thought of the first day I had met Harold. There had been so much to do in preparing the small, rented house to function as a doctor's office. I immediately noticed his spasticity, which seemed only mild when he was standing still. He had asked whether he could trim the hedges for me, and after reassuring me that he had done that type of work for others, I readily assented before returning indoors to see how the paneling of the exam rooms was progressing.

I forgot all about Harold until I stepped back outside some two hours later to observe the most bizarre, chopped up, mutilated hedgerow I had ever witnessed. Standing before the last shrub, Harold was busy whittling away, forearms jerking, legs unsteady as he tried repeatedly to make a straight cut across the top. Every whack instead slanted in one direction or another, until there appeared to be no way, short of removing the shrub altogether, to repair the damage.

Harold was so excited to see me that he whirled around and excitedly proclaimed, "This sure is something, ain't it, Doc?"

I could only shake my head in amazement and chagrin before answering, "It sure is!"

That had been in July, and much of the violated hedge had recovered by now.

Entering the office again I greeted Donna and Christine, my nurse and receptionist. "How's the schedule coming? Any new patients for the afternoon?"

Christine surveyed the appointment book before answering, "Still only nine, but we should get some more appointments before the day is over. I believe your first patient is just coming up the sidewalk now."

Grabbing my stethoscope, I headed through the former dining room to wait in the kitchen for Donna's evaluation of the patient. My office was quite small, with a back bedroom situated just off the kitchen serving as a larger examination and treatment room. The dining room had been partitioned into a smaller, wood-paneled exam room, with the rest of the area serving as hallway to the kitchen and bathroom. My waiting room was the former living room.

I sat down in the kitchen, which served as a multipurpose area—including a lab for doing simple blood work, such as examining urine and other specimens with a microscope, and a small area reserved for enjoying snacks and sodas—to await my patient.

Within about fifteen minutes Christine had the patient registered and Donna had situated her in the smaller examining room. As Donna approached me, she was chuckling to herself. "Your patient is ready. You don't need the bigger room for this one."

I quickly entered Exam Room 1, as we had christened it, and extended my hand to Mrs. Jones in greeting. "How do you do, Mrs. Jones? I'm Dr. Matlock. How can I help you today?"

"It's my boys, Doc—Jimmy and Jack. I want you to give me some medicine for them."

"Oh yes. I believe I met them last week when they came in for school physicals."

"That's right, Doc."

"They didn't seem to be sick. In fact, they looked quite healthy and fit." I tried smiling at her as I recalled the rambunctious ten- and eleven-year-old brothers who had broken the flower vase in the waiting room while wrestling one another. In the back of my mind I hoped they weren't in the waiting room right then.

"Well, they aren't sick. Not yet, anyway, but they will be."

"What makes you think that, Mrs. Jones?"

"Worms, Doc."

"Worms?"

"Yes, Worms. I mean they're full of them."

"How did you find them?"

"Every time the boys play in the fields and woods near our house, they pass them."

"That's unusual; I mean to only pass them when they play outside."

"I know. I was afraid you wouldn't believe me; so I brought in some samples." With that, Mrs. Jones withdrew a large plastic sack from her ample purse, from which she proceeded to extract two pairs of jockey shorts, which she held up to the light with a triumphant expression.

Shaking my head, I stood up to examine the underwear more closely, finding them to be full of little bits of dried grass and weeds. There was no sign of a parasite in either of the boys' underwear.

"There's nothing in these but grass and weeds, Mrs. Jones. Your boys are fine."

As I stood there feeling somewhat foolish, I glanced up from the shorts to see that she was highly offended by what she considered my slighting of her knowledge. She sat rigidly, fists clenched, red-faced, and head tilted back, looking down her nose and literally glowering at me.

"I know worms when I see them, Doctor."

Initially at a loss for words, I took a deep breath while trying to decide what to do. Finally I just dumped out all the "worms" on the examining table and mumbled an observation I hoped would appease her: "None of these are moving, as you can see."

"Of course not, Doctor. Any fool can see that. They're dead now and can't hurt anything. I'm not worried about them; I'm concerned about the live ones inside my boys."

At a total loss now, I weighed whether to really insult her by insisting on my level of knowledge being superior to hers, as opposed to continuing to feel foolish while perpetuating some kind of compromise ploy. Finally I attempted to placate her with, "Perhaps if you could bring in stool specimens, I could send them to the lab. You no doubt understand that I have to identify parasite eggs or living parasites in order to prescribe the correct medication."

Mrs. Jones responded to this rather heatedly, exclaiming loudly, "Doc, if you think I'm going to dig these specimens out of our toilet bowl, you have another think coming."

"No, no. I don't mean toilet stool specimens. I mean fresh movements. I can give you specimen cups for collecting them at home."

"If you want to help my boys, you're going to have to quit flauntin' your book learning with big words. What kind of movements are you talking about?"

"You know, of course: bowel movements."

Seeing the blank look on her face, it dawned on me that she truly didn't know what I meant. Feeling increasingly frustrated, I finally blurted, "You know—their poop!"

"Well, why didn't you say so the first time? I still like you, Doc, but you have a lot to learn. Just drop your high-falutin' words and talk common, like folks around here do. Now you just get those whatever-you-call-it jars for me to put the specimens in."

Realizing that this wasn't going to end well, I dispatched Mrs. Jones on her way with the specimen jars, all the while hoping she wouldn't come back with them.

Fortunately, the rest of the day went well, as I met a couple of new patients and visited with several returnees. We were finishing by six o'clock when I looked up to see my wife and two-year-old daughter standing in the doorway to our lab.

Janet was about five months pregnant, and her OB doctor, the same one who had delivered Cindy by Caesarean section, practiced in Indianapolis, about forty miles from our home. My wife informed me now that she was feeling a good deal of movement and wanted to make certain everything was alright.

She took her place on the examination table as I retrieved my OB fetal stethoscope to listen to the heartbeat. Palpating the abdomen to determine the fetal position—which can be challenging early in pregnancy—I found myself confused by what I was finding. I listened in the upper left abdomen and detected a perfectly regular rhythm of 160 beats per minute. Then, just for curiosity, I listened in the right lower abdomen—only to hear another regular rhythm, this one of 120 beats per minute. Thinking I had done something wrong, I kept placing my fetal scope first in one position and then in the other, all the while observing my watch and counting.

"Is something wrong, honey?"

"What did you say? I didn't quite understand you because of the scope in my ear."

"I just wondered if something is wrong. It seems like you're having some difficulty hearing the heartbeat."

"No, the heartbeat is good and strong. Nothing's wrong, but I just want to check once more."

For probably five minutes I continued to shift my OB stethoscope back and forth on the abdomen, counting and recounting all the while. Finally, I looked up and smiled at my wife, who was becoming more and more anxious.

"Guess what?" I announced. "You're going to have twins. There are two distinct heartbeats, one fast and one slow— perhaps a girl and a boy based on such a large difference in the heart rates."

Having delivered many babies already, it was my observation that quite often boys have a considerably slower heart rate than girls prior to birth. Without doubt the heartbeats were different enough to easily detect two babies.

"Your OB doctor is going to be surprised. He only found one heart beat the last time."

"That's right, Carl, but he only listened in one area of my abdomen. You aren't playing a joke on me, are you?"

"Not at all, my dear. We need to pick out two names now—two for twin girls, two for twin boys, and two for likely boy and girl twins."

Now it was my turn to be concerned, as Janet looked perplexed for a minute or so. "What's wrong, honey? Are you okay?"

"I'm fine, my dear. Just shocked, that's all. I thought you were teasing me, but I see you're serious. Actually, I'm very happy about having twins. Aren't you?"

"Janet, I couldn't be more pleased. You've made my day."

A MAN OF MANY TALENTS

nother of my first patients and subsequent friends, Art
McKay, a man of many talents, will live in my memory
always. Fifty years of age, with thinning brown hair
and a pear-shaped body, he weighed in at three hundred
plus pounds, supported by a body of five feet three inches
in stature; he would never admit the degree to which he
exceeded the three-hundred pound mark.

Art, a naturally nurturing individual, owned the only
funeral home in Glen Oaks. At his own expense he had
started an emergency service by equipping one of his vehicles
as an ambulance, complete with oxygen, bandages, splints,
and a few other basic emergency supplies. Art had of his own
accord become an EMT, leading a crew of six other volunteers
who had all undergone some training. In the seventies many
a rural funeral home doubled its functionality by providing
one or more emergency rescue units. If this combination

suggested a conflict of interests, no one thought anything about the matter in those days.

Emergency rescue units in that era had a much lower standard of care than that to which we have become accustomed, our current standard defined by a rising breed of emergency physicians beginning to agitate for recognition as specialists. Art, well loved and appreciated by the community as he was, repeatedly won re-election as county coroner. An outgoing, friendly man, Art naturally attracted a loyal following.

I remember my initial meeting with Art, who came in for an appointment in July 1973, shortly after my opening day.

"Hello, Doc. I just thought I should come get my blood pressure checked and make your acquaintance. I really look forward to working with you. My prayer for the last four years has been that we would get a young doctor to care for our citizens. Old Doc Langley in the next town is no longer up to the rigors of private practice; he's only available about three hours a day now."

"It's a pleasure to meet you, Art. I know what you mean about Dr. Langley; he was one of the people who recruited me to come here. He wants me to help him as he slows down his practice."

"Old Doc has been good to us here. If you follow in his footsteps, you won't go wrong."

As I continued my exam, peppered with an easy exchange of small talk, I noticed that Art's blood pressure was too high at 180/105.

"Are you taking blood pressure medicine now, Art?"

"Yes, I am, Doc—when I don't forget to do it."

After completing my exam, I retook Art's blood pressure and shook my head in concern. "It's still 180/100, even after you've been sitting here for a few minutes. Do you use much salt in your diet?"

Grinning sheepishly, Art responded enigmatically, "Well, I don't salt ham."

Looking up questioningly, I went on, "No, really, do you use a lot of salt?"

"I'll admit I like the taste of salt. Food just doesn't taste right without it."

Patting his ample abdomen, Art continued, "You can see that most of my food tastes very good—so I guess I use a lot of salt."

"One of the first things you can do to get your blood pressure down is to limit your sodium intake. Begin by hiding the salt shaker, and then watch the salt content of your food."

"I know, Doc. Remember, I'm the coroner. I see what happens when people overeat and use too much of anything, but I just can't help myself. Food is my crutch for the stress of the work I do."

"Do you take enough time off to rest, Art?"

"Doc, you know this is a big rural county. What would happen to all my good friends and neighbors if I took a couple of weeks off? Someone might die without my crew to get him or her to the hospital. I just couldn't live with myself if that happened."

"Okay, Art. Have it your way for now, but I'd like to recheck you in about two weeks after you start watching the salt in your diet. Also, be sure and bring in your medicine next time so I can review your therapy."

Looking somewhat doubtful, Art smiled and responded, "I'll try to be careful of the salt, but I don't know if I can do it, Doc."

Standing up to leave, he shook my hand and continued, "Doc, they have a ham sandwich special at the drugstore today. Come on over with me for lunch and I'll buy. We won't even need any salt."

"Why not? I don't have any more appointments this morning, so I'll be right with you, Art."

Several weeks had passed since Art's initial appointment, and his blood pressure

remained too high even though he had come in to see me three or four times already. On Saturday mornings I maintained office hours for the convenience of working men and women who couldn't get off work to see me during the week. I had just dismissed the last patient on that particular morning and had mentally prepared to enjoy the rest of the day off when the phone began ringing. Turning to me, Donna called out, "Wait, Doc—don't leave yet. It's your neighbor, Linda Castle. She says her husband, Ted, is really sick. She'd like you to come over right away, if at all possible. She thinks he might be in shock."

I didn't have to think twice about the request; the couple were not only neighbors but also good friends. Ted and Linda were in their mid-sixties and retired. They had immediately fallen in love with our two-year old daughter and did occasional babysitting to give my wife and me a rare night out.

"Donna, tell them I'll be right over. Could you and Christine please lock up for me and take the deposit to the bank?"

Christine smiled as she answered, "I was just going to suggest that. You go ahead to see Ted; he and his wife are favorites of ours."

I grabbed my black medical bag and headed out the door, hoping this would prove to be nothing serious. Jumping into my Ford, I punched the accelerator and squealed away from the curb. It would take me all of three or four minutes to get to their house. As I laid rubber in the street, I saw Art and two of his crew readying the ambulance for an emergency run. Art had already activated the revolving red light on his roof and was backing out into the street. Turning left at the next corner, I heard the undulating wail of his siren close behind me.

Arriving just ahead of Art, I bounded up the steps of the small porch as Linda opened the door. As I entered their neat living room, my heart sank at the look of apprehension that replaced her usual cheerful demeanor. Glancing over my shoulder, I saw Art pulling into the drive beside their bungalow, siren at full blast and red light rhythmically rotating in circles.

"What's wrong, Linda? I came as quickly as I could."

"I don't know, Doc. Ted was up all night vomiting and complaining of shoulder pain. He didn't want to worry you, knowing how little time you have with your family, this being your Saturday afternoon off, but for the last hour he's been listless. When he started breathing hard, I decided to call anyway."

"You did right, Linda. Where is he?"

Leading the way, she motioned for me to follow. "He's right in here, Doc, in our bedroom."

The bedroom door opened off a small hallway from the living room. As I followed Linda down the hall, an urgent pounding on the front door brought Linda to a halt.

"That'll be Art and his crew. They were following close behind me." Stating the obvious, with the high-pitched siren just fading to silence in the driveway, I motioned her back to the living room and hurried in to see Ted.

Linda disappeared back down the hallway, wringing her hands. "I called Art, Doc. I hope you don't mind. I thought he might bring his oxygen for Ted."

The bedroom was rather small but very neat with its flowered wallpaper, high plastered ceiling, pair of French provincial chairs, mahogany vanity, and sturdy oak nightstand. From the regular sized double bed Ted looked up from beneath the pile of blankets covering him to his neck. He tried to smile but ended with more of a weakened grimace.

Ted had never been a large man, weighing in at about 145 pounds and, like Art, standing no more than five feet three inches tall. He had retired from his factory job with General Motors in Glen Falls two or three years earlier and had been in for a check-up shortly after I set up practice; at that time no general health problems had been apparent. He had been the picture of health, in fact, even yesterday morning as he had waved to me while reading his newspaper on their porch from his usual perch on the green cushioned glider.

Today, everything had changed. Ted indeed struggled for air, though propped up on three pillows. His face and lips were a dusky blue, his respirations forty and shallow, his chest heaving, his abdomen bulging with every breath, and beads of sweat on his forehead.

"Are you able to tell me what's going on, Ted? Are you in pain?"

In hesitant, gasping sentences Ted began, "Just my left shoulder—it has a funny ache in it. Mostly, I can't breathe."

Art entered the room with Linda at that point. As I pulled my stethoscope from my medical bag I looked up at Art. "It looks like Ted needs to go to the hospital. Can you get oxygen and your cart back here so we can load him in the ambulance?"

Although already flushed and panting, Art managed to respond, "Sure, Doc. I'll be right back with the other fellas and our equipment."

I checked Ted's blood pressure, which was 102/70 with a slightly irregular pulse of 130. Noticing his distended jugular veins, I heard moist rales all across his chest through my stethoscope, a sign of fluid in his lungs. A prominent third heart sound, an S3 galloping rhythm characteristic of congestive heart failure, could both be heard and palpated over the left chest wall, where a prominent lateral displacement of the heart indicated enlargement. Upon gentle palpation of the abdomen, I found the liver to be about three centimeters below the right rib cage, another sign of heart failure. Last of all, I uncovered his legs long enough to detect only minimal swelling.

Hearing a loud wheezing in the hallway, I stood up as Art and one of his crew members, Ollie Stone, lumbered into the room with the cart, upon which was positioned a large tank of oxygen. I stared in alarm at Art as he wheezed, his fat cheeks alternately puffing in and out, his face reddened, and his own chest heaving, struggling as he was to maneuver the cart into the small room.

"Are you okay, Art?"

"Fine, Doc. Just winded. Cart's heavy."

Not wanting to embarrass Art by continuing to stare at him, I turned back to Ted. "I think you've likely had a heart attack during the night. You're experiencing congestive heart failure and will have to go to the hospital now."

Noting his look of apprehension, I quickly added, "You'll be alright, Ted. I'll ride with you in the ambulance if it's okay with Art."

Art smiled and nodded his affirmation. He continued to ready the oxygen with the help of Ollie, a twenty-year-old man with a high-pitched, feminine singsong voice. Ollie, who thoroughly enjoyed his job as volunteer EMT, fairly danced about the room, wheeling out an oxygen line, attaching it to the tank, and chattering away, announcing each step he was taking in preparation for the ambulance ride.

They made a good combination, Art concerned and caring but too winded for conversation, and Ollie cheerful—happy, even—energetically jumping about the room, a nonstop torrent of meaningless words flowing from his lips.

After Ted had been loaded onto the cart with the oxygen flowing, his head elevated, and blankets piled to his neck, we started for the ambulance. I followed anxiously, as Art had once again begun grunting, breathing hard as he rolled from side to side, balancing his ponderous body on his small feet while loudly blowing through his lips, gulping in air, and then repeating the blowing like a winded horse.

I began to wonder what I would do if Art were to break down physically before we could get Ted to the hospital. As we exited the front door his other EMT, Willie Robertson, a forty-five–year-old, lean but muscular man, held the door and assisted in getting the cart down the steps. Willie was a good soul who volunteered for anything and everything in the community. He sold insurance for a living but was always ready to jump in and help a neighbor.

Once Ted's cart had been latched into place in the back of the ambulance, Ollie situated himself in the front passenger seat and put on his radio headset so he could jam to the Oldies while we rode to Glen Falls. Art climbed into the driver's seat, mopped sweat from his forehead with his handkerchief, glanced back to see Willie and myself seated next to Ted, and saluting us with his index and middle fingers began backing the ambulance out of the drive while reactivating the siren and flashing red light.

As we headed for the interstate I relaxed a little, glad that the oxygen was providing some relief to Ted. In those days the ambulance consisted of little more than a converted hearse painted white, with a logo of some type added and siren and lights attached. Paramedics were a rarity in many locales—totally unknown in Glen Falls and Glen Oaks. I had no IV to start, no diuretic to administer for the congestion, and little other than oxygen and prayer at my disposal prior to our arrival at the hospital.

In three miles we arrived at the interstate and merged with traffic, pulled into the passing lane, where I now believed we would make good time to the hospital. To my amazement Art settled into a steady fifty-mile-per-hour cruising speed, in the passing lane, on an interstate where the speed limit was marked at seventy for cars. Within seconds traffic started to pile up behind us—until the first driver summoned the courage to pass us along the right side. From there until we exited the interstate a steady stream of traffic flowed around us in the driving lane, while we maintained our much slower speed in the passing lane.

I hunched over, trying not to be too visible to the passing drivers and hoping no one would recognize me in this embarrassing predicament. Willie leaned over and patted me on the arm in encouragement.

"Don't worry, Doc. Art always does this; it's just his way. I keep telling him he should lose weight and exercise, but he never seems to get started on his own health. He says he has to care for others first; then he gets out here and drives like he has all day."

As we neared the Glen Falls interstate exit, Art turned around to yell back, "I'm going to get the sheriff on the CB to see if they can give us an escort at the intersection; it can be really busy."

I shook my head in wonder as traffic continued to flow unobstructed around us in the driving lane. Interestingly, the police deemed themselves "too busy" to come to our aid. I couldn't help but wonder how often this scenario had played out in the past.

Finally arriving at the hospital, Ollie reluctantly took off his headphones to assist with the stretcher cart. Willie smiled and clapped me on the back as we all piled out and made our way into the emergency room.

I was pleased to see Nurse Kilgore, a middle-aged woman from Glen Oaks, on duty. Once we had Ted taken care of with continued oxygen, IV Lasix for diuresis, and nitroglycerine for pain, he rapidly improved. An EKG indeed showed that he had experienced a myocardial infarction, or heart attack.

We were not routinely using aspirin for heart patients in the early seventies. The advances in cardiac therapy for heart attacks—angioplasty, stents, and CABG surgeries, cardiac rehab with excercise—were for the most part awaiting future developments. Indeed, a heart attack in that day confined a patient to a slow recovery with bed rest for sometimes as long as ten days, followed by slow, progressive ambulation. No doubt we created many cardiac cripples back then, emphasizing as we did the disability of a heart patient.

After Ted had been transferred to an ICU room, I settled down in the emergency room to dictate his chart and finish his orders. Nurse Kilgore approached, smiling and offering me a cup of coffee.

"Here, Doc. You look like you could use this. That 'fast ride' with Art was no doubt harrowing."

"You're right about that; I thought we were going to be run over by the cars speeding around us."

"When you all went by in the ambulance, I was just combing my hair for work. I left about five minutes later and still beat you here. How about that?"

"I don't doubt it. I'm just glad we got here in one piece. I know Ted was glad to see a familiar face in the ER when he saw you would be his nurse. I think he was too sick to worry about the ride."

"You'll get used to Art. I know he has a good heart, and everyone loves him."

"You're definitely right about that. I really do appreciate his dedication. He asked me if he should stay to take me home, but I told him my wife would pick me up so we can get our grocery shopping done while we're in town. She likes to shop at Kroger, so this worked out well enough."

"Well, you have a good afternoon off, Doc. Ted looks much better. Linda's here with him now, and they sure appreciate your dedication too."

I'm happy to report that Ted survived the heart attack and continued to be my patient for a few more years before finally succumbing to congestive heart failure.

VALLEY OF THE SHADOW

On one of the first days of my medical school training a professor I greatly admired talked to the assembled students about our chosen profession. He doled out a good deal of grandfatherly advice, but one thing he said I'll never forget: "You have chosen a profession in which you will walk through the 'valley of the shadow of death' many times during your career." The purpose of the lecture was to emphasize the necessity of our own mental health maintenance.

I have certainly found this to be true during my forty plus years of medical practice. One never gets used to the finality of death; this outcome invariably seems to defeat our purpose as medical practitioners. It isn't easy to admit that all of our treatments are, in the final analysis, doomed to failure: the mortality rate in this life will always remain at one hundred per cent.

The field of medicine takes quite a toll on the practitioner; depression and suicide are higher for doctors than for the general population. Many doctors are perfectionists who don't deal well with failure of any kind. Dealing with death in medicine is one of the greatest challenges I have ever faced.

Raymond, a seventy-five-year-old man, looked the picture of health the first time I met him in my office. We initially engaged in small talk, a technique that usually puts a patient at ease before getting to the issues of real concern.

"Doc, I think I have a problem that might force me to see a surgeon."

"What kind of problem, Raymond?"

"Well, you know, it isn't easy for me to talk about private things. I really don't know where to start."

"Just take your time, Raymond, and start from the beginning. What's bothering you at the moment?"

"I'm having some type of rectal pain—this is so embarrassing, Doc."

"It doesn't have to be embarrassing. God designed our bodies the way they are. I'll need more information if I'm going to be able to help you."

Taking a deep breath, Raymond plunged into his story: "For several months now I've had pain when my bowels move. For the last two months or so I bleed with every movement. I think I have hemorrhoids; at least, I hope that's what's wrong."

"Have you noticed anything else that's different?"

"Different? Like what, Doc?"

"I mean like abdominal pain, weight loss, or poor appetite?"

"Now that you mention it, I've lost about twenty pounds in the last six months. I seem to fill up quicker these days, but I needed to lose a little weight anyway. I really don't have abdominal pain, unless you count some cramping in my left side at times."

"Has there been any change in your bowel movements besides the blood? Also, what color is the blood?"

"My bowel movements are smaller, string-like most of the time. The blood is bright red and colors the water. I came in because I'm worried about how much I'm losing."

"One good thing, Raymond, is that it doesn't take much blood to color the commode water red. Please put on this gown and take everything else off except your stockings so I can examine you thoroughly. I'll step out for a minute while you get ready."

Stepping back into the exam room, I saw that Raymond was ready but quite anxious as he sat fiddling with the string tie on the gown.

"Are you ready, Raymond?"

"As ready as I'll ever be, Doc."

Proceeding with the exam, I noted that Raymond's conjunctiva and palmer creases were a little pale, raising concern regarding possible anemia. His general exam, however, was otherwise normal . . . until I got to the rectal evaluation.

"Please lie on your left side with your knees pulled up toward your chest."

Waiting until Raymond was in position, I proceeded to do a rectal exam with a disposable glove and plenty of lubricant. After pulling a sheet over his legs and thighs, I pulled up the gown and stopped short in amazement. My heart sank as I saw the ugly, three-centimeter linear ulceration of his perineum, extending from his anal canal toward the scrotum.

Pausing before the digital exam, I asked, "Are you in much pain now, Raymond?"

"No, I'm okay, Doc. Go ahead with whatever you have to do; I just want to get this over with as quickly as possible."

Gently I probed with my index finger, noting a slightly enlarged but otherwise benign prostate. Failing to find any nodules or other masses, I removed my finger, noting the bright red blood on the glove and worrying about the obvious narrowing of the anal canal and distal rectum, in itself indicative of probable tumor involvement.

Raymond had stoically tensed but visibly relaxed as I completed the examination. Rolling over onto his back, he looked up at me, forlorn hope in his questioning eyes. "What's the verdict, Doc? Do I have hemorrhoids?"

Hesitating, I sat down beside him, trying to decide how to proceed. As he slowly changed to a sitting position, I began, "I'm afraid you have a more serious problem than hemorrhoids. It appears that you have some type of tumor involving your anal canal and rectum. That's what's been causing the pain and bleeding."

Raymond dropped his head and admitted, "I was afraid of that, Doc. Well, what's next?"

"You need to have some blood tests for anemia and a general check-up. Also, I want you to see a surgeon as soon as possible."

Sighing deeply, he conceded with resignation, "Anything you say."

○

Two weeks later I found myself scrubbing in as assistant to my good friend, Rob Hendrick, the general surgeon. Reviewing our findings during the scrub-in, I hoped aloud that we would be able to remove the aggressive anal carcinoma Raymond had tried to ignore for too long.

"His hemoglobin is up to twelve grams after the two units of packed cells I gave him last night. His EKG and other tests all look good; I hope the cancer hasn't spread any further in his abdomen. At least his liver functions tested normal; maybe he'll be in luck. What do you think, Rob?"

"I don't know; he's let this go too long already. I don't know how he put up with this as long as he did."

"I believe he was afraid to find out the truth, though I think he knew the news would be bad."

Rob was preparing to do a major abdominal-perineal resection, a procedure that involved extensive abdominal and rectal surgery with removal of the anal canal and the distal rectum, along with attaching a colostomy bag to the abdominal wall to handle bowel movements following the bowel diversion procedure.

"What if you find metastatic disease in the abdomen? Will you still do a major surgical repair?"

"Yes, Carl. I'll still do the procedure because this is so advanced he's in danger of eroding into major blood vessels—not to mention that he's about to obstruct the outlet completely. I had a long talk with him about it last night; he knows his chance of complete cure is poor."

About three hours later we exited the surgical suite. Raymond had tolerated the procedure very well for a man of his age, yet it was difficult for me not to be discouraged. The exploration had found extensive lymph node involvement in his abdomen, indicating no chance of complete removal of all the tumors. The tight anal-rectal tumor responsible for the initial bleeding and pain had been dealt with, but the disease was incurable.

Over the next nine months I became much better acquainted with Raymond, who maintained a stoical front for the world to see, though inside he was quite depressed and anxious. I watched him endure chemotherapy and radiation with little apparent benefit and cared for him when he came in vomiting and dry heaving from the treatments. I was privileged to become his good friend, as well as his physician.

As our relationship evolved, he gradually opened up more and more to me, voicing his fears, his concern over his family, and his awareness of the finality of death. The last time he came in he was markedly dehydrated from vomiting. In spite of high doses of narcotics he was in agonizing pain.

"Raymond, I believe it's time for you to go back to the hospital where we can hydrate you and give you IV pain medication. Is that okay with you?"

He managed a faint smile as he clasped my hand and answered, "It's okay, Doc, but I want you to know—no heroics. I'm at peace with dying now. I'd like to be in less pain, but please don't do anything to prolong this. I want to thank you for all you've done for me."

"You're very welcome, Raymond. I'm just sorry I couldn't do more."

"I know, Doc. I should have come to you sooner. There's something I want you to know before I die, since you're a praying man. I haven't always been one myself, but I'm glad God gave me this time to prepare to meet him in eternity. I promised God I would take all the suffering he could give me if he would just save my soul. Since that prayer I feel a lot better about what's happening to my body—I just wanted you to know."

Briefly overcome by emotion, I gripped his proffered hand, searching for the right words with which to respond. Finally, I could only reply, "I'll continue to pray for you and give you all the relief I can." I couldn't help but think that though his theology might not have been orthodox, his heart was all right.

"That's all I ask, Doc. That's all I ask."

Raymond was admitted to the general medical ward for what turned out to be the final week of his life. His quiet demeanor and obvious gratitude for even the smallest favor quickly endeared him to the nursing staff. His ongoing suffering was so apparent that the nurses made it their goal to administer pain medication before he even asked, trying to make his last days as comfortable as possible.

On the Friday following his admission six days earlier, I was just preparing to go to the hospital when I received a call at home. The choked-up voice on the other end was that of Susie, one of Raymond's nurses. "You'd better come quick if you want to see Raymond alive; he's very low right now. His kidneys have shut down, and his blood pressure is only 90/60."

"I'll be right there—tell him I'm coming."

Twenty minutes later I walked onto the medicine floor, only to be met by two weeping nurses. "He's already gone. He quit breathing five minutes ago."

"Was he conscious at all before he died?"

Susie stood dabbing tears from her eyes as she answered, "Just before he breathed his last he opened his eyes, raised both hands up to the ceiling, and smiled so beautifully. He saw something or someone, Dr. Matlock—something not of this world. His struggle is over now. He died very peacefully."

I sat down in a corner of the nursing station, pretending to look at his chart; with his having been pronounced officially deceased, I now had paperwork to complete. It took me some time to finish that task, however. My mind kept reliving the last several months, reviewing the good friendship that had developed between myself and this elderly, gentle soul I would miss a great deal.

Raymond had helped me put death into better perspective. Although I had been defeated in my initial attempt to keep him alive, and later on even free of pain, I had been successful in keeping faith with him; in doing my best; and, ultimately, in seeing him off to eternity, to a better place of abode than this world has to offer, to final victory as a man prepared to meet his Maker.

HOUSE CALL

Belle Skinner stood in my waiting room, her eyes dull, her cheeks sagging, her forehead wrinkled, and her expression stolid. A peculiar odor emanated from her clothes and body. Up until mid-morning the day had been proceeding slowly, routinely—so much so that I found myself with some time before my next appointment. Since no other patients were in the office at the time, Donna had asked me to step into the waiting room to discuss a request for a house call.

"Let me get this straight, Mrs. Skinner: you say that something has fallen out of your mother-in-law's body?"

"That's right."

"Also, she's bedfast due to a stroke a few years ago, her Doctor no longer makes house calls, and you'd like me to take her case?"

"Right."

"How long ago did she have the stroke?"

"I dunno; maybe five years ago."

"When did this body part fall out of her?"

"Oh, 'bout three weeks or so ago."

"What makes this an emergency now?"

"I don' think it's an emergency; she's just tired of it. She wants it fixed."

Stroking my chin while glancing at the clock on the wall before briefly perusing the appointment book, I turned to Mrs. Skinner and conceded, "I can come by after my next appointment if that fits with your schedule."

"Okay, I'll be there to let you in."

With that, Mrs. Skinner trundled about and shuffled to the door.

Turning to my staff, I raised my eyebrows and mused, "I wonder what I just got myself into."

Christine tried to look serious, but the twinkle in her eyes betrayed her mirth as she replied, "I'll bet it will be interesting. Did you notice that odor?"

"Yes. I don't know what it indicated, but I'm sure I'll find out soon enough. It really burned my nostrils. I tried not to let on."

Donna laughed aloud. "I noticed you were trying to breathe through your mouth until she left. Does that really help?"

"Well, at least it stopped the nasal burning for a little while. I hope I wasn't too obvious."

One hour later I turned my Ford station wagon down the last street in town beside the railroad tracks, swerved to avoid the deep chuckholes before slowing along a seedy area of dilapidated housing searching for the house number. I noticed rusted vehicles without tires jacked up on cement blocks, piles of trash bags, broken glass littering the street, and waist-high weeds in yards in which the homes had been boarded up.

Arriving at 23 Waterford, I braked to a stop, eased my car into the rutted driveway, and cut the engine. An ancient hound slowly rose from the small stoop that served as front porch, bayed loudly twice, then promptly collapsed back down on the stoop before losing interest or energy and closing his eyes. Since he didn't look too dangerous, I carefully made my way to the front door, dodging debris on the bare path to the house.

Stepping over the dog, which now ignored me, I started to knock on the screen door hanging askew from a single top hinge, took a deep breath, and wondered what the inside would be like. Before I could knock, however, the door opened to reveal Belle, a full-length soiled apron covering her obese midsection and a wan smile on her face.

"I heard our old hound bayin' at ya, Doc. Thanks for comin."

Stepping into the room, I was once again assailed by the noxious odor I had noticed in the office when I had met Belle—only now it was much more pronounced. Glancing about the room, I discovered the source of the odor: cats—cats everywhere, big cats, little cats, kittens, tabbies, calicos, blacks, whites, mixed colors, . . . and the list could go on. There must have been twenty-five or thirty of them, sitting on frayed overstuffed chairs (though less stuffed, I noted, than they had once been) or an old green couch and even climbing on the kitchen table. Un-emptied litter boxes attested to how well those felines had been dining.

Belle turned to shoo one of the tabbies off the table, where it had been helping itself to what appeared to be her own unfinished lunch. Picking up the chicken leg it had been gnawing on, she proceeded to finish it off with more gusto than anything else I had as yet seen her do.

The room was a large, multipurpose one; there would have been no other way to describe it. The kitchen table stood in the center with the sink and chipped enamel stove on the right. The left side of the room contained an accumulation of aged furniture belonging more appropriately to a living room, had there been one. Near the back left-hand corner of the room a pot-bellied black wood stove glowed red from the logs even now being devoured by the flames. In the very center of the back wall a long, old-fashioned, iron-posted daybed featured the patient, an elderly woman buried beneath piles of quilts. In each back corner doors led to darkened areas I assumed to be family bedrooms.

Belle nodded to the back of the room to indicate the patient, all the while continuing to munch on the chicken leg retrieved from the jaws of the tabby cat. Shuddering at the sight, I nodded in acknowledgement and moved forward to meet my newest patient.

The old woman smiled weakly as I approached her side. Waving my hat at a large white cat perched on her bed in a futile attempt to chase it off, I heard it hiss and felt it spit at me before fleeing to the security of the couch, engaging in a brief fight with one of its fellows over the coveted position on the worn armrest.

Hearing a loud scraping on the wooden floor, I turned to see Belle pushing with her foot a dark brown kitchen chair over the rough floor in my direction. She continued eating from the plate, which she now sheltered in her hands from the aggressively ravenous cats surrounding her legs and mewing loudly for her attention.

I briefly inspected the proffered seat prior to accepting it; spotting no vermin or other filth, I gingerly sat down. "What's your name?"

As silence greeted me, Belle stopped eating long enough to inform me, "She can't talk—the stroke, you know. Her name is Mary Skinner. My husband is her oldest boy."

"Mary, I understand you have a problem with something falling out of your body."

She nodded with what I hoped was understanding of my explanation, prompting me to continue, "My name is Dr. Matlock; I'm going to examine you with the help of your daughter-in-law. Hopefully there's something I can do to help you. Is that okay with you?"

As she again nodded, I turned to Belle for assistance. Belle, it appeared, was indeed preparing to assist—by replacing her plate on the table, wiping the chicken grease from her mouth with the back of her right hand, and shooing away the cats by swishing her apron in their direction.

"I'm comin', Doc. She probably don't know a word you just said, so let's get on with it."

I stood back as Belle turned back the covers and pulled up the worn blue gown, exposing Mary before gently rolling her onto her right side toward the wall. Next, she pulled up Mary's legs, placing her in the fetal position. It was obvious that the old woman's right side was completely paralyzed, rendering the poor soul helpless.

I couldn't help but be impressed by the skill Belle exercised in caring for her mother-in-law. Hygiene was certainly lacking, but her care and love were apparent in her handling of this elderly invalid and matriarch of the Skinner family.

I retrieved a pair of disposable gloves from my bag and looked with consternation on the prolapse of the uterus, lying on the old sheets in the midst of cat hair and bits of stool. The vaginal tissue was dehydrated, excoriated, and stretched where it enclosed the womb, and the entire mass protruded about five or six inches from the outlet of the vaginal canal. I had never seen a more severe prolapse in my brief career. Still, nearly fifty years later, it ranks among the worst I have ever seen.

Belle retrieved a bed pad and placed it beneath Mary, allowing us to first cleanse the area with tepid water in a slightly more sanitized field. Explaining to Belle what I was going to do, I retrieved some lubricant from my bag and applied it liberally to the dry tissue. Carefully palpating the mass and finding no undue tenderness or gangrene, I prayed silently as I gently pushed. Observing Mary's hunched up figure for signs of pain or stress, I slowly reduced the mass up into the vaginal canal and held my breath, hoping it would work.

Mary stirred briefly as the mass disappeared into her body . . . and stayed there. Gently we rolled her to her back and did our best to make her comfortable once again beneath her pile of blankets. Mary smiled at both of us as though thanking us for caring.

For the first time the dull light in Belle's eyes gave way to a sparkle as she nodded her approval. "Thanks, Doc. I know that was worryin' her a lot."

"Belle, does she get up much? If she does, it may fall right back out."

"Naw, Doc. She just stays in bed. Been there about two years now."

"How can that be? She doesn't have any bed sores."

"I turn her a lot, Doc. She likes to be where she can see the cats. They belong to her; they're her babies."

"I thought they were your cats, Belle."

"Naw Doc. I can't hardly stand them. They're hers."

In amazement I prepared to leave. I had been there long enough that the foul odor no longer bothered me much; however, I knew I wouldn't have wanted to live with it. As I bid Belle good-bye, I had a new appreciation for a woman who would so solicitously care for her incapacitated relative, regardless of the personal inconvenience it might cost her.

Driving away from that poor section of town, I found myself passing a stately old home belonging to the wealthiest family in the county. As I glanced at the well-kept grounds, the sprawling brownstone two-story house, and the carefully trimmed firs lining the drive, I couldn't help but contrast the two families.

In the Skinner home was abject poverty, filth, and cats galore, but there was also a rough but recognizable love and concern for family—in particular the matriarch. In contrast, I knew, the patriarch of the family of worldly means—that large, well-to-do clan—now resided in the sterile environment of the foremost nursing home in the county. A bitter man, who also had been the victim of a debilitating stroke—though one that had left his harsh, complaining voice intact—never allowed me to finish a visit without taking the opportunity to regale me with a thoroughgoing denunciation of the family that had left him in this hated place to finish out his life.

Driving back to the office, I contemplated the marked contrast between the two families. The Skinner family could have easily placed Mary in a chronic care facility; her Medicaid would have covered the cost. The other family could just as easily have paid for in-home help to keep the old gentleman in the comfort of home through his declining years. The difference amounted to love and devotion to family.

If individuals might be given a choice of families, I wondered, which would they choose? Personally, I would rather not live in squalor, but neither would I prefer to live in the absence love. Thankfully, those extremes don't constitute the only choices.

A GROWING FAMILY

By the seventh month of my medical practice my life had already become much busier, the days longer, and the cares greater. Not only was I putting in long hours in the office, making rounds of hospitalized patients, and making house calls, but still more significant demands on my time, in my roles as father of Cindy and husband of Janet, required my attention. Janet was near the eighth month of a difficult pregnancy, expecting the birth of twins in early February; however, she had experienced several episodes of false labor. Each time we were emotionally drained, worrying about the possible complications of prematurity in our twins.

Just after New Year's Day in 1974, as I finished another grueling day in the office, Christine called me to the phone.

"Dr. Matlock, it's your wife. She says she needs to speak with you right away."

With shaking hands that I hoped weren't noticeable to my office staff, I took the wall phone in the lab off the hook, attempting to answer in a calm voice: "Hello, sweetheart, are you okay?"

I'm sure my face paled as I detected the fear in Janet's voice. "Please come home as soon as you can. I think it's starting again."

"Are you having contractions?"

"I'm afraid so. Maybe we should go to your mom and dad's for the night."

"I'll be right there. Just stay calm."

In reality I was assailed by my own inner fear, to which I immediately gave counsel. Only a fellow physician could appreciate the turmoil playing out in my mind. When a physician sees a loved one suffer, that reality always brings to mind the horrendous possibilities of anything and everything that could go wrong. At such times knowledge becomes a curse, as the mind detours into visions of potential complications and problems.

As I turned my yellow and brown Ford station wagon toward home, I attempted to don my usual mask of security and calm; it was yet again time for me to masquerade. This is one of the great burdens of being a physician: the necessity of remaining in control even when everything feels as though it's falling apart around you. When it comes to family, this can be a nearly impossible task—accounting for the well-known advice against physicians treating their own close family members. Wearing such a mask, even in the best of cases, takes a toll on the sensitive nature of most physicians, who are often called upon to witness unspeakable tragedy and death.

Upon my arrival I was met at the door by Janet, a relieved smile on her face. "The contractions have stopped again. I feel better now."

"Let's get ready anyway. I don't want to take a chance; twins usually come early."

After a late supper at Mom's that night, we turned in, with Cindy tucked safely between Janet and me. I planned to get up early to get to the hospital and office, a forty-mile drive from my parents' home in Indianapolis. The added complication of a major snowstorm would make the task somewhat difficult but not impossible.

After only a few minutes of sleep, however, I became vaguely aware of my wife shaking me, calling me back from a dreamless sleep of exhaustion.

"Carl—wake up, honey."

"Hmm?" was all I could manage at first.

"I'm in labor, for sure. My water just broke."

Sleep instantly fled, as I was startled into a full-on state of awareness and alarm. "What? You say it's started? Really?"

"Yes, really!"

Jumping out of bed and groping for the light, I frantically dressed, rushed to the bathroom, and splashed cold water in my face. Looking at the clock, I noticed that it was about 12:30 in the morning of January 5.

With Dad staying home with the slumbering Cindy, Mom accompanied Janet and me out into the fury of the snowstorm. My car was parked across the street from their house in Indianapolis, where the pavement was buried in six inches of snow with more on the way. Windblown snowflakes created a white curtain beautifully illuminated by the faint glow from the streetlight.

Fearing for my wife's safety on the treacherous, snow-slicked street, my mother and I positioned ourselves, one on either side of her. I took her left arm while Mom clasped her right. Gingerly we set out to make the hazardous crossing, stepping carefully.

Halfway across the street, however, despite my best effort my right foot slid forward and my left backward, and I started careening sideways toward the ground; fortunately, my wife gripped my arm, preventing me from going down in a heap. Here I am, I thought ruefully, the typical nervous expectant father, relying on my wife for stability. I was thankful it was too dark and stormy for any of the neighbors to witness my clumsiness or detect the chagrin on my face.

Two hours later I found myself ensconced within the sterile, brightly lit environment of an operating room awaiting the delivery of our babies while trying to comfort my wife, anxiously hoping for the anesthesia to take effect and relieve her acute distress, her contractions now being nearly continuous.

With little warning I realized that the room around me seemed to be reeling, the horizon beginning to tip crazily. A strange ringing in my ears warned me that all was not well, so I began to give myself a pep talk: You can do this, Carl. You're a physician. You regularly assist in general surgery cases. You'll be embarrassed if you end up on the floor. Get a grip!

Noticing my distress, Janet's doctor focused his concern on me. He had just scrubbed in, ready to operate as soon as the anesthesiologist gave the signal.

"Carl, are you okay?"

Noticing my hesitation, he continued, "Perhaps you should take a seat out in the hallway."

I bravely replied, after only a little hesitation, "I'll be fine. Just a momentary weakness. I'll sit down if I feel faint again."

He replied, "I don't have time to take care of you if you pass out. Please take a seat over by the infant warmers. You can help with the babies."

Smiling weakly behind my mask, I resolved not to make another display of weakness. I made my way to the area he indicated, being careful not to watch the actual incisions necessary for the Caesarean section. I felt briefly ashamed of the weakness I had so obviously displayed and determined not to do anything else that might get me expelled from the surgical suite. In those days fathers weren't permitted to observe Caesarean operations; an exception had been made for me, a physician, who had been taught obstetrics by the same kind physician who would now be performing the operation.

In less than five minutes I forgot all about my temporary weakness as the nurse handed me Baby A, Diane Elaine. She was beautiful, and I was totally distracted at first sight by an overpowering love. I carefully suctioned the remaining amniotic fluid from her nose and made sure she kept warm.

One minute later Baby B, David Kent, followed his sister into the world. My cup ran over with love and gratitude as I gazed into the face of the little boy I would teach to fish and hunt and eventually influence by example to become a family physician.

I wish no offense to my readers, but there could never have been a more beautiful pair of twins born into the world. Assured by the anesthesiologist that my wife was doing well, I accompanied my new daughter and son to the nursery.

As I stood a few minutes later admiring the additions to our family, the doctor joined me, announcing, "Carl, your wife is doing very well. I'm glad, though, that we did the repeat section and didn't give her a trial of labor. The lower uterine segment had thinned out so much at the site of the previous C-section that it appeared ready to rupture. As you know, that could've been catastrophic for her and the babies. Over all, I'm pleased with how everything went. She'll be in recovery until she's awake and alert. I anticipate that she and the babies will be in the hospital for about a week. Do you have any questions?"

"No, I don't believe so. We're very grateful for your help."

As he entered the nursery to examine the babies, I felt a momentary return of the former weakness. Uterine rupture, a dreaded complication, could have been fatal for all three. I wondered how I could ever have raised Cindy without the beautiful, loving presence of her mother. Standing now outside the nursery, my eyes grew misty as I leaned against the wall and offered a silent prayer of thanksgiving to Almighty God for watching over my family. He had indeed been merciful to us. I was glad that we hadn't waited before proceeding to Indianapolis. My parents' home was only about five miles from the hospital, not the forty miles from where we lived.

Arousing myself from the reverie, I went to summon my mother so she could see the babies. I could hardly wait for her response.

"Mom, both babies are healthy. Each one weighed five pounds and one ounce. Diane is short and chunky, and David is long and thin. I know you'll agree with me that there has never been a more beautiful set of twins."

After Janet awakened from the anesthesia, I visited her for a few minutes before returning to my parents' home, accompanied by my mother. Dad was anxiously awaiting our arrival. Our twins had been born at about 3:30 in the morning, and the winter sky was still dark as we shared an early breakfast, rejoicing that Janet and the babies were safe and healthy.

I was due in the office in about two hours, so after bacon, eggs, plenty of black coffee, and buttered toast, I bid Mom and Dad goodbye and prepared to drive back to Glen Oaks. I first stepped quietly into the bedroom that had been mine as a child growing up in Indianapolis. Before setting off to work, I wanted to catch a glimpse of my strawberry-golden-haired daughter still lying in peaceful oblivion beneath the warm blankets. Tiptoeing to the bedside, I softly kissed her forehead and tucked the covers around her.

Assuring Mom and Dad that I was fully awake, I departed for work equipped with the full mug of coffee Dad had prepared for me. It was a clear, bitterly cold morning as the snow vacated the deep blue sky, chased away by the sun peeking over the horizon. Fierce winds from the north made the zero-degree temperature feel much colder.

To help me stay awake I tuned in to WIBC, cranked up the volume, and sipped my coffee from time to time. I drove carefully over the icy, snow-encrusted roads, avoiding the back roads that had become impassable due to drifting snow. Within minutes, as though I had requested a special song, the Carpenters populated the air space, thrilling me with the strains of "I'm On Top of the World." A warm glow suffused my body as they sang that familiar song, perfect for the occasion. I couldn't have been happier, more content, or more in love with my wife and family. I was profoundly thankful that Janet, Cindy, and the twins were all safe and healthy. I was truly blessed.

Arriving at the office I found that my mother had already apprised the staff of the happy news. A prominent sign announced the birth of David and Diane. Although I'd had little sleep, I felt as though I were walking on air, and the day flew by.

"HELP, DOCTOR — I'M SICK"

A tall row of pines cast long shadows across the lot behind my office as the late winter sun reflected brightly across the cement parking lot filled with vehicles belonging to my patients. The exam rooms were full and the waiting room overflowing, with standing room only, as I paused to glance wistfully out the laboratory window, wishing to be finished for the day. My practice had quickly outgrown the two-exam-room office; I could now boast a much more adequate working area with a good deal more examination and treatment space.

Influenza season was in full swing in Indiana that year, as hacking coughs resounded throughout the office, and I did my best to keep up with the influx of patients, especially those who hadn't had flu shots. Although the injections weren't one hundred per cent effective, I was certainly glad I had taken mine before the flu season began.

Before I could make my way into the next exam room, my reverie was interrupted by a disturbance in the waiting room. Muffled shouts of help, accompanied by the slamming of the front door, resounded to the back of the building.

I hurried to open the door leading to the waiting room, where to my astonishment I witnessed Donna and two husky young fellows heaving a flaccid Lydia Isaacs into our wheelchair. Lydia looked ghastly with her eyes closed, her head thrown back, an uncombed mop of white hair, and an open mouth, a saliva rope making its way down her chin, her arms hanging limply over the sides of the wheelchair.

Holding the door widely open, I shouted above the din for Donna to bring her back to the lab, which currently held no patients. Donna started on a run, closely followed by Lydia's oldest daughter, racing toward the doorway with the evidently unconscious patient; it was at that point that I noticed the precarious position of Lydia's limp, dangling arms.

"Watch out for her arms. They're about to slam against the door frame."

Donna stopped short at my warning as we watched Lydia of her own volition quickly drawing both arms into the safety of her lap. No other observable change occurred in her posture during the episode, but her reaction to the warning didn't escape either Donna or me.

With a knowing smirk on her face, Donna remarked, "Perhaps we should slow down a little. I wouldn't want Lydia to get hurt."

Sighing deeply, somewhat relieved yet irritated at the same time, I answered, "No, we certainly wouldn't want her to get hurt."

Matilda, the middle-aged daughter who still lived at home caring for her parents, urged us on as she wrung her hands in the hallway. "Please hurry and do something for Mother; I think she's dying."

"Matilda, come on back with us. Your mother will be fine. Donna and I will take good care of her, and you can help us."

Blinking back the tears brimming in her soft blue eyes, Matilda followed Donna closely as the waiting room door swung shut behind them. She obviously hadn't seen the behavior we'd witnessed during the dramatic entrance of her mother.

Wheeling Lydia into a corner area, Donna grabbed a tissue, handed it to the sniffling Matilda, and retrieved smelling salts to hold beneath Lydia's nose. I had to watch the rest of this little drama unfold as I leaned back against the wall, folded my arms across my chest, and waited for the action to commence.

Within seconds Lydia began turning her head away from the smelling salts, even lifting her left hand to push the bottle away when Donna continued to track it close beneath her now wiggling nose. Lydia's eyes fluttered open as she sneezed loudly, finally brushing Donna's hand away as she exclaimed, "Wha'—what happened? Whe'—where am I?"

Sobbing with mixed joy and anxiety, Matilda appeared near collapse beside her mother as I quickly scooted a chair beneath her.

"Here's a chair, Matilda. Sit here by your mother. Donna will get you both some ice water. As soon as we get a room free, we'll give your mother a good check-up. She looks a lot better now."

With an angelic smile Lydia gazed up adoringly into my face, reached for my hand, and squeezed it gently while replying, "How can I ever thank you for saving me like that, Doctor? You were really wonderful."

I winked at Donna and Christine, who had also entered the room to see how Lydia was doing. "Your gratitude is reward enough for me, Lydia; I'm just glad you're better."

Donna screwed the lid back onto the smelling salts with a look of disgust on her face, hesitating before replying sarcastically, "I don't know why I even came to work today. It seems as though I really didn't do anything."

Without the slightest hesitation, Lydia looked up at Donna and intoned, "Never you mind, honey. You just keep working with Doc long enough, and he'll teach you everything you need to know for an emergency."

Inhaling deeply, Donna turned to walk away from Lydia, but not before Matilda joined in, "That's right, Mother. Doc saved you from a stroke or something worse. I'm sure we're very grateful for what he did."

Donna stalked away, muttering to herself, while Matilda took her mother's proffered hand and lovingly held it between her own while patiently waiting to be placed in an examination room.

Two hours later we were finally able to lock the front door and straighten up the office for the next day. Lydia had made such a remarkable recovery that she had been able to walk out of the office under her own power. That is, she made it to the waiting room before she began to lean heavily upon her daughter's arm all the way out to their car.

Christine, though not medically trained, was an astute observer of humanity. When the last patient had departed for the night, she raced back to the laboratory and in her best whining voice began, "I'm sure glad you saved me, Doctor. You knew just what to do while that worthless nurse just stood there torturing me with those awful smelling salts."

While we both doubled over with laughter, Donna stood glaring at us until she couldn't take it any longer, collapsed into the nearest chair, and laughed herself until she cried.

Following a rare leisurely dinner with my wife and children, I returned to make late evening rounds, having to check on a patient admitted through the emergency room earlier in the day.

As I sat on 2 North studying patient charts, Nurse Kilgore stopped by to talk. Tonight she was functioning as house supervisor as well as emergency nurse.

"How are you this evening, Dr. Matlock?"

"I'm fine, thanks. And you?"

"I'm hanging in there. I heard you saved Lydia today, Doc."

"You've got to be kidding me. How did you hear about that?"

"Glen Oaks is a small town, Doc. You'll get used to it."

"Tell me, does she do that sort of thing often?"

"How long do you have, Doc?"

"I don't think I want to hear this."

"I'll spare you some of the details, but you should know that she faints at the county fair every year, . . . but only in crowded locations. And that's only the yearly episode. She also . . . "

"Stop! I think I'll listen to this when I have more time, but I appreciate the heads up."

Smiling pleasantly, Ann Kilgore turned to continue her rounds. "Don't say I didn't warn you, Doc. Once she gets started, she's good for several more tries before she tires of it."

"I appreciate the information, Ann. Let's just say I've been warned."

Thinking that Ann Kilgore must certainly be exaggerating, I soon forgot all about Lydia while I examined my new patient, who had been admitted with congestive heart failure earlier in the day. After determining that he had been stabilized with oxygen, diuretics, and digoxin, I prepared to go home for the night.

Draping my stethoscope around my neck, I had started for the first floor exit when Ann Kilgore turned the corner, stopped, and smiled enigmatically before saying, "You need to see a patient in the ER before you leave. The emergency doc wants to see you too."

With an exaggerated sigh I turned in the direction of the ER, trying to ignore her seemingly upbeat attitude in light of my own discomfiture.

Arriving in the ER, I greeted Jerome Hayden, one of our ER docs: "How are you tonight, Jerry? What's up?"

"I have one of your patients here. You apparently saw her today but for some reason decided not to admit her."

Alarm bells began ringing in my head as he continued with his dissertation. Jerome always enjoyed practicing one-upmanship.

When I didn't respond, he went on, "As I said, for some reason you didn't admit her, and now here she is in serious condition."

"Who is it, Jerry? Might this by chance be Lydia Isaacs?"

"Yes, that's exactly who it is. I think we should transfer her to Indianapolis for a neurologist to care for her. Don't you agree? You apparently missed something today in the office."

"Follow me, Jerry. Let's take a look at Lydia first."

Upon entering the room I saw Matilda sitting beside her mother, who was supine on a hospital cart. Lydia again had her eyes tightly closed and appeared unresponsive.

Nurse Ann Kilgore followed us into the room. Making her way to the opposite side of the cart from us, she looked across and asked, "Would you like this, Dr. Matlock? I heard it did wonders for her today."

Dr. Jerome Hayden looked on in mystified silence as he observed her handing me a bottle of smelling salts. Hesitating only briefly, he began, "Really, Nurse, I don't believe that's at all appropriate."

"Now, just a minute, Jerry. I think Nurse Kilgore is on to something. This might just work again."

Dr. Hayden watched in irritated silence as I uncapped the bottle and held it up to Lydia's nostrils.

This time Lydia didn't so much as hesitate; she reached up and batted the bottle out of my hands before sneezing three or four times. Then she gazed up with a beatific smile before crooning, "Oh, thank you, Doc. You did it again. I already feel better."

I glanced at Dr. Hayden and noted with satisfaction that he was now regarding me with a respectful, if bemused, expression. "I would never have believed it."

"Jerry, you just have to know how to use this wonder drug. Isn't that right, Lydia?"

"It sure is, Doc, and I thank you again."

"Jerry, I'll tell you what: if you don't mind writing a few orders for her care tonight, I'll see her again in the morning and try to sort out what's going on. Is that okay with you?"

Quickly regaining his composure, Jerry answered, "Sure. I'll be glad to get her admitted for you. I agree that she can be admitted here tonight. No sense bothering a neurologist now."

"None at all, Jerry. Thanks for your help—and Lydia, I'll see you in the morning."

A STROKE AND NOT A STROKE

The insistent jangling of the alarm clock in the still darkened room startled me from the peaceful land of repose. Quickly rolling over in bed, I noticed that it was already 5:30 a.m.— another all too short night. Groping to turn off the alarm, I instead sent it flying to the floor with a loud crash. Duly "alarmed," my wife sat bolt upright in the bed.

"Go back to sleep. It's okay. I accidentally knocked the alarm clock off the nightstand."

"What time is it? I thought it was one of the babies. Scared me to death."

"No, it's just me. I guess I didn't get enough sleep again last night. Late night rounds at the hospital are killing me," I groaned.

"I told you you're taking on too much. I know you want to take good care of your patients, but you have to start with yourself."

Stumbling off to the bathroom to splash water into my sleepy face, I tried to make as little noise as possible.

"Sorry, honey. I didn't mean to wake everybody up. Just clumsy this morning. You are so right. I need to get more rest. Nine months of practice and I'm already exhausted. Oh well, such is life. At least I didn't stay up all night in labor and delivery. As you know, Mary Jane is due at any time for her third child."

In a small town everyone knows everything about everybody. In those days privacy was neither a major topic nor its lack a potential hindrance in the practice of medicine. I don't recall that many of my patients were greatly concerned about the issue.

People didn't live and die on smart phones in those days; interaction was always face to face. Families really got to know one another, and people didn't text across a restaurant table. The birth of a baby was a big deal in a small town. My wife had attended the baby shower for Mary Jane, so I didn't have to worry about mentioning her name.

As I prepared for work, trying to be as quiet as possible, I heard the comforting sound of rattling pots and pans from the kitchen, soon to be accompanied by the enticing fragrance of bacon frying on the stove. I dearly loved a hearty breakfast, accompanied by a hot mug of black coffee and a refreshing glass of milk.

Making my way softly through the hallway, I tiptoed past the nursery, hoping its residents would remain soundly sleeping, but standing there in the doorway, clutching her

Teddy bear, stood my darling two-year old. Catching her up in my arms, I whispered, "Are the twins still asleep?"

"Uh-huh. Dey are."

"Good. You come with Daddy to the kitchen. We'll see what Mommy's fixing that's sure to taste good on a cold winter morning. I'm sure she has something very good for Cindy and Daddy."

Maintaining a measure of quietness to avoid arousing the babies, we sat down to a tasty breakfast while discussing the plans for the day. The kitchen was small in this, our third home, but also bright and cheery. I once again congratulated myself on having found such a wonderful companion and cheerful homemaker to serve as the example and guiding light for our children to emulate.

Janet did everything she could to make things better for the family while I struggled with practicing sixty to eighty irregular hours each week to build my practice and support our growing household.

Following a sumptuous meal, I prepared to drive to the one-hundred-bed county hospital where I did my inpatient practice. Picking Cindy up, I kissed her on the cheek while I drew Janet into my other arm, kissing her and thanking her for a wonderful breakfast. As I sat Cindy down, I instructed her, "Now you be a good girl for Mommy and help with the babies. Okay?"

"Okay, Daddy. I will, I will."

Pulling on my overcoat and grabbing my medical bag and hat, I hurried out the door, drawing a quick breath as I encountered the blast of cold air; an anemic looking sun was just peering over the horizon. I dearly loved those quiet mornings with the twenty-minute commute, passing farms with frost still on the fence posts and waving at farmers trudging over the frozen ground to care for their livestock.

The commute, in fact, constituted one of the few instances of solitude in my day, a time to ponder the Scripture verses I had just read, to plan, and to commune with God, expressing my gratitude and admiring His creation.

Arriving just before 7:00 a.m., I parked behind the hospital in the doctors' parking lot and made my way up to the third floor. By this point my adrenalin was surging with my usual sense of workday urgency; I was due at the office at 9:00 a.m. and couldn't afford to waste any time. I didn't always succeed in this endeavor, but I made a concerted effort every day not to convey a sense of urgency to my patients.

This morning I had two post-op patients to check on, one having had a gall bladder surgery and the other an emergency appendectomy. In our small hospital I regularly assisted with surgeries on my own patients and helped the surgeon check on them post-operatively. Laparoscopic surgery was an innovation for a future day. Most patients were hospitalized after gall bladder surgery for seven days or longer.

Picking up the first chart from the rack, I listened as the overhead page clicked on, making its peculiar popping sound as the operator activated the system.

"Dr. Matlock, Dr. Carl Matlock, please call the operator."

There it was. The first interruption in my day. I soon learned that Annie Smith was in the ER and that my presence was urgently requested.

Retracing my steps via the elevator to the first floor, I hurried to the emergency room to see about Annie, my mind traveling back to the first time I had seen her in the office.

Annie was a short, plump lady of fifty-five who lived alone and had never married. To say that she was eccentric would be an understatement. Annie collected things: old newspapers, pennies, dogs, cats, and injured animals. She had inherited a three-story, seventy-five-year-old farmhouse from her grandparents.

All of her family members had passed away except for some cousins who looked in on Annie periodically to make sure she had adequate clothing, food, and wood for her stove. If she had any other friends, I had yet to meet them. She had difficulty learning and had dropped out of school as soon as she had turned sixteen. She hadn't been able to negotiate her way past the eighth grade and was self-conscious about her shortcomings.

She had come to the office for the first time only a few weeks earlier. It seemed like only yesterday that she had sat in front of me, hands carefully folded in her lap and nervously clearing her throat, dressed in a clean but ancient appearing farm dress. I replayed the visit in my mind as I hurried to see what was wrong with Annie.

"Hello, Doctor. My name is Annie. I—I'm not very good with words, but something ain't right with me. My cousin Elmer said I should come see you."

"Hello, Annie, I'm glad to meet you, and you did right to come."

I shook hands with her—hers were tremulous and sweaty—attempting to set her at ease.

"How may I help you today, Annie? What seems to be the trouble?"

After a long pause Annie began, "I don't know what to say, Doc. I'm not very good with words, and I'm afraid you'll laugh at me."

"Annie, don't worry. I would never laugh at you. Please tell me what's bothering you, and don't worry about proper words."

Sighing deeply, she finally began: "It's like this. It's just like swimmin.'"

"Go on, Annie. You're doing fine. Tell me some more about how you feel."

"Well, It's like swimmin'—I guess I don't know how to tell it very good."

"When do you feel like you're swimming, Annie?"

"I have a pain."

"A pain?"

"Yeah, that's it—a pain."

Seated across the small examining room from Annie, I took my cue from her, laying down my pen and chart, clasping my own hands together, and nodding my encouragement. One of the most valuable lessons I had learned in medical school was that a patient will usually divulge his or her own diagnosis if one will only take the time to listen. That's the hard part of medicine—learning to be a good listener.

"Well, Doc—it's okay to call you Doc, ain't it? I mean, it's not disrespectful or anything, is it?"

Smiling, I nodded again, "It's fine, Annie; lots of people call me Doc. By the way, I should have asked you: Is it okay to call you Annie? Or should I say Miss Smith?"

"Shucks no, Doc. Just plain Annie. That's all I am or ever hope to be."

Finally she seemed to relax a little; flashing her quick smile, she launched into her story.

"It starts in the mornin', when I get out of bed. I feel like I'm swimmin'. I can't hardly walk at first. Seems like I'm gonna fall over. I sit back down on the bed real quick like until my head quits swimmin'. Sometimes it takes a mite of time. What do ya think it might be, Doc? Could be it's serious, maybe?"

It had all finally come out in a rush, probably the longest monologue in which she'd engaged in some time. She leaned forward, looking expectantly at me for an answer.

"What about the pain you mentioned earlier, Annie?"

"Oh yeah, 'most forgot. Sometimes the back of my head pains in the morning and when I'm working. Feels like a hammer in there."

A brief examination disclosed a blood pressure of 250/145, dangerously high, at a stroke level. I advised hospitalization, but Annie politely refused, asking, "Who would take care of my animals, Doc? I could never go to the hospital and leave my friends."

☙

Arriving now in the ER I spied Jim Conner, one of Annie's cousins. in a cubicle at the side of her hospital cart.

"Morning, Doc. It's Annie. Found her like this early this morning. She lives just across the road from me, and I knew something was wrong when I didn't see her in the yard tending to her chickens. There she was, just a layin' on the floor like she had fallen and hit her head. She was out like a light, so I called for the ambulance. She ain't woke up yet, and the ER doc says it's serious, but I wanted your opinion."

It was Annie, all right, and she was comatose and unresponsive, her blood pressure 220/120 and breathing deeply, with labored respirations. I once again thought back to our office chats. She had finally seemed to trust me and was more relaxed when recounting her ailments after the first visit, though she had never consented to hospitalization for testing and stabilization.

I tried everything we had in those days, but the available drugs were for the most part less effective than those we have now. Annie had failed to respond to a diuretic, to Hydrochlorothiazide, and to numerous other drug classes, including Aldomet and Apresoline in various combinations. The lowest I'd been able to get her blood pressure in the office was 180/105—not at all satisfactory—but she still refused to leave her animals. And now this: my patient was likely dying, I conceded, feeling a sting of remorse over my inability to convince her to accept inpatient treatment before a hemorrhagic stroke.

As recently as the seventies medicine was primitive by today's standards. We didn't have CT scanners for instant diagnosis and treatment, and Annie was already deeply comatose and flaccid in all four extremities. She obviously didn't have long to live.

With a heavy heart I wrote admitting orders, basically for palliative care. There were no significant signs of trauma on her head or body to suggest a subdural hematoma on the brain, a medical problem treatable by surgical evacuation. Nuclear brain scans weren't nearly as accurate in diagnosis as today's, and carotid angiograms of the brain carried significant risk to the patient.

Jim Conner was a tall, raw-boned farmer, somewhat gruff but still soft-spoken and kindly. He and I discussed his cousin's disposition, as he was her nearest relative.

Jim stood beside me in the ER hallway away from the traffic, head bowed as a single tear coursed down his cheek. He kept turning his straw hat nervously in his hands as we discussed the best course of action.

"Jim, I could send her to University Hospital in Indianapolis. They could run the latest tests, but I have to be honest: she's in grave condition."

"Naw, Doc. She wouldn't want that. Looks to me like she's had it. Funny thing, though: last night she asked me to see to her animals should anything happen to her. I promised, and I'll do it. 'Peers to me like she had a premonition. You just keep her comfortable and do your best for her, as I'm sure you will. Did she bleed in her head, Doc?"

"It appears so, Jim. She may have ruptured a berry aneurysm, a swollen blood vessel, at the base of the brain, but now she's already developing dilated pupils and unstable vital signs. I'm afraid she won't survive. I couldn't get her to have any tests; she didn't want to be away from her home, and she was afraid of the cost."

"I know, Doc. Don't blame yourself. She's a stubborn woman. And if she doesn't make it, . . . well, Doc, she wouldn't want to live. If she couldn't care for her animals, that would just kill her. She wants to be a whole woman—or no woman at all. She never had much, but she believed in God and Jesus—always went to church. I believe she'll be in a better place with her ma and pa and lots of animals to care for."

Indeed, Annie "didn't make it," as her cousin Jim had predicted. She lingered for several hours in a coma and died peacefully.

She was a simple, plain woman, one who loved animals and practiced her simple faith. I didn't know her long, but somehow she touched my life. She represents in my mind and heart all the "Annies" of the world. They're all around us, standing in the shadows trying in their own ways to reach out to others, even though we don't often notice. I try to be more observant of the needs of others now, because of Annie.

That was a busy day in my life. I had just finished the orders regarding Annie's care when I was paged urgently to one of the general medicine floors, 2 North.

A new graduate nurse, Shannon Freeman, was working that day when she found Lydia Isaacs barely responsive following her admission of the night before.

"Hello, Shannon. What's going on with Mrs. Isaacs today?"

"You'd better hurry, Doctor; she's taken a turn for the worse. I believe she's had a stroke for sure."

Sighing, I followed her to Lydia's room, wondering what Lydia might be up to now. The problem with people who cry wolf all the time is that no one believes them when something serious really does happen. I kept telling myself to remain objective.

Lydia Isaacs was stretched out in bed, eyes closed and tongue protruding from the side of her mouth, moaning softly. Shannon stood by, breathlessly awaiting my order.

"Let's examine the patient first, nurse. Tell me her vital signs again."

Shannon whipped out her notebook and began, "Temp 97.8, pulse 85, respirations 16, BP 140/90. I found her like this ten minutes ago. She doesn't seem able to talk or move her left side. What else would you like to know?"

"Well, Shannon, she's been having these attacks quite frequently, but usually they're just simple fainting spells. Could you please get my medical bag from the dictation room while I begin checking her?"

"Certainly, Doctor. Anything else?"

"No, that will do.

Oh, wait, . . . you might bring a vial of smelling salts if there are any in the nursing station."

Shannon had just started out the door when she heard my second request. Whirling about, she put her hands on her hips and glared at me.

"What did you say? Smelling salts? Really, Dr. Matlock, I hardly think . . . "

Shannon was so flustered and offended that she couldn't complete her thoughts, at least not in a civil manner. Instead she pivoted and took off for the nursing station, audibly muttering to herself.

Ann Kilgore was pulling a double shift due to a shortage of nurses that day. She had quietly observed the proceedings from the hallway and decided to join us for the evaluation. Anne was one of those senior nurses who knew everybody and everything. In her career she had seen it all, yet somehow managed to retain her sense of humor.

"I'm afraid I upset your new nurse. Shannon doesn't know about Lydia's health problems yet."

Chuckling softly, Ann replied, "She'll learn. Be patient with her. I believe she's really going to be a good nurse. She just isn't familiar with some of our chronic patients."

We had both noticed the fluttering eyelids and the eyeballs involuntarily trying to track our position in the room. Meanwhile Shannon reappeared with my bag, an offended look still on her face.

Smiling briefly, I began my neurologic evaluation. Pupils equal and reactive to light. No blood in ear canals. Mouth and throat clear and moist. Keeps tongue slightly protruded to the side. Neck supple and no sign of trauma. No bruits: abnormal sounds over the carotid arteries of the neck. Heart regular. No heart murmurs. Lungs clear. Abdomen soft and no masses felt. Eyelids continue to flicker during the general exam. Extremities with normal reflexes, 2+ and equal upper and lower. Babinski reflexes: toes pointing down with stimulation, normal with no sign of upper motor neuron damage. Left arm drops to bed when picked up and released. Right arm floats down normally. Left leg drops. Right leg normal, eases gently to the bed.

Now for the tuning fork test. Placing the tuning fork on the left of the sternum after first striking it to obtain a vigorous, loud vibration, I spoke to Lydia.

"Do you feel this, Lydia?"

Shannon looked on in amazement when Lydia fluttered her eyes open and moaned while shaking her head no.

"She actually heard you, Doctor."

Anne Kilgore smiled and whispered something to Shannon, who continued to observe the evaluation with a mixture of surprise and relief.

Next I moved the tuning fork to the right of the sternum and repeated the procedure.

"Can you feel it now, Lydia?"

Once again a moan accompanied by the flicker of a smile as Lydia nodded in the affirmative.

"One last test, Lydia." I gently raised her left arm, flexed it at the elbow, and dropped her hand toward her face. Instantly Lydia reacted, rotating the arm down to strike her chest instead of her nose.

Turning to Shannon and Anne Kilgore, I motioned for them to follow me to the hall where we could discuss the case in privacy. Anne Kilgore was all smiles, and Shannon looked perplexed, but calm.

"Do you understand what you just saw, Shannon?"

"I think so; she seemed to be putting on."

"Correct. I'm not sure why she does this, but I have my suspicions. Do you understand the tuning fork test?"

With a smile Shannon answered. "The sternum is all one bone. If she felt it on one side, she would have to feel the vibration on the other side. But she doesn't know that, does she."

Anne Kilgore chuckled out loud now and enthused, "Go to the head of the class, Shannon. You're a quick study.

"Dr. Matlock, I told you she would make a good nurse."

"I totally agree. Good job, and you did right to alert me. You don't know this patient as we know her. Anne will have to tell you about her antics at the county fair every year."

"One thing, Doctor: you mentioned that you thought you knew the reason for this behavior. Can you tell us what you think is going on so we can better understand her and reach out to meet her needs in the right way?"

"Right, Shannon, and I agree that you have the makings of a great nurse. Lydia lives with her middle-aged daughter and her invalid husband. He is profoundly handicapped and spends his days in a wheelchair. I don't know how they do it, but they transfer him to bed, to the commode, and to his recliner when he tires of the wheelchair. Lydia doesn't get much attention at home most of the time, and I believe this is her way of compensating. I don't even know if she understands the psychodynamics of her problems.

"She has a lot of emotional needs that are difficult to comprehend and treat. I recently made a house call to her home, and she claimed to need her 'pain medicine' refilled.

She handed me a pink tablet with the word 'Lilly' and some numbers on it. Her former doctor gave her these from the office, and she informed me that this was 'Dr. Langley's strongest pill.' She's been on it for years.

"Naturally, I had no idea what it was but promised to research it for her. On arriving at the office I got out the Physician's Desk Reference and started looking at pictures of pink tablets for pain. Imagine my surprise when I discovered the name of the medicine. It was Eli Lilly's 325 milligram aspirin—just a simple adult aspirin she could take every four hours, as needed for 'severe pain.'"

We all had a good laugh, and I was finally able to depart for the office for an eight- to nine-hour stretch of nonstop patient visits. Perhaps Lydia's old doctor with all the mysterious packages and labels had been on to something: aspirin for "severe pain," Benadryl for "breathing or allergy" problems, antacid tabs for "upset stomach," . . . and the list went on. Over the years I was to encounter many such packaged pills, most of which could be obtained over the counter, but when old Doc prescribed them they seemed to take on a mystical healing power that was indeed impressive for many of his patients.

All in all, it was an instructive day. Sadly, I saw a patient with a very real and devastating stroke; I also saw one with psychological problems and symptoms that could only be labeled as something quite otherwise.

ONE SPRING DAY

pril 3, 1974, started out as just another typical day in my medical practice—hospital rounds at 7:00 a.m., followed by my commute to the office. After a bleak, cold winter, signs of new life were everywhere.

Driving through the farmland following my usual route, I took note of hay fields just turning green, newborn black Angus calves, and a sorrel mare with her new colt frolicking in the field. The morning was bright and cheerful with a few clouds in the sky; all in all, it was a great day to be alive.

The weather forecast that morning had warned of possible severe afternoon storms, but living in Indiana I wasn't particularly worried. Strong spring storms are just a part of life in the region, but with the temperature already at seventy degrees and slowly rising to a predicted high of eighty, it had started out to be a glorious morning, with only a few fluffy cumulus clouds in the sky and mild westerly breezes.

Our day progressed smoothly with the usual blood pressure checks, spring colds and coughs, late flu season cases, and patients with multiple chronic diseases. We were working steadily through our list of patients for the day when I stepped into our back office for a quick break. This was a large area with multiple functions, including a small lab, an area to draw blood, and a separate area with table and chairs where staff could sit and relax between patients or for brief breaks. I had ceased taking time out for lunch, and it was here that I would eat a sandwich as quickly as possible, hurrying to get back to work.

I enjoyed gazing out the large picture window in the back of that office, looking out over a field with horses grazing peacefully. The fence came within fifty feet of the back of our office, and over it the occupants liked to stick their heads, gazing in our direction.

During a momentary lull Donna and Christine both joined me for coffee and a brief snack. The next patient was due in fifteen minutes.

"How is everything going out front?"

"Just fine. The usual questions, insurance forms, 'Do you have my medical excuse ready?' and so on. Nothing new."

"Christine, do you have the school physicals scheduled for today or for tomorrow?" asked Donna.

"I believe they're all tomorrow. Just routine checks the rest of the afternoon."

As I listened to the girls talk, I enjoyed keeping an eye on the horses in the back field. Watching farm animals grazing in green pastures has always instilled in me a sense of peace and well-being.

"How was Mr. Jones today, Doc?"

Although Christine worked in the front office, she loved our patients and wanted to make sure they were okay.

"He still has some congestive heart failure, but he's better. He's even got his sense of humor back; he wanted to know if we could swap hearts."

I turned to look out the window once again as the ladies resumed their conversation . . . and found myself instantly perplexed.

"Now, what do you suppose could be wrong with those horses?"

"Whatta you mean?" asked Donna.

"They're going wild—look at them run; I think they're going to jump the fence."

We all stood up to gaze out the window, watching the strange behavior, when suddenly Christine gasped, "Oh look—just look!"

Shifting our gaze about one-half mile across the field, we instantly recognized the source of their terror. The skies had noticeably darkened, thick black clouds were rolling in, lightening streaked across the sky, and the wind was obviously picking up. One of those old red barns, about one hundred feet long and sixty feet wide, was about to be engulfed by a massive funnel cloud, later said to be over one-half mile wide.

Christine was wringing her hands and Donna had her hand over her mouth; both were visibly trembling. There being no basement in this building, we had no place to go for shelter. With a deafening crash, lightning hit nearby, splitting apart an old tree near the back fence.

Heart racing, I realized instantly that the tornado would either miss us or likely kill us, depending on its trajectory. Already I could see boards and all kinds of debris circling along its edges. The decrepit barn never had a chance; it simply exploded, its rubble flying in all directions.

"Lie down on the hall floor and hold on to something if you can," I shouted, struggling to make myself heard above the now raging wind. Instead, all three of us remained standing, transfixed by the realization that there was little we could do if the monster kept coming our way.

With mixed emotions we observed the twister veering off forty-five degrees and heading out through open fields, destroying whatever fences, buildings, and old farmhouses were unfortunate enough to find themselves in its path. We felt profound relief, of course, at the realization that it was no longer headed our way but were appalled at the damage we were observing firsthand in what we would later learn was an F4 tornado with wind speeds of well over two hundred miles per hour.

It was only then that I had the presence of mind to set down my coffee cup, my hands shaking so badly I nearly spilled its now cold content. Then, as we watched debris scattering across the fields, with unbelievably large objects being tossed about as though by giants at play, we heard the drumming roar of one-inch hail pounding the roof. Ten minutes later a blinding downpour accompanied that onslaught.

Hurrying out to the front office, I stood mesmerized before the picture window in the waiting room. By now the power was off, and our vehicles were being mercilessly pummeled by the hail, accumulating on the ground like snow.

"Oh no, would you just look at that!? As if the tornado wasn't enough by itself. Now this," I shouted above the din.

It was only then that it hit me: my wife and children—and our home—were only about a half-mile from the office, though not in the path of the tornado. It would be hours before I could check on them, and the phone lines were all down.

The hail continued for at least five minutes, after which the rain slacked off and the sun once again appeared, beaming benignly while revealing devastating destruction. The schools had just been dismissing when this storm hit, and within five more minutes the office began to fill up.

"Doc, Doc!" Mrs. Wright wailed. "Please look at Billy's head. I think he may be hurt bad." The ten-year-old had been caught out in the hailstorm, but though terrified and tearful he had thankfully been spared severe injury.

As I stood in the center of our spacious waiting room, I glanced over Billy's head as the door opened again to reveal more parents with hail-battered children.

"Billy's fine; he'll just have a headache. Give him some Tylenol and be sure he rests for a while."

I went down the line, palpating bruised heads and reassuring children and mothers until the first group began to filter out of the office.

Just then Harold Woods, an insurance agent with Farm Bureau, held open the door for Betty Brown, ushering her into the office. Betty had a homemade sling on her right arm and was walking unsteadily.

"Doc, I just saw Betty outside her home on the edge of town. The house was gone, and she was wandering about in the yard holding her right arm with the left one. It looks like a bad break. I don't know how she survived."

"Yes, Harold, this is a bad open fracture of the forearm." The radius and ulna were both protruding from the wound. "Set Betty down here while Donna gets her a tetanus shot and a pain injection; we'll get a better sling for her. She'll have to go to the hospital, of course—not much I can do here."

Betty was unnaturally quiet, only moaning once in a while and gazing up at me fixedly as I carefully picked out the worst of the debris from the open wound with a pair of forceps. She appeared to be going into shock.

Harold stood by, highly concerned over Betty's precarious condition. A longtime friend of the family, he knew Betty well.

"Harold, I wonder if you could do something else for Betty. I have no way to contact the ambulance service. Phone lines are all down. Do you think you could take her to the hospital in your vehicle?"

Harold was obviously excited and anxious, but he answered without hesitation: "Sure thing, Doc. And I'll tell her husband, John, as soon as I have a chance. But first, to the hospital."

Donna and I helped Harold get Betty into his car. Her vital signs were all normal, though she was suffering from emotional shock, still saying very little. There was no active bleeding, her circulation was otherwise good, and Harold was ready to go.

"Thanks for your help, Harold; this isn't in your normal line of work, I know."

Harold smiled briefly before gunning his engine and heading in the direction of the hospital in Glen Falls.

Hurrying back inside, I noticed Christine comforting several other people as they congregated in the office.

"Good job, Christine.

Folks, as you all know this is a serious emergency. Donna and I will quickly check all of you, and then we'll see what else we can do to help our neighbors."

Everyone sat down in the reception area, illuminated only by its own large picture window, calmly awaiting their turns. Christine followed Donna and me, jotting down names, administering tetanus injections, and cleaning minor cuts.

After the unexpected burst of activity, the office seemed almost eerily quiet when it finally emptied.

"It sure is quiet in here with the power off, no air conditioner running, no noise from the centrifuge, and no patients to talk to," I commented to my nurse and receptionist. "Before Harold left he told me he heard over the CB that the little town of Brownfield got hit hard. The storm did veer right toward it, and we have a lot of patients from Brownfield. Are either of you game to come with me and see if we can do anything there?"

"You don't need to ask twice—of course we will. I'll get some bandages, a blood pressure cuff, my stethoscope, and anything else that might be useful," Donna put in with alacrity. "Christine, you grab a notebook and whatever you think we could use. I'll also bring some syringes and a vial of tetanus toxoid."

Christine nodded to Donna, and both hurried to gather supplies while I retrieved my medical bag and stethoscope.

We listened to the local news reports while driving toward Brownfield. Glen Falls had escaped major damage, but there were power lines down, signs overturned, and minor injuries throughout the area. The town had been hit mainly by powerful gusts of wind.

Driving toward Brownfield on Highway 3, though, I was flagged down by an Indiana state trooper.

"I'm sorry, sir—only local traffic allowed now. The town is mostly destroyed."

"I know, officer. I'm Dr. Matlock from Glen Oaks, and this is my staff. We just wondered if we could help. We have a lot of patients in Brownfield."

"Sure, Doctor. Just let me look at your credentials, and you can go on through. Emergency vehicles are allowed. I don't know if anyone's hurt bad up there, but it's sure possible."

After reviewing my wallet medical ID, he pulled out his Motorola radio and cleared me on through the checkpoints ahead.

"Just drive with care, Doctor. There's debris all over the road. You may even have to detour out through a field up ahead. Good luck."

His prediction proved accurate. We found it necessary, in fact, to detour around tree limbs, toppled road signs, a collapsed garage that had blown onto the road, and overturned cars. Power lines were down everywhere, making the trip a hazardous undertaking.

Arriving in Brownfield I was stunned to witness the carnage on Main Street. Highway 3 went right through the middle of town, which appeared to be seventy to eighty percent destroyed. Homes were collapsed everywhere, and frantic people were rushing here and there, lifting debris and shouting down into basements in an attempt to locate potential victims. Two ambulances had made it through as well, and the medics were busy loading them with the injured.

Brownfield had been a picturesque little town of about four or five hundred people. Giant oak trees had lined either side of Highway 3 all the way through town; every one of them, without exception, had been chopped off like a matchstick, with only ten to fifteen feet of its trunk left standing. What had taken a hundred years to grow had been destroyed in mere seconds.

Brownfield looked like a disturbed anthill with the inhabitants running aimlessly in all directions. Just then I spotted Johnny Russell, a stocky eighteen-year-old high school senior. He was as busy as everyone else, searching for victims, trying to help.

"Hey, Johnny. Are you okay? Are your folks okay?"

Johnny hurried over as we exited the car.

"Thanks for coming, Doc, Donna, Christine. Yes, I'm okay, and my folks are, but our home is gone. It's a miracle, Doc. So far no deaths, but lots of injuries. We're still looking."

"I'm glad that you, at least, are okay, Johnny."

Johnny's clothes were soaked, his face was smudged, and his black curls plastered against his scalp. His jeans were torn in two or three places, and he was covered with grime.

"You'll have to excuse me, Doc. I need to get back to work."

"You go right ahead, Johnny. Just let me know if you or your family needs anything."

We walked gingerly along the street, alert for downed power lines, carefully stepping over boards with protruding nails, and looking for anyone we might be able to help. About halfway through town I spied Ben Watson supervising a rescue. A girl was being pulled from the wreckage of a home. She had made it under a kitchen table, and that, I was to learn, was all that had saved her.

Ben, a sixty-year-old school bus driver and cattle farmer, stood six foot three and, though he easily weighed two hundred fifty pounds, was all muscle with very little fat.

"Hello, Ben—glad to see you're okay."

"Hey Doc, thanks for coming. Did you hear about the school?"

"No, Ben—what about the school?"

"I was in line to pick up kids when we heard the sirens. Sally Fairfield already had her bus loaded ahead of me. I ran to her window to make sure she'd heard the sirens. Of course she had. She was already supervising the unloading of her kids back into the school. It was sure the right thing to do, Doc.

The other drivers were just getting there to pick up kids, and we all herded them into the basement and hunkered down to wait the storm out. I kid you not, it sounded like five or six locomotives went through that building all at once. The top of the school is gone, but we didn't get a scratch down there in the basement. Not much of that school is left other than the basement, though."

"It looks like the Lord was watching over those kids today, Ben."

"He sure was, Doc. It was a miracle none of them were killed. The bus that was loaded is smashed to a pulp, partly wrapped around a tree behind the school. The ones in that bus would've been killed for sure if we hadn't gotten them out in time."

"Who was hurt here, Ben?"

"Kathy Wagoner was trapped under a table. She's bruised and hurts all over, but I believe she'll be all right; she's talking to us and moving everything. They say she was expecting."

"I sure hate to hear that. After losing that baby last summer, this'll be hard on her."

"You're right about that, Doc; she's a real good kid."

As the rescuers eased Kathy out of her entrapment under the table, they placed her on a door that had blown down and carried her to a waiting station wagon. There was no more room in the ambulances, but an off-duty medic volunteered to escort her. I hurried over to check on her as they prepared to head for Glen Falls and the county hospital.

Kathy was pale, tremulous, and bruised all over. I took her left hand in mine and stood there trying to comfort her. Kathy, an exceptionally bright, cheerful seventeen-year-old, was married to eighteen-year-old James Wagoner. Although very young, they were a responsible couple.

"Are you okay, Kathy?"

"I think so, Doc, but I'm really worried about the baby."

"I know. You're still very early in this pregnancy, I hope everything turns out good for you and James this time."

"You'll be in to see me soon, won't you, Doc?"

"Of course I will, Kathy, as soon as I can. It may be a few hours because there are a lot of injured folks, but I'll be there."

An hour or two later my staff and I realized there was nothing we could really do beyond comforting people. So far no deaths, but lots of trauma.

"Donna, Christine, I think we might as well go back to the office and then go check on our families. Harold told me my end of town was okay, but I still want to see how they are as soon as I can. I'm sure you want to see your families just as much."

"Doc, will Kathy Wagoner be all right? I mean, she's had so much heartache for such a young girl."

"I sure hope so, Christine. I sure hope so."

As I tried to relax later that evening, I tossed and turned in bed, unable to block out my vivid memories of the events of the day. The phone lines had finally come back up, and I had been advised by Ann Kilgore that the patients were all taken care of for the time being; all was under control until I could see them tomorrow. So far there were twenty new admissions to the hospital from the storm, five of whom were my patients.

Tomorrow, Thursday, was to be my regular day off, though no doubt I would be busy in the hospital for most of the day, since my census was now up to fifteen patients.

I quietly turned back the covers and slipped out of bed, trying not to awaken my wife. The luminous dial on the clock told me it was already 12:15 a.m. I tiptoed carefully down the hallway, making my way to the kitchen, before preparing a cup of hot chocolate and resting with it in the family room in my recliner.

The pallid, anxious face of Kathy Wagoner seemed to hover over me as I tilted back the chair, trying to rest. The Wagoners, including her parents, were such a nice family; her mom and dad were middle-aged, hard-working people. My mind went back to the first day that I had met the Wagoners—Kathy, James, and her mom and dad, Nancy and Mark Johnson—who were among my earliest patients:

August 1973 had been a particularly warm month. I had practiced medicine only since July 1, when during a momentary lull in seeing patients I made my way into the waiting room to converse with the staff.

"Christine, how are we doing today?"

"Not bad. All but three of the patients have paid their bills. We've seen twelve people so far. There are at least seven more scheduled—all new patients."

"How do we stand for supplies? I understand one of the patients is a burn injury from the emergency room who'll need dressing changes. Do you know where we stand with Silvadene cream, Telfa pads, and Kerlex gauze?"

Donna thought for a minute before replying: "I think there's plenty. We may not have enough for repeat dressing changes, but Indiana Surgical is sending a rep tomorrow to go over our supplies. I'll see what we need and show you the list before ordering."

Before I could ask any more questions, our door crashed open and the Wagoner family—all of them—rushed in: Kathy, James, and Kathy's parents, Nancy and Mark, Kathy cradling a tiny bundle in her arms. Although we hadn't met them before, we were soon to learn their names.

"Please help us, Doctor. It's my baby. I don't think he's breathing."

She thrust the little bundle into my arms, pulled down the blanket for me to see the tiny cyanotic face, and began to sob.

"Please help him, Doctor. He's only nine weeks old. He was born prematurely and has pneumonia. We just came from the pediatrician's office in Mount Pleasant. He got a shot of penicillin there, and we came to fill a prescription for him across the street at the drugstore. Mr. House, the pharmacist, told us to bring him here."

I turned to run to the back room with this precious little one, calling over my shoulder, "Donna, grab our emergency supplies, and come quick. Christine, have the others wait in the outside room while this young lady and her husband come with me. I'm sorry; folks; the room is small."

As an afterthought I shouted back, "Christine, call Art McKay right away. He's just down the street by the bank; tell him to bring the ambulance. If there's anyone else the family wants called, please help them do so."

Arriving back in the exam room, I prepared to place the baby on his back for resuscitation when I was interrupted by the mother's screams: "He can't lay on his back. He can't lay on his back. He has a meningomyelocele. The pediatrician said never lay him on his back."

"I'm sorry, but in an emergency like this it's the only way to help him."

I was horrified as I uncovered the tiny body; the little tyke couldn't have weighed more than six pounds. He probably hadn't been out of the hospital very long.

Donna rushed into the room with the few emergency supplies we had at our disposal—and there wasn't much. I hadn't counted on attempting to resuscitate a newborn during my second month of practice. We had adult strength epinephrine, known to the uninitiated as adrenaline, needles, and syringes for injection, but not much else.

"What's his name?" I was trying to calm the family, not to mention myself, when my medical training finally went into auto pilot after the initial, mind-numbing shock of being handed an apparently deceased infant.

"His name is James Junior; we call him Jimmy."

"That's a fine name." I was rapidly examining the child while trying to listen to the near hysterical mother relate her story.

My examination disclosed a normal fontanelle, commonly called the soft spot, with no evidence of meningitis based on abnormal bulging and no unusual sagging to indicate dehydration. Examination of the eyes revealed unreactive pupils. Using a tongue blade, I carefully opened the mouth to visualize the throat. No obvious obstructions.

In the background I could hear Donna questioning the parents. No, he hadn't choked. Yes, he'd been responsive when they'd first entered the drugstore. Yes, he'd had a slight fever at the pediatrician's. They had waited thirty minutes after the shot before leaving, and there had been no reactions. Little Jimmy had seemed to be doing all right in that office, though he hadn't been interested in his bottle on the way back home, which was a little unusual.

Meanwhile, I was proceeding rapidly with my evaluation. No breath sounds. No heartbeat. Extremities all cyanotic. No spontaneous movements. Carefully looking at his back, I noted a meningomyelocele four centimeters in diameter.

It seemed as though hours had passed, when no more than one or two minutes had gone by since their arrival at our door.

"Folks, why don't you take a seat? If you don't mind watching you can see what we do. If it bothers you, though, please go back to the front waiting area with the rest of your family. As you can see, I already have him on his back, I'm using my index and middle finger to push on his chest, attempting to pump blood through his little body, and we'll be sending little puffs of air into his mouth. My nurse, Donna, will assist me."

The young husband shook his head in resigned consternation, put his arm around his wife's shoulders, and gently turned her toward the door and the outer waiting room. "Kathy, I don't think you oughta watch this. I'll take care of her, Doc."

Reluctantly the young woman allowed herself to be guided from the room by her insistent husband. I was sure this was for the best.

Donna and I continued with CPR, for we had no other recourse. We hoped, of course, for a miracle but had no emergency supplies for such a disaster as this.

"We had better time what we're doing, Donna. I don't have a good feeling about this, but we need to be as professional as possible."

Donna nodded in tacit understanding, and I noticed tears trickling down her cheeks. She continued administering intermittent puffs of air to allow the little chest to rise—the lungs to expand—whenever I motioned to her.

About ten minutes into the cycle I glanced at the doorway as a tall, kindly appearing man entered the room.

"Hello, folks. I hope you don't mind, Doctor, nurse, but I'm the Wagoners' minister. My name is Rev. White. I promised I would have a prayer for the baby and for you while you work. I'll just sit over here in the corner out of your way. I appreciate what you're doing."

"It doesn't look good, Reverend. We can use all the help we can get. We don't have a lot to work with here, and this baby is in grave condition."

"I know, Doctor—I know. But just you go ahead while I pray."

Donna kept track of the minutes, and I lost track of time. I knew in my heart that our endeavors were futile, but I had so little to work with in a physician's office intended for outpatients . . . where this kind of tragedy isn't supposed to happen.

About fifteen minutes into the resuscitative effort I turned to Donna. "Do you think you could draw up just one-tenth of a milliliter of the epinephrine. I know it isn't for babies, but we have nothing else; it's the smallest dose we can give now."

Donna still couldn't answer aloud, but she nodded affirmatively and began drawing up the medication. She remained professional throughout, cleansing the top of the epinephrine vial with a clean alcohol pad before inserting the needle on a one-milliliter syringe, carefully drawing up one-tenth of a milliliter, and preparing to administer the injection.

"Just inject into the lateral thigh, and we'll hope for a response."

Following the injection she quickly resumed her position at the baby's head, where she continuing sending puffs of air. Unfortunately, there was no response other than a brief muscular jerking.

Pausing briefly to listen, I quickly determined that there was still neither heartbeat nor spontaneous respiration.

We resumed our resuscitative effort, as time seemed to stand still. I knew it was futile but I couldn't get myself to stop. Rev. White observed us sympathetically before finally voicing the obvious: "I don't think he's going to survive—do you, Doctor?"

"No, Rev. White. I don't believe he will. I wish there were more we could do."

"Doctor, you and your nurse have made a fine effort. I know you've been trying for over a half hour, but sometimes the Lord just wants to call his little lambs home to be with Him. This is a good family; they won't blame you."

"It's just that I never expected anything like this. Sure, I knew my patients would sometimes die, but to lose a tiny baby in my second month in practice—it's overwhelming."

Rev. White nodded sagely and assented, "Death is never easy, Doctor. You and I have chosen to deal with it often in our respective ministries. I try to heal souls, and you try to heal bodies. I'm glad to hear you're also interested in the souls of your patients. Whenever you think it appropriate, I believe we can talk to the family."

Rev. White was a wise man. He wasn't, I realized, there only for the family, but also for me and my staff.

Donna and I stopped all resuscitative efforts and stood in stunned silence for a few moments. I listened one last time in the vain hope that I had missed any heartbeat or respiratory effort, but there was nothing—nothing at all.

As we made our way down the hallway I tried to rehearse what I would say. It's never easy to break news of death to a family, especially when a child is the victim. But I didn't need to say much; my expression told the story, for Kathy took one look upon our entering the room and collapsed into her husband's arms. James held her close, rocking her gently as she wept.

Their minister made his way to Kathy's side, placed his hand gently on her head, and offered a brief prayer of comfort. Her parents were visibly affected as well; Nancy cried softly, while Mark stared at the floor, head bowed and hands folded.

Words seemed superfluous now, but I felt compelled to say something. Pulling up a chair beside the young parents and seating myself, I maintained silence until they had become somewhat composed.

After several minutes they both looked expectantly, awaiting whatever it was I might have to say.

"I'm so sorry for your loss. I want you to know that your baby didn't suffer during our efforts. He never showed any signs of life returning, so there was no pain. Nothing I can say or do will bring him back, but I want you to know I'm here for you and your family if you have more questions, or if I can help in any way."

By now the waiting room was filling up. Art McKay had arrived with two EMTs; the ambulance was idling at the curb with red lights flashing.

"Thanks for coming, Art, but little Jimmy passed away."

As it happened, Art was also the county coroner, meaning that he still had work to do. By now Christine had canceled the rest of the afternoon appointments and rescheduled the patients for the next day. This was a wise decision, since we would be here for a while.

The pediatrician's office had to be contacted, Art McKay had legal documents to fill out, and the family remained in the office in the initial throes of their grieving. Art spoke briefly on the phone with the other physician's office to confirm the cause of the sudden death.

Pneumonia was confirmed to be the diagnosis, along with prematurity and meningomyelocele, a condition typically resulting in paralysis of the lower extremities due to the spine being incomplete, allowing a herniation of the spinal cord and nerve roots externally onto the back. If Jimmy had lived, this would have required surgical closure, as the condition poses a high risk for meningitis.

My expectation was that the family would never again want to see me, let alone darken my doorway, but to my amazement the entire extended family, including uncles, cousins, and others, became some of my most faithful patients.

As for Rev. White, he extolled our praise all over town, speaking highly of my staff and myself for caring so much for this young family.

The first gray light of morning was just filtering through the window when I blinked my eyes open, gazed around the room to regain my bearings, and realized I had finally slept a little. With a groan I pulled the recliner upright and heaved myself out of the chair.

Remembering Kathy once again, I hurriedly dialed the hospital operator and asked for Ann Kilgore. I knew she would be on night duty as supervisor and would be aware of everything that was happening.

Following the storm there was a little static on the line while I waited, but finally her familiar voice came over the phone.

"Hello, Ann. This is Dr. Matlock. Do you know how Kathy Wagoner is doing?"

"I don't think she's awake yet, since it's only 5 a.m., but she has done well during the night. But there is one thing: she's losing the baby. No excessive bleeding, though. She's young and will recover quite nicely. The whole family has camped out in the waiting rooms and cafeteria. I don't think they'll leave until you give your verdict, so we'll be glad to see you. I can't keep enough coffee on for that gang."

That episode occurred more than forty years ago now. I cared for that family for many years, but as far as I know Kathy Wagoner was never again able to carry a baby to full term. I sent her to various gynecologists before talking adoption with the family. The couple was finally able to adopt a little boy, and I'm sure he was greatly loved. They eventually moved away, perhaps to escape the scene of so much sorrow, so I don't have all the details.

SHOULDER PAIN AND DEMON WHISKY

A ndrew Morgan was a thirty-four-year-old gentleman who came to see me for the first time for shoulder pain. Andrew worked for one of the pharmaceutical companies located near Glen Falls. He was neatly dressed in casual business attire with gray slacks, a light blue shirt, and a dark blue tie. Andrew stood five feet eight inches tall, had dark brown hair, was clean shaven and somewhat pale, but had a pleasant, if somewhat anxious, countenance.

"I'm glad to meet you, Mr. Morgan. What can I do to help you today?"

"Just call me Andrew, Doc. That's how I'm known to my friends."

I nodded at him, smiled, and indicated that he should go on.

"Something's wrong with my shoulder—just the right one. The problem is, I'm right-handed. I work in the office— no heavy lifting or anything like that—but I'm having trouble just lifting light boxes. I never had anything like that before."

I glanced down at his chart before setting it back on the rack. (Each of my examining rooms has a pull-down rack at just the right height for me to stand while writing and making progress notes. I try to do most of this after each patient conversation, however. Patients tend to get distracted if the doctor isn't making eye contact.)

"I see by your information that your pain isn't always the same. Can you describe it more fully to me?"

"That's true. There's a dull ache that I feel a good deal of the time around the top of my shoulder, not particularly over the joint but more over the top of the rib cage. At other times I get a stabbing pain with certain movements of my arm; it even goes down toward my elbow a little ways. Sometimes it gets better if I reposition my arm right away. I also wake up at night with pain—not every night, just some nights. And I have a slight nagging cough. If I cough too hard—boy, is there a sharp pain in the shoulder around the collarbone!"

"Have you had any injuries that you can recall?"

"No sir, I've wracked my brain and can't think of anything unusual. No heavy lifting, no collision with a doorway, no recent weekend sports—nothing at all."

"From your information, I also see that you smoke cigarettes. Have you been doing that very long?"

"I'm ashamed to say, it, Doc, but I started when I was fourteen—really stupid, wasn't it? My older brother was smoking, and I thought it looked cool. I've been a two-pack-a-day man since the age of twenty, and I don't seem to be able to quit. Maybe you can help me after we find out what's going on."

"I'll be happy to. First, let's just examine you. And one more thing: Have you lost any weight?"

"Strange you should ask, but I just noticed this week that my pants are looser. I had to tighten my belt another notch. If your scales are any indication, I might be down twelve pounds."

I ran through an otherwise negative review of systems with Andrew before instructing him to get him into a gown while I stepped out of the room.

"All set, Andrew?"

"All set."

"I'll do a general physical exam to evaluate your overall health, as well as check this area that you're concerned about."

My general exam follows a routine; I find the details much easier to remember and record if I'm systematic and consistent in my approach. Especially with new patients, I sometimes detail out loud what I'm doing, giving them an understanding of the evaluation.

Thus, I began, "Eye motion and pupillary reflexes are normal. Mouth and throat clear. Teeth appear in good condition. No postnasal drip. Neck palpation normal. No spine tenderness over the posterior neck or upper back. No enlargement of the thyroid. No abnormal masses felt. Chest clear to auscultation and percussion. Evaluation of the heart reveals no murmurs or gallops. Heart rate and rhythm are regular. Abdominal examination normal. No apparent enlargement of the liver or spleen. Genitalia are that of a normal adult male. Rectal exam to be completed at next visit per your request. Extremities normal. Reflexes normal in upper and lower extremities. Right shoulder with full range of motion but with pain precipitated. Tenderness over right clavicle laterally and perhaps over upper rib cage on the right. Once again, I'm going to feel the soft tissues of the neck and armpit. This might hurt just a little; I'm checking for lymph nodes to be sure they're normal—that is, if I can feel them at all."

I spent a little time carefully palpating the neck and then the axillary lymph nodes, particularly on the right side. It isn't unusual for a patient to have swollen axillary lymph nodes. This is the body's way of filtering out bacteria that might enter through a wound—even a superficial one—of the involved extremity. Finally, I went back over the anterior and lateral neck and clavicular area. I noted that he was tender over the distal right clavicle, and somewhat over the right upper rib cage as well. He flinched every time I pushed with any pressure at all in a couple of locations.

"Why don't you get dressed while I step out and write some orders for you. There are some lab tests and X-rays you'll need to have done. I'll be back momentarily to discuss what might be going on."

Donna anticipated my next move and had already prepared X-ray and lab forms with his name, address, and identifying information on them. All I had to do was check off the orders and sign the paperwork. A good nurse is worth her weight in gold, as Donna was in the habit of proving on a regular basis.

"Thanks, Donna. Are there any more patients to see?"

It was nearing the end of the day, and already I was planning for evening rounds at the hospital—but not before a home-cooked meal with my family.

"No, Doctor. This will wrap it up. Christine and I are already straightening up the other rooms in preparation for tomorrow. Anything else you need done?"

"No. You ladies think of everything. Thanks so much. He won't need anything else besides a prescription for pain and basic instructions. He'll be out shortly, and we can lock up for the night."

Knocking on the door, I reentered the room upon hearing Andrew's reply that he was dressed. I sat down across from him and began, "Other than tenderness over your clavicle, or collarbone, and upper rib cage on the right, as well as some pain with movement of your shoulder, I didn't find swollen lymph glands or anything else I can diagnose with certainty.

"Your problem could be the result of a minor injury or could stem from a deeper problem in the bones or lung tissue. I didn't find any abnormal lymph nodes or glands in your neck or under your arm. That's a good thing.

"You'll need to have some tests done. This form is an X-ray request to evaluate your right shoulder and chest. I want a PA and lateral chest X-ray. The PA view is taken from your back but gives an excellent picture of your entire chest structures. The lateral view is taken from the side for completeness to look behind the heart and other areas that are harder to see on the first view. The technician will also do special X-rays of your shoulder.

"This other form is for blood work. You'll need a complete blood count and a panel of chemistry tests to check your electrolytes, renal, and liver functions.

"If you can get the tests done right away, you can make another appointment for three or four days from now to go over everything together. I also want you to have some pain medication. Since you're in a good deal of pain and have indicated no allergies, I wrote out Tylenol with codeine, 30 milligrams, that you can take every four hours, as needed. Since you work for a pharmaceutical company, I'm sure you know this could make you sleepy, so you may not be able to take it while you work. If you would like a note to be off for the next couple of days, I can do that for you. The only other alternative is to just use Tylenol during the day and take the combination pill at night.

"Do you have any questions?"

"No, I believe you've answered everything for me. I'll try to go ahead and get the tests tonight if the X-ray and lab are still open. And I don't need a note. I'll just use Tylenol during working hours. I don't like to miss."

"Of course, the blood work won't be fasting, but for what we're testing it should be okay. The blood sugar won't be diagnostic unless it's extremely high, but there wasn't any sugar in the urine dipstick the nurse checked a while ago. So I'm not expecting diabetes at this point. If you get the tests tonight, by late tomorrow afternoon I'll probably have the results; you can make an appointment for two days from now if you'd like."

"I'll do that, Doc. I'm beginning to get worried. Thanks for being thorough, and I'll see you in two days."

❖

At about 7:30 that evening I made my way to the radiology department following brief evening rounds. My hospitalized patients were all stable, and I wanted to check whether Andrew had been in for his shoulder and chest X-rays.

Approaching the X-ray department, I met Tracy hanging up X-rays in the film room for viewing by the radiologist the next day.

"Hello, Tracy. Do you know if my patient Andrew Morgan has been in yet?"

"Yes, he's been in. I'm just now hanging up X-rays on a different patient, but if you'll give me about one minute, as soon as I make sure these are okay I'll let this patient go and put his X-rays up for you."

"Go right ahead, Tracy. I'm anxious to see them."

"He was sure nervous about these films. He wanted me to read them for him, but I told him I'm only an X-ray technician. I'm not allowed to give formal readings, but you need to see these films."

"I suspected something serious."

"Your suspicions were right, Doctor. Just a second, and I'll be right back."

Within minutes Tracy and I were staring at the chest X-ray. There was no doubt about the source of Andrew

Morgan's pain. An obvious tumor in the apex of the right lung had already eroded the distal end of the right clavicle or collarbone. It was an irregular, fluffy mass without any well-defined borders, the classic picture of cancer.

"Well, Tracy, you were right. That's a Pancoast tumor—unfortunately, not a very promising prognosis. And he's only thirty-four years old. I'll have to get him to a cancer specialist right away. Thanks for your help, Tracy."

I was just about to leave the hospital when I was paged overhead by the emergency room. One of my patients was there and wanted to see me. All I wanted to do was go home to my family, but with a sigh of regret I made my way to the emergency department.

Ann Kilgore, the evening supervisor, was assisting in the emergency department as they were quite busy, and the regular emergency nurse couldn't handle everything by herself.

"Good evening, Doc. Kyle Edwards is here, and he insists you take care of him. He's in Room 3. Good luck."

I didn't like the silly grin on her face when she said that; now I was sure something unpleasant awaited me. Reluctantly, I entered the room to greet Kyle.

"Hello, Kyle. What in the world did you do to yourself?"

Kyle had multiple lacerations to both of his upper arms and forearms. There had been an attempt to clean them up already with saline solution, but he had apparently thrashed around and had all the dressings back off, half of them in the floor. Blood trickled down his arms and hands, and there was blood all over the sheets, cart railings, and floor.

Ann Kilgore entered the room, still smiling, and scolded Kyle.

"Kyle, I told you to lie still. Now look at the mess you've made. I'll have to clean you up all over again." She was trying hard not to laugh.

"I'm shor, shor, shorry nurse. Didn'a mean to make a mesh—I mean mess."

Ann had donned a gown and gloves to protect herself. This occurred well before what would come to be known as the AIDS epidemic; that medical disaster waited in the future. However, we understood that blood had infectious potential—not to mention that it could ruin clothing!

Unfortunately, Kyle had nineteen significant lacerations that needed suturing, some as long as six or seven inches. It was going to be a long night.

While Kyle was having his wounds cleansed a second time, housekeeping mopped the floor, and I donned a gown, gloves, and shoe covers.

Finally, we were all set to start, and I had several packs of suture laid out to use. I selected a 5-0 suture with a cutting needle, drew up a large vial of one percent lidocaine for local anesthesia, and prepared for a lengthy process.

As I began to work I asked Kyle once again, "What happened, Kyle? You still haven't told me."

"Doc, my sis made me mad. I jus' got even with 'er."

"I hope you didn't hurt her, Kyle."

"Nope. Shucks. Would na' hurt Sis. But I got even."

"How did you get even, Kyle?"

"She has this storm door she is too proud about. Jus' rammed my arms through it. Made beautiful mesh. Yes sir—I got even."

We had Kyle reclined at about a thirty degree head elevation while I sutured one extremity at a time.

Without warning he sat bolt upright, nearly tossing everything onto the floor, and announced, "Doc, know what's wrong wis me? Too much Jack Daniels."

Laughing uproariously, he lay back down on the cart while we attempted to maintain a sterile field—nearly impossible with this patient.

"Kyle, please try to stay still; this isn't an easy job, and you're making it harder."

But Kyle was really plastered. About every three to five minutes he would ask whether I knew what was wrong with him, sitting up and repeating with finality, "too much Jack Daniels." In his fogged brain he couldn't remember having filled me in on the answer over and over again.

After about ten or twelve repetitions I began losing my patience. When yet again he asked his infamous question, I decided to answer, perhaps not in my calmest voice! "Too much Jack Daniels!"

Unfortunately, he sat up yet again, a look of utter astonishment on his flushed face and surgical instruments flying to the floor with his thrashing. Gazing at me with new respect, he exclaimed to Ann Kilgore, "Boy, he sure knows his whiskey!" After that he stayed relatively quiet and allowed us to finish the procedure.

Evidently Kyle surmised that I could tell what he had drunk by the odor on his breath—and thought highly of one he believed to be a fellow drinking man—which I most decidedly am not. But since he was quiet I let it go.

After all of 139 stitches, Kyle was ready to leave. Slightly more sober now that two hours had passed, he hadn't forgotten that I had correctly answered his whiskey riddle and now wanted to shake my hand: "Doc, you shore know your whiskey—best diagnoser I ever saw."

As Kyle exited the department with his buddies, Ann Kilgore and the ER nurse began to laugh hysterically. I knew I was in for some long-term ribbing.

Once again I was seated in my examination room with Andrew Morgan. It's always hard to relate bad news to people, to tell them the last thing they want to hear. I've been amazed at how often people stoically take whatever information I might convey, some even seeming not to hear my words or register their meaning. Andrew was new enough to my practice that I had no idea what his response would be.

My patient sat stiffly upright in his chair in the examining room, awaiting the inevitable, hands tightly clasped together and nervously swallowing and clearing his throat.

"Hello, Andrew. Would you like some water to clear your throat?"

"Yes, that would be nice. It feels all dry."

After a drink of cool water, he seemed to relax just a little.

"Thanks. That helped a lot."

"You're welcome, Andrew."

Hesitating, I pulled out the lab test and X-ray results from his file so I would make certain not to miss anything. It's easy, I've found, to make a mistake during a tense situation.

"Andrew, your lab tests all look good except that you're a little anemic. Your hemoglobin is down at 12.5 and should be at least 14.0. Your blood sugar, electrolytes, liver, and kidney functions are all normal. That's all good news, except for the slightly low blood count.

Unfortunately, there's a tumor in the apex or top of your right lung. That's probably what's causing all the pain in your chest and shoulder."

Andrew sat as stiffly as a board, not blinking an eye; the only indication he had heard what I said was that he began clasping and unclasping his hands.

"Are you all right, Andrew?"

Heaving a ragged sigh, he relaxed, slumping in the chair. "Yes, Doctor, I'll be all right. I suspected something like this all along. I'm not really surprised."

I remained silent to give him time to process the information, and then he asked, "Well, what's the next step?"

"First, you have a tumor that's likely malignant. I'll need to get you to see an oncology specialist as soon as possible. Do you know any oncologist you'd like to see?"

"No—whoever you say will be fine."

"You might want to think about it. There are centers that specialize in cancer treatment, but all oncologists are highly trained in the treatment of tumors. Second, you'll need to remain as optimistic as possible about your care. Science is making great strides in the treatment of cancer, and this may well be curable. They have options for radiation, chemotherapy, and good general medical care that weren't available ten or fifteen years ago. The important thing is to get started right away."

"I'll take your advice and start right in with therapy. Let me talk to my wife and family tonight; I'll call tomorrow and let you know about going to a cancer center or receiving treatment by an oncologist in Indianapolis. At least I assume that's where I'll have to go."

"Yes, that would be a good way to handle this."

Andrew was my last patient of the day, and I walked him to the door. Before he left I shook his hand and counseled, "Andrew, don't give up. This may be a highly treatable situation. Please know that I'm here for you if you need anything—and I'll pray for you."

"Thanks, Doc. I appreciate it. Maybe I should take the advice you gave me the first time and quit smoking."

With that Andrew was out the door. He and his family elected treatment in a major medical center that specialized in cancer therapy, but I'm sorry to report that he didn't reach the age of thirty-six, succumbing to his lung cancer—one that is most often the result of smoking.

This particular form usually doesn't affect one so young, but our bodies are all different due at least in part to inherited traits, and we all handle noxious stimuli differently. I have cared for many who have smoked into their eighties, often developing COPD at the very least, but I've also witnessed many dying at a relatively young age from cancer of the lung.

A CHRISTMAS GIFT

I had been making late evening rounds in the hospital when the emergency department paged me, informing me that one of my patients was there. On this evening I had several elderly people in the hospital, at least one of whom, Mr. Brown, was very unstable with congestive heart failure.

I was studying his chart, noting the medications given and the amount of diuresis, or fluid output of the kidneys. Since I had been in to see him early in the morning he had made very little progress; his heart was utterly worn out.

I had just finished talking with his fragile, anxious wife for the second time since 9:00 a.m. when I heard the page. As the voice of the switchboard operator again sounded over the PA system, I placed Mr. Brown's chart back on the rack with a sigh and picked up the telephone.

My patients were definitely learning my habits. It seemed as though I couldn't make hospital rounds any longer without someone showing up in the emergency room. A wave of self-pity swept over me as I learned that a young man was waiting to see me. Why couldn't he be satisfied to see the emergency physician? Why did he have to see me? Why did this always happen to me?

Striding into the emergency department, I found Nurse Jensen on duty.

"Hello, Dr. Matlock. Your patient is in Exam Room 4. Here's his chart."

Scanning the data, I saw that the patient was Mark Bradshaw, a twenty-nine-year-old male complaining of chest pain. I vaguely knew who he was since his family had been coming to me for a while. He had three children, ranging in age from three to eight, and a wife who was also in her late twenties. I noted that the nurse had recorded a normal set of vital signs for Mark. With a final sigh of resignation I made my way to Room 4.

The young man lying on the hospital cart clutching his chest appeared sad and apprehensive. His head was propped up as he anxiously studied the cardiac monitor attached to him. A continuous rhythmic beep announced every heartbeat as he nervously rubbed his pectoral muscles. Becoming aware of my presence, he gave an embarrassed cough and looked up at me with haunted eyes.

"Hello, Doc. Thanks for coming. My chest hurts real bad. I don't know if this is a heart attack or what. My dad died with a coronary, and I know I smoke too much. It feels just like a knife is cutting into me."

I couldn't help but notice Mark's uncombed hair and disheveled clothing. He wore faded blue jeans with holes in both knees and had on a pair of old tennis shoes with the soles torn about halfway off, revealing well-worn stockings, also with holes. His body gave off a faint odor of perspiration, and he appeared to be the picture of abject despair. Taking a shallow breath while splinting his chest muscles with his hand, he looked up at me pitifully, as though resigned to what he assumed would be my response.

As I gazed at him lying there in utter hopelessness, I no longer felt so sorry for myself. Surely, this man knew the meaning of trouble.

"When did you first notice the pain, Mark?" I asked while trying to collect my thoughts.

"About two days ago, Doc. I was trying to pick things up around the house when this awful stabbing in my chest began. It hurts worse to take a deep breath; everything gets black for a while. Then these pains get a lot worse."

While I examined Mark, I couldn't help but wonder what was going on in his life. He didn't have a fever or cough of any significance, and the constellation of circumstances didn't make medical sense. What he related didn't sound like true cardiac symptoms, but it was apparent he was under severe duress.

As I listened to his heart with my stethoscope, I noticed that he took intermittent deep sighing breaths, after which he exhaled with a sobbing sound. His hands were visibly shaking, and tears were welling up in his eyes as he struggled to compose himself.

"Mark, I'm going to have the nurse run an EKG to be sure, but I don't believe you're having a heart attack. Tell me, what's been going on in your life recently? Are you under any stress?"

Like pent-up floodwaters bursting forth from a breached dam, great sobs of grief racked his body as tears coursed down his cheeks, and he trembled with emotion.

"You know, Cathy left me and the kids, Doc. Two days ago—she told me she couldn't take it anymore. She took all her clothes and things and left. The kids were all crying and everything, and I begged her to stay, but she said she wouldn't be back."

It was a little while before I could trust my voice to speak again as I shared in this young man's agony. I really didn't know what I could say that might alleviate the depth of his sorrow, so I finally asked, "What happened to cause her to leave?"

"Dr. Matlock, I've been out of work for six months now. I don't want to accept charity, but I had to get food stamps to feed my family. My work was only seasonal anyway, so I couldn't get unemployment. I didn't finish high school, and I've never been anything more than an odd job man.

"Bill collectors took our beat-up old car back a long time ago. The telephone company disconnected our phone because I couldn't pay them. At least they can't call to hassle me now. But what really hurts, Doc, is that before we at least had each other. Now that's gone too."

He broke down again, evidently too overwhelmed to continue. But then he went on: "What's even worse is that she let the kids know she didn't want them either. That's what hurt me the worst of all. She hurt our sweet kids. Please, Doc, please say that my heart's all right. If something happens to me, my kids won't have anybody."

Muted sobs again racked Mark's frame as he lay on the hospital cart trying to control his emotions. I noticed that his body was altogether too thin; it didn't look as though he was getting much of the food purchased with those food stamps. The only luxury he apparently allowed himself was the generic cigarettes he smoked.

He and I both knew he shouldn't abuse his body with tobacco, but for the life of me I couldn't bring myself to mention the obvious to him just then.

Excusing myself, I stepped back out of the room and made my way to the main desk. Handing the chart to Mrs. Jensen, I asked her to do an EKG on my patient. I also ordered a chest X-ray to rule out pneumonia or the collapse of one lung, a not unusual occurrence in smokers.

How helpless I felt in the face of such sorrow. I knew I had little to offer, but I could at least reassure him about his heart. The heart trouble he was experiencing wasn't a type I could do anything about.

I felt a sense of utter helplessness steal over me, a feeling that was becoming all too common, not just for me but within the practice of medicine. I have no doubt many other physicians have experienced the same desolation over the years when confronted with immense sorrow or loss far beyond the scope of their ability to assuage.

Over in the corner of the department, I noticed an EMT entertaining three youngsters with children's books. This had to be Mark's children, for it went without saying he had no money for a babysitter.

"Bless you, John, for caring," I whispered under my breath. Three precious children had momentarily forgotten their own problems, having been transported vicariously into the wonderful world of childhood imagination as John read to them of dragons, knights, and fair maidens.

Reviewing the EKG and chest X-ray as they became available, I realized that the situation was just as I had suspected: normal chest X-ray and EKG, but a brokenhearted man. It's a priceless human experience to work with people who really care. This was quickly brought back to me as Nurse Jensen emerged from around the corner.

"Doctor, we have some free samples of mild sedatives and some snacks from the cafeteria for Mark and the kids. It looks like he needs food and medicine, and I doubt he can afford a prescription right now."

"Thanks, Mrs. Jensen. You are so right."

It seemed very little for us to do, but at least Mark knew some people who were concerned about him and his family.

I was all too quickly caught up once again in the relentless pace of my vocation and practice. Once in a while something would remind me of Mark Bradshaw and his plight, but I ruefully admit that I was too preoccupied for any personal involvement with his family.

Once again I was making late rounds in the hospital when the familiar voice of the telephone operator came over the PA system, requesting that I call the emergency department. Since I was nearby reviewing an X-ray, I just decided to walk over.

"Hello, I believe you were paging me," I announced, noticing that John, the EMT, and Nurse Jensen were both on duty again.

"Oh yes," replied Mrs. Jensen. "Do you remember the young man whose wife left him and the children? Well, he's back again and says he has something in his eyes."

A bitter, blustery wind carrying wet snowflakes blew in as the automatic doors opened, announcing the arrival of yet another emergency patient. The blowing snow reminded me that it was almost Christmas; as usual, my shopping wasn't nearly finished. I would have to step on it if I wanted to finish on time. I had several requests from my own three children as to what they wanted Santa to bring them only a few days hence.

As I entered the eye examination room, I saw Mark seated in the exam chair wearing a tattered light jacket and the same torn jeans he'd had on before. He sat in the chair rubbing his reddened eyes, which were draining and irritated.

"What happened, Mark?"

"I was rummaging through some trash cans behind the lumber yard, and the wind blew some wood dust, ashes, and maybe some chemicals into my eyes. The nurse washed them, but they still hurt like something's in them."

A brief examination did disclose that there were still tiny particles in his eyes. Placing some topical anesthetic drops in each eye, I asked, "What were you trying to find at the lumber company? There are probably a lot of harmful chemicals in those old wood scraps, not to mention the discarded ashes that blew in your face."

Briefly pausing, I continued, "These drops will take effect in a few moments, but they'll burn briefly at first. After a minute or two I'll have Nurse Jensen do a more thorough irrigation of your eyes. You just couldn't tolerate the degree of pain with the first irrigation to allow her to finish. I want to get all of the particles out, as there could be some harmful chemical mixed in with the wood scraps.

As I pushed the buzzer summoning Nurse Jensen, Mark haltingly began a subdued explanation of what he had actually been up to.

"Well, Doc, you know it's almost Christmas. My kids told me they would be happy if they could have some building blocks to play with. I told them I was sure Santa would at least bring them some blocks, but I guess it wasn't very smart of me to make that promise. Now I don't know what to do."

His face clouded over as he continued, "If those blocks have chemicals in them, I don't think I'd better try that again. Wouldn't want my kids to be sick from chemicals."

Silence filled the room as Nurse Jensen coughed quietly from the hallway to announce her presence. As she entered the room, I could tell at a glance that she had heard the conversation. Her face was strangely pinched as she worked, and I couldn't help but notice the moisture in her eyes. For that matter, I had an uncomfortable lump in my own throat; I seemed to have lost all power of speech.

Once again I noticed Mark's shabby clothes. He wore an ill-fitting shirt beneath the light jacket, both stained with ashes from his latest endeavor. His face was drawn from misery and self-doubt. His wife had been true to her word; he hadn't heard from her since the day she'd walked out the door.

In the hallway I could once again hear John's sonorous voice reading children's books aloud. He was just finishing the story of a poor baby born in a stable in Bethlehem some two thousand years ago. How appropriate.

My eyes wandered back to Mark as he sat there looking so forlorn, clad in his cast-off clothing that someone at least two sizes bigger must have discarded or left in a church box for the poor. I noticed that his socks were soaked where snow had melted on the insides of his torn tennis shoe soles. It didn't look like as though he had shaved in several days; perhaps he was growing a beard to help keep his face warm.

Sadly, his children weren't much better off—with the exception that they were always cleaned up when he brought them in. It seemed as though he had simply lost interest in his own appearance, or perhaps the daily struggle to survive and care for his family preoccupied his thoughts.

Trying to sound casual, I asked, "Any luck finding work yet, Mark?"

Shaking his head, he mumbled, "No, no luck." Then, in a quavering voice, he added, "But I'm still trying."

Mark didn't cry during this visit, except for the tearing induced by the eye irritants. The truth was that he looked as though he had run out of tears.

When we finally finished and he'd been relieved of his pain, he gathered up his brood, motioning them to follow him out the door. Once again the automatic doors opened as the forlorn family marched resolutely out into the wintry night. Icy wind intermingled more snow within the warm atmosphere of the emergency department.

The four thin figures leaned as one into the icy wind, hunched over and heads downcast, inadequately clothed for such an inhospitable night.

Temporarily transfixed, we gazed out the window as the swirling snow quickly hid them and erased their footprints, blotting out any evidence that four destitute, desperate human beings had ever been there.

Nurse Jensen, John, and I found conversation uncomfortable for several minutes; there being no other patients to be seen at the moment, we simply sat in silence in the work station.

"I guess that's the end of the kids' Christmas," I finally began, but I found myself unable to complete the thought. Glancing up, I noticed a questioning look on John's face.

"Well, why not?" he exclaimed.

"Why not what?" Mrs. Jensen and I asked almost in unison.

"We've already taken up some funds for a few other needy families we know about. It's not too late to add them to the list. I just didn't think of it before."

"That's a great idea," Mrs. Jensen responded enthusiastically. "I'll leave word for the other shifts that we know of an especially needy family who won't have any Christmas without help. This'll be fun. I'll shop for the children myself."

"That's a wonderful idea. You two are special people. I want to help with this too. I know about what size clothes Mark wears. John and I can go to the men's department at Penney's together and find Mark some clothes and shoes."

"I'm game," put in John. "We'll do it!"

"I believe Mark is a worthy young man," I reflected, "—a little rough around the edges, perhaps, but nonetheless a basically good man trying to provide for his children and keep the family together. I take care of some men who are much better off than Mark who never do as much for their children."

"You're right about that, Doc. A lot of the people we see in here don't appreciate what they have," observed John.

And so it was done. The Bradshaw family was added to the list for Christmas just in time.

On Christmas morning I made early rounds to be able to spend the rest of the day with my family. I purposely made my way to the emergency department to wish the staff a merry Christmas. Upon entering the department, I saw John leaning against the counter, looking quite sleepy following a long night of holiday duty. On seeing me, however, he beamed a cheery smile in my direction and exclaimed, "Merry Christmas. I hope you have a little time off today."

"Merry Christmas to you too, John."

"Guess what, Dr. Matlock? We took a Christmas tree over to Mark Bradshaw's house last night, set it up for him, and loaded the place with packages all wrapped up. You should have seen those kids. It was the best Christmas gift I've received this year to see their sad little faces light up with such delight.

"I think I saw Mark Bradshaw smile for the first time since his wife left home. He was simply overcome with gratitude—kept repeating that he hadn't known anyone cared. I let him know these gifts were from a lot of other people at the hospital who care as well.

"He looked really great when he got all dressed up, and the kids' outfits were really something. I'm active in a church group, and I'm having Mark go to a class supper with me tomorrow night. He's actually looking forward to it.

"Also, the ER nurses prepared them a great Christmas dinner, and we got that all set up too."

John was barely pausing for breath, all evidence of drowsiness gone from his eyes. "You know, Doc, we help a lot of people here. But sometimes we get so caught up with our work that we forget the bigger picture of life.

"This was an especially wonderful holiday season—I'll never forget being able to touch the lives of needy people in our community. We plan on keeping track of this family, and I have some tips for Mark about a janitorial position that'll be opening up here at the hospital. I'm going to personally recommend him for the job.

"Our department has adopted the family as our special project, and we'll do all we can to make their lives a little more bearable. Well, Merry Christmas, Doc. Hope you have a great day with the family."

"Merry Christmas to you too, John. I hope you can introduce the poor child of the Bethlehem manger to Mark and his family through your church group. Human entanglements can make it tough to straighten out life's problems, but the answer to all human need is Jesus. It all comes down to sin, after all, and He's the One who came to save us from our sins."

"You're so right about that, Doc. Have a good one."

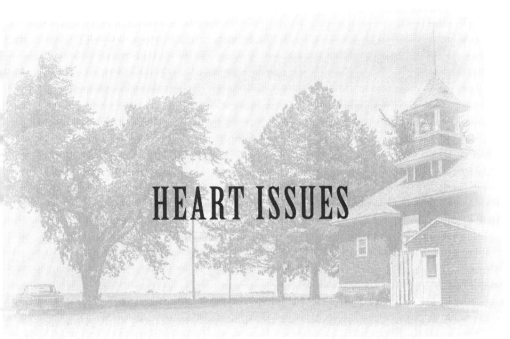

HEART ISSUES

Evelyn Wycoff was a pleasant, silver-haired lady when I first met her in the office. She had to be brought back and placed in a room ahead of several other patients after experiencing dizziness in the waiting room.

When I entered the room, Donna was at her side helping her get up on the examining table. Evelyn was pale, diaphoretic, and tremulous.

"Hello, Mrs. Wycoff. It looks like you aren't feeling very well today. Are you in pain or having trouble breathing?"

"I just felt a little faint, Doctor. And you can call me Evelyn; it sounds more natural to me."

"Very well, Evelyn. Are you feeling better now?"

"Thanks to your kind nurse, Miss Donna here, yes. I'm feeling better after being able to lie down on your examination table and have some sips of water."

I studied her chart for the vital information: "Age 73, widowed, lives with her unmarried 55-year-old son, doesn't want to have heroic rescue efforts in case of sudden serious illness or death, prefers palliative measures."

"I see by your chart that you haven't seen a doctor in over twenty years. You must have been very healthy for most of your life."

"Yes, Doctor. The good Lord has been very good to me."

"What kind of problem brings you in to see us today?"

I had already read Donna's notes that the patient was experiencing blackout spells, but I wanted to hear about it in her own words. I'm absolutely amazed at how often a patient will tell a nurse one thing and then turn around and tell the doctor another story altogether.

"I'm having strange sensations in my head sometimes. I was afraid maybe I would have a stroke, so I decided to get a check-up. If something's seriously wrong, I want time to make preparations."

"What's your urgency about making preparations, Evelyn?"

"Doctor, it's my son, Jimmy. He was born with birth defects—cerebral palsy, the doctor who delivered him called it. Now Jimmy—well he can walk, but he's clumsy and can't cook for himself. He wasn't able to get beyond the second grade in school and wouldn't be able to make it alone without my help; he just isn't educated enough. He doesn't have even a vague idea about money and the value of things. Jimmy's fifty-five now, but he needs someone to care for him."

After hearing her story, I was apprehensive about the situation, almost willing myself not to find anything serious.

She was obviously very nervous, and Donna stayed at her side, holding her hand, throughout the visit.

"Evelyn, I need to know more about your problem. In what situations do you feel like you'll pass out?"

"It usually happens if I get up too fast, walk too fast, or try to climb the stairs to my bedroom. I started sleeping in the recliner downstairs about a month ago. I feel better sitting up a little anyway; I can breathe better that way."

"So this has been going on for a while?"

"That's right, Doctor. But it seems to be getting worse."

"How so?"

"It happens more often now and with less exertion. All I did was walk for several feet from my car to your office, and I nearly went out in your waiting room. I was so terribly embarrassed. I wasn't trying to get to the head of the line."

Donna patted her hand, softly assuring her, "Now don't you worry about that. Everyone was glad you got here to get help. No one was unkind about it in the waiting area."

"Yes, your neighbors understand. So tell me more about your problem. What happens first, and is there any pain with the feeling of potential blackouts?"

"Well, once or twice there was some pain in my chest and throat, but it didn't last long."

"Did you ever have seizures?"

"No, I never did."

"What about rheumatic fever or a heart condition?"

"When I was very small, a doctor came to our house and advised my mother to keep me in all summer. I didn't get to play much. It was very boring for me."

"Do you know why that happened?"

"I had scarlet fever in the spring of that year. He said something about it affecting my heart—something about a murmur."

"Do you remember if you had any other symptoms? Possibly arthritis, rashes, or unusual jerking movements?"

"The only thing I remember was having a lot of aching for several months. But it finally all went away. Of course, now that I'm older I have some aches and pains. It's only to be expected when you get to be as old as I am now."

After several more questions I explained that I was going to conduct a general examination, after which we would discuss a further course of action. She nodded in understanding and squeezed Donna's hand tightly, glancing up at her as though for confirmation.

With Donna smiling and nodding back her approval, the patient looked back at me and sighed in resignation, "I guess we might as well get this over with."

Donna had already checked Evelyn's vital signs; her blood pressure was 100/80 lying down. Due to her dizziness Donna hadn't yet tried to get it from a standing position. The patient's pulse was 109; she was afebrile and breathing normally at rest.

We had the head of the examination table elevated a little, and I noticed mild jugular venous distention, or congestion of the great veins of the neck. Examination of the head, eyes, ears, and throat proved unremarkable for a woman of her age. Her lungs had a few moist rales at the posterior bases as we rotated her from side to side to listen, but it was her heart that drew my attention.

There was a loud, harsh systolic murmur occurring with each heartbeat; it was loudest at the upper right and left sternal borders and radiated toward the lower left chest as a softer murmur. Also, there was a soft, blowing type of murmur at the very apex of the heart, which I could hear best with her lying on her left side. I also noted a dynamic heaving of the heart muscle with each beat. Finally, I heard an intermittent soft third heart sound—called a gallop rhythm, meaning that three or more beats were present instead of the usual two.

The rest of the exam didn't take long. Her liver edge was slightly swollen below her right lower rib cage, and she had a little edema in her legs, along with obvious signs of both left and right heart failure. What really worried me, however, was the rapid heartbeat in conjunction with the fairly low blood pressure, even lying down.

Hesitating momentarily, I asked, "Do you feel well enough to stand up just long enough with our help so Donna can check your blood pressure in that position?"

"I feel a little better since lying here. I believe I can do it okay."

Even with our help, however, Evelyn struggled with getting up, to the point that I noticed her lips getting a little cyanotic with the effort.

"Are you sure you can do this?"

"I'll be fine, Doctor. Do whatever you have to."

Her blood pressure dropped to 85/70, with a pulse rate of 120, and we quickly returned her to the semi-reclined position on the exam table.

I drew up my chair beside the cart, and Donna remained standing at Evelyn's side. I wanted to be sure she understood everything I was about to say.

"Mrs. Wycoff," I began, but paused when I saw her frown. "I'm sorry—Evelyn, that's what you want to be called, isn't it?"

She smiled at me then and squeezed Donna's hand more tightly.

"I'll try this again. Evelyn, you have a condition known as congestive heart failure. Your heart is weak for some reason and isn't pumping enough blood to help you maintain consciousness in the upright position. That's why you faint or black out. I wish a simple pill would solve the problem, but from listening to your heart I believe you must have had rheumatic fever as a child and that it damaged your heart. I'm guessing that you've had problems for quite a while now but that they're just getting a lot worse. Am I right?"

Reluctantly, she gazed back at me and then once again looked to Donna for reassurance. Buoyed by my nurse's encouraging smile, she finally answered, "Yes, you're right. I've been slowly getting worse for many months now. Yesterday my heart raced so bad I thought I was going to die. But I just couldn't do that now, could I?"

"We sure don't want you to die, but what do you mean?"

"My son—Jimmy. There would be no one to care for him. See what I mean. I knew I couldn't die just then. So I sat in my recliner chair, had Jimmy turn the fan on me, leaned back, and prayed for all I was worth. I guess the Lord heard me, 'cause here I am."

This was going to be more challenging than I had suspected. My patient needed urgent admission to the hospital, but what to do about Jimmy . . . ? I knew I had to answer that question before she would likely consent to admission for treatment.

"This isn't going to be easy for you, but you need to be admitted to the hospital right away. I mean tonight."

"I know, Doctor. Believe me, I know. But I don't know how that's possible. Who would take care of Jimmy?

In those days before the government became extensively involved in the practice of medicine, life was much simpler. Social admissions were permissible in extenuating circumstances—something that would never occur legally in this regulated aspect of our current economy.

"Evelyn, listen carefully. Jimmy's at home by himself, I assume."

"That's right, Doctor."

"Does he know Art McKay very well?"

"Oh yes, Art has always been very kind to Jimmy. He even picks him up sometimes and lets him do odd jobs at the funeral home to make a little money. Then he takes him to the drugstore for an ice cream treat before dropping him back off at home."

"That's wonderful. Art's a prince of a fella. Now here's my thought: I can have Art come here to pick you up right away, and then swing by your home to get Jimmy. I know we have several bed vacancies right now, and I'll admit both of you. We'll check Jimmy out because at fifty-five he probably has a few minor problems of his own. We'll get you on the same medical unit so he can be nearby.

"I have a former teacher and friend who's an excellent cardiologist. He lives in Indianapolis but does consults for us in our county hospital; I'll get him to come and see you. He's very good and can help us figure out what to do for you."

"You think it's my heart, then? An old rheumatic fever-damaged heart?"

"That's correct."

"One more thing. Can you tell what this has done to my heart? I mean, what's the chance it can be fixed?"

"I believe you have a bad aortic valve with a condition we call aortic stenosis. That means it has become very narrow and isn't letting enough blood through at a time. That in turn causes your blood pressure to be low since not enough blood is pumping, and it results in blackouts if you try to do too much. In addition, the mitral valve has been affected, either by rheumatic fever or by a buildup of pressure because not enough blood is being let out of the heart.

Seeing her temporary confusion, I asked, "Donna, could you get that model of a heart out of the other exam room, please? It will make understanding simpler for her."

In less than thirty seconds Donna was back with the life-sized heart model to demonstrate the problem to Evelyn.

"Do you see that the heart has four chambers, two on each side?"

I waited for her to study the model and resumed when she indicated understanding. "Now, the left side of the heart is the power pump, and the right side is the volume pump. The left side has to pump the blood all the way to the feet and head. That's why it's the stronger side in normal people.

"The right side handles the basically same volume, but it mainly has to get the blood into the lungs—not nearly as hard a job."

When Evelyn was satisfied that she understood, I proceeded with my brief demonstration. "Your problem is mostly on the left side, I'm pretty sure. The outlet valve on the left, the aortic valve, is too tight; hence, blood is backing up. Then what we'll call the inlet valve on the left, the mitral valve, isn't closing enough. So it in turn is letting some of the blood that's supposed to flow to the body and head back into the lungs. That makes you short of breath. That's called left heart failure. Finally, the volume pump is feeling the back pressure, and your liver and legs are just beginning to swell up. That's what's known as right heart failure.

"It's a little more complicated than that—actually, a lot more complicated—but that's the basic explanation of what's happening to your body. This has to be resolved in order for you to live much longer. Do you understand what I'm trying to get across?"

"Yes, you've made it very plain that I have no choice but to do what you ask. So yes, I'll go to the hospital."

"Good. Donna will stay with you, and I'll have Art bring the ambulance right down. It shouldn't take him long to get here. He'll have oxygen to help you breathe better."

Following admission and gentle diuresis with Evelyn in bed, she was seen by my cardiologist teacher and friend. As disclosed later on through her cardiac catheterization in Indianapolis, she did indeed have both damaged aortic and mitral valves.

Procedures weren't as advanced at the time as they are today, but she was able to tolerate a brief operation to open the aortic valve and allow more blood to flow through to the body, followed by a more serious surgical effort—an aortic valve replacement. That relieved pressure on her only mildly damaged mitral valve, reversing the pressure that had caused her lungs to begin filling with fluid.

Amazingly, she had relatively normal coronary arteries; it was wholly a valvular problem that had led to the heart failure. Following her treatment in Indianapolis and a prolonged recovery, she would be able to be up and about without developing extremely low blood pressure and fainting. The pain had been anginal, or coronary induced, but only because of inadequate blood flow through the coronary arteries due to the tight aortic valve.

And Jimmy—well, no serious problems were diagnosed other than his cerebral palsy; he stayed with Art while his mother was hospitalized in Indianapolis, helping out around the funeral home and keeping the ambulance clean.

Evelyn would be our patient for several more years. Although she had a very damaged heart physically, it was helped along in the healing process by the loving nature of her mother's heart for Jimmy, her beloved son.

OBSTRUCTION

nother fine spring morning—robins trilling merrily in the treetops, grass turning green, Easter lilies poking their heads above the recently frozen soil, . . . and a full schedule in the office. It was OB and well-baby day; indeed, there was evidence of new life everywhere.

"How's the schedule for today, Donna?

"This morning we have seven established OB patients and two new OB patients scheduled. There are also three well babies to see—two you have delivered and one referred from the obstetrician in Mount Pleasant."

"How about the afternoon schedule?"

"It hasn't filled up yet, but we have seven so far."

I had learned by experience that a great way to build a practice was by practicing obstetrics. We'd had no obstetricians in our county for several years, and the patients had to travel miles if the family doctors were unwilling to deliver the babies. I was enjoying this part of the practice—except, of course, for the middle-of-the night deliveries. That was truly the hard part: learning to work all day and sometimes again all night.

During my training I had functioned as an intern on an OB floor for two months, although I had been only a senior student at the time. Still, I'd gained invaluable experience, including forceps deliveries, which family doctors used to be taught.

I enjoyed assisting new life into the world and preferred having the fathers in the room, an unusual practice for the 1970s. Nevertheless, our younger medical staff had been able to convince the older physicians and the hospital administration that this was appropriate. Most of us felt that the fathers would be more empathic after the deliveries, better able to appreciate what their wives had gone through, if they took part in the birth. Interestingly, only a few fathers declined that privilege. Most were happy to be there, supporting their wives and being introduced in this way to their children.

So far I had delivered normal babies without birth defects, or so I thought. That was about to change, though I had no inkling of it at the time. The morning went by quickly; all of my patients were doing well, except for one expectant mother who had been gaining too much weight. I sent her to the hospital for dietary consultation, as the problem appeared to be mainly due to excessive caloric intake; she had no appreciable edema, and all her vital signs were normal, with no signs of toxemia. She was suffering the effects of an eating binge that had likely been induced by her abnormal cravings during pregnancy.

To finish out the morning we regularly tried to schedule well-baby appointments. I preferred not to mingle obstetric patients, infants, and sick people in the waiting room at any given time. We attempted to have those who were ill or older come in the afternoon.

It was to be the last visit of the morning that would challenge my diagnostic abilities. Mary Abner, with her new baby, Ronnie, came in immediately before the lunch hour. Christine checked them in and helped Donna weigh little Ronnie to begin the appointment. As they conversed in the hall, I noticed that both Christine and Donna appeared concerned.

"Dr. Matlock, this baby is sick. His mother is very young—only seventeen—and probably should've brought him in yesterday, if not before. He's eight weeks old now but has been vomiting for a week. Now he's somewhat listless and less interested in his bottle. She's bottle feeding formula, by the way."

Little Ronnie, who had weighed eight pounds at birth, now tipped the scale at only eight pounds twelve ounces. "I realize this isn't the same scale as the hospital," Donna went on, "but he doesn't look well."

Donna tapped the chart, calling to my attention the notes she had made, not wanting to repeat them in the mother's presence. She had written, "Mary failed four-week postpartum check. Failed four-week appointment for

Ronnie. Not weighing him at home. Has no idea about his weight, other than she believes it is less now than a week ago."

I knew immediately that this was going to take a little more time than the ordinary well-child appointment. Little Ronnie did indeed appear ill. Mary was seated with her baby, rocking him gently in her arms.

"Hello, Mary. How are you and the baby doing today?"

"I'm okay, I guess, Doctor, but little Ronnie is sick. I think he has the stomach flu. He started vomiting earlier in the week. but it got a lot worse two days ago."

"I noticed that you didn't make it in for your own checkup."

"No. I'm okay, and I knew you were too busy already."

"Mary, we're never too busy to work you in at some point for your postpartum exam. We'll be glad to schedule it for you while you're here today, if that's okay with you."

"No, I don't think it'll be necessary. I'm really fine. You did a good job for me. I'm just worried about my baby."

"Whatever you say, Mary, but you ought to think about it. I can't give you any birth control pills without examining you again."

"That's okay. I really don't have any money. I'll go to Planned Parenthood for that. I haven't finished paying you yet, and I didn't know if you'd see me or not."

"I'd be glad to see you any time. We haven't been putting pressure on you for the rest of the money; you can pay it over time. Right now your health is what's important. But that's up to you. Now we'd better look at little Ronnie. Can you tell me what's been going on with him?"

Mary hesitated for a while, searching for words. She had dropped out of school early and was self-conscious when speaking to me, apparently sensing her lack of education. She was inordinately shy and diffident in her approach to other people as well. Her husband, William Abner, was nineteen and worked at the feed mill. He had finished high school, though just barely.

"He started spitting up a lot two weeks ago. Well, he spit up ever since he came home, and Ma said that isn't unusual."

"That's right; babies can spit up for several months. But vomiting and not gaining weight are definitely unusual. Can you tell me more about what's been going on the last two weeks?"

"He started spitting—more like vomiting—last week, and this week it's been real bad. He vomits all over himself. I ain't ever seen anything like it before."

"Does he have other symptoms, like diarrhea or fever?"

"No, just vomiting."

"His vital signs here are fairly normal; he has no fever, and his pulse is about one hundred. He seems to be breathing all right, but we need to get to the bottom of this as soon as possible. Babies can dehydrate very quickly and go into shock."

"I know. Ma said I better bring him today. I kept thinkin' he'd get better, but maybe not. You think he'll be okay?"

"We'll sure do our best to find out what's wrong and help him get better. Can you tell me how much formula he takes?"

"He did take four ounces at a time, but now he only takes one or two before he starts crying. He pulls up his little legs and acts like it hurts."

"How does he vomit—does it just run out of his mouth, or does it fly out?"

"It mostly flies out now. He even vomits down to his toes."

"Does he ever vomit anything that looks yellow, like bile?"

"No. Just formula."

"Could you give him a bottle now, and have us see what happens?"

Donna and I watched as the young mother opened her diaper bag and got out his formula. She seemed nervous and tense, as though she anticipated failure. The baby hadn't been fed for a little while, and he began to suck vigorously for a short time, after which he rejected the nipple, pulled his little legs up toward his abdomen, and began to cry, shaking all over. Mary sat him up to comfort him, and he began forcefully vomiting, beyond his feet and onto the floor.

"I wouldn't try anymore just now, Mary. That's what we call projectile vomiting. I suspect he may have a condition called hypertrophic pyloric stenosis—something that needs to be surgically corrected.

Donna, please help her get him undressed except for his diaper, and place him on the examination table."

I was pleased to note that Ronnie produced tears when he cried, a favorable sign that he wasn't severely dehydrated . . . yet. His mouth was moist, but he'd just had a bottle. The anterior fontanelle, the soft spot on the scalp, wasn't sunken in, as happens in dehydration—another good omen. However, I thought I detected a soft knot in the upper abdomen. Unfortunately, his diaper was dry—a less positive sign.

"Mary, he'll need to go to the hospital. We need to do a special X-ray, an Upper G.I. The radiologist will give him a very small amount of dye so he can swallow it. Then we can see what happens in his stomach. If something needs to be done, we have a surgeon who's very experienced in pediatric surgery. If it's okay with you, we'll have him take a look at your baby too."

"Okay. Can I call my ma? I want her to go with me. In fact, she'll have to take me. My husband has our car at work."

"Do you want to call him?"

"No. We need the money from his work. I'll have him come to the hospital after work. You won't do surgery right now, will you?"

"No. Ronnie will need to have some tests first to rule out early dehydration. We'll also try to get the X-ray done today. In addition, he'll get a small amount of IV fluids. If he needs surgery, it'll probably be tomorrow."

I have no doubt it was a long day for Mary and her husband as we awaited the results of the testing on their newborn son. As I suspected, the Upper G.I. revealed an obstruction at the pyloric valve of the stomach. Normally, the valve functions to close the stomach during early digestion and then opens to allow the passage of food and liquids.

In the case of pyloric stenosis, for some reason the valve becomes hypertrophied or enlarged, obstructing most of the flow through the valve. The condition typically affects newborns—especially first children, and boys more often than girls. Theories have proliferated as to the causes, but the etiology was poorly understood at that time.

At about 8:00 p.m. I found Mary and William in the hospital room with the baby. Both sets of parents were also there, all awaiting the report. Dr. Hendrick had been in and examined the baby; Doctor Rob had the perfect bedside manner, and the family was well pleased with him.

I introduced myself to the rest of the family and sat down to discuss the test results. I began, "Little Ronnie has a condition known as hypertrophic pyloric stenosis. That's a mouthful for such a little guy. It's a benign condition— no sign of cancer or anything permanent. However, it will require surgical correction. The good news is that the rest of his lab studies are very close to normal. He had only developed minimal dehydration. It's fortunate you brought him when you did.

"For reasons we don't completely understand, the outlet valve of the stomach to the small intestine enlarges and causes an obstruction so food can't go through properly. When that happens, the baby vomits forcefully and loses weight. If this goes on too long, it can cause serious dehydration, shock, . . . and even death, so we have to do something. I know he hasn't gained much weight, but you must have gotten enough down to keep him from getting dehydrated.

"I just stepped into the lounge area in the OR and spoke to Doctor Rob by intercom. He was doing a late emergency surgery but has already seen the films. He said he would stop by to see you after surgery, perhaps within an hour. He agrees that surgery is necessary. Do you have questions for me now?"

The family indicated understanding, so I excused myself, stating before leaving the room, "I'll be here early in the morning and will be with Doctor Rob in the OR when he does the surgery. I believe little Ronnie will be eating normally very soon."

The next day I assisted by holding retractors to expose the area of obstruction, but the procedure itself was brief. Dr. Hendrick was indeed an excellent children's surgeon. He easily located the pyloric valve, which was quite enlarged for a baby; made a simple incision in the muscle to allow the valve to open properly; and then quickly closed the surgical wound.

One of the most valuable and educational activities for my practice overall has been assisting in surgery on a weekly basis. I have found it helpful to see the pathology that has caused the patient's illness, in correlation with the presenting symptoms. In this fashion the information gleaned has been imprinted on my mind.

Little Ronnie Abner responded very favorably to surgery and was soon gaining weight. At my last contact with the family he was a healthy young boy.

Driving home from the hospital that day I had time to think about my medical training. I remember the day we began studying pediatric congenital abnormalities, especially those that could be corrected surgically. Little did I realize that I would be seeing several of those in my own practice. To me, and to most of my fellow students who weren't choosing pediatrics for a career, most of these cases seemed like red herrings—situations we would be unlikely to encounter frequently during our professional lives.

To my amazement, however, within a three-month period I delivered three boys with pyloric stenosis, each of whom had the condition surgically corrected by Rob Hendrick. Nor was that the end of it. I was to see several other congenital anomalies show up in the children I delivered, and I was more than grateful for the excellent education afforded me by Indiana University School of Medicine.

Indeed, red herrings seemed to be everywhere—the norm rather than the exception.

IT'S A MYSTERY

Mae Allison was among my first patients, having come to the office in Glen Falls during my initial week of practice, presenting as a delightful seventy-six-year-old widow—always upbeat, smiling, and frequently recounting the adventures of the cat she had named Webster. Mae had mild hypertension and hypercholesterolemia but was in otherwise excellent health. She enjoyed visiting in the office, appearing to consider each appointment a social call with my staff and me.

She was the first patient on a sunny June morning.

"Hello, Doctor; it's sure a fine summer morning. I woke up at 5:30 with a robin singing outside my window. Webster had perched in the windowsill, and I'm sure glad the screen kept him away from that beautiful bird. He's such a naughty cat."

"Sounds like it, Mae. But I know you love him anyway."

"You are so right. I keep him mostly indoors. He's such good company for my sister Emma and me. That big old farm house we were raised in would be awful lonely without his company."

Mae and Emma were the last of their generation of the Blackburn family still living in that three-story Civil War-era mansion with the high end gables reaching up to an attic with small rectangular windows, rounded turrets with conical roofs at each end of the house; and Grecian-style columns and rails connecting the turrets with a roofed balcony, lined with hanging plants and flowers. The blacktopped circular driveway led to the entryway, where even larger Grecian columns graced the porch, extending upward to support the balcony above.

The house was mostly of red brick, characteristic of that earlier era, and looked as though it belonged in the Deep South instead of the Midwest. The initial Blackburn patriarch had built and owned railroads extending from coast to coast and had lavishly constructed this sixteen-room house, which featured a ballroom and servants' quarters.

The sisters closed off much of the house during the winter months. The grounds were maintained by a fifty-year-old gardener and general handyman, Jeff Bowers; though lame in one foot and hampered by a mild learning disability, he was able to get along reasonably well, making his home in a separate servants' quarters behind the house. There was even a greenhouse, available during all four seasons, attached to the back of the mansion.

"What can I do for you today, Mae?"

"I just would like for you to check my blood pressure and listen to my heart again. A person my age can't be too careful, you know."

"Of course, Mae, but is anything bothering you right now?"

Following the usual focused review of her heart and lung systems and general health, the examination had thus far been essentially normal for a lady of her age.

"Your blood pressure is 135/80—very good, well controlled with hydrochlorothiazide and a small dose of reserpine. You're doing great. Your next lipid test is due in six more months. I think we can see you in two months for the next visit."

A look of apprehension spread over Mae's face as she reached to take my hand.

"Well, Doctor, I don't know. Don't you think you should see me in two more weeks? At my age, just about anything can go wrong."

I was feeling guilty about charging her every two weeks for seeing me in the office. She had been doing very well, and such frequent visits seemed unnecessary in her case. I started to say as much but then noticed her hand trembling as she grasped mine. Her apprehension was all too apparent.

Instead, I replied, "Oh, certainly. Sure thing, Mae. You come back in two weeks, and we'll go over everything again. And Mae, you can come any time you need to see me. We're always glad to see you for any problems."

With an evident sigh of relief, Mae started for the door. I stood quietly in the hallway listening to Christine checking her out; Mae's preference for such frequent visits piqued my interest. I continually learn a lot about human nature from my patients. Some people require a lot of reassurance, while for others an office visit is a social highlight of the day.

"It's good to see you're doing well, Mae. When did Doctor say to come back in for a follow-up?"

"Oh, he said two weeks, but sooner if I need to see him earlier. A lot can happen at my age, you know. And how are you getting along with that nice young man who accompanied you to the drugstore the other day? He was very nice looking. Are you getting serious? You two remind me of myself when Robert and I were first dating. I hope you'll be as happy as we were. I still miss him so."

Holding up both hands to stop the running monologue as it pertained to herself, Christine entreated, "Please, Mae. He's only a good friend. We have no plans at the moment."

"Oh, my dear, I know better. I could tell by the way he looked at you and held the door. He certainly looked love-struck to me."

And so it went with Mae's visits. I felt grateful that she thought so highly of us, evidently both individually and collectively, but still felt a little guilty about her paying me so often for such minimal effort.

This pattern with Mae had been consistent throughout our acquaintance, but I rarely saw Emma, her younger sister of seventy-two. Emma, who was also a widow, had an entirely different personality. Both ladies had grown children in another state, but only one other surviving sibling nearby, a brother named Steve Blackburn. Steve was a sixty-five-year-old gentleman, a patient himself, along with his wife and extended family.

I was making rounds in the hospital about 7:30 one morning when the PA system sizzled to life with its brief click and soft humming, followed by, "Dr. Matlock, Dr. Carl Matlock, please call the emergency room."

I had only completed half my rounds, but I headed for the emergency department immediately to see what was happening. Such an announcement often preceded another admission. Glancing at my watch, I sighed. Likely another late start at the office, . . . but not much to gain by pondering it for long.

"Hello, Mrs. Jensen. Who's the patient today?"

Handing me a chart, she smiled and replied, "Emma Barnes. She's in Room 2."

"Anything serious?"

"I really don't know. Dr. Hayden is in with her now, but it's a curious case. He couldn't come to a definite diagnosis, but she does look very ill."

Emma was cut from a different cloth altogether within the Blackburn family from either Mae or Steve. She had to this point visited me only once, and that because Mae refused to give her any peace until she did. Her blood pressure had been elevated at 185/100, but she had refused medication, advising me that though she appreciated my concern she felt just fine. That had been nearly a year ago, and she had failed to keep her subsequent appointments. For her to appear in the emergency room, I surmised, she must be seriously ill.

Greeting Dr. Hayden and Mae as I entered the room, I approached the hospital cart to greet Emma.

"How are you today, Emma?"

The lady I observed before me looked nothing like the robust picture of health I had seen in the office months earlier. Emma opened her eyes and tried to look up and focus on me, but her eyelids drooped briefly before she relinquished the effort and allowed them to close again. Her respirations were shallow, and she remained very still on the cart.

"What do you think, Jerry? Are any tests back yet?"

Jerome Hayden was nothing if not opinionated, and he wasn't bashful about stating his diagnosis and plan of action. "She's apparently had a stroke. Nothing focal—she can move everything—but she's extremely weak, with slurred speech and shallow breathing. I already have bed control working on a room for her, . . . with your permission. If you want I can send her on to Indianapolis instead. They'll be able to diagnose her case there."

"Emma, how about it? Would you prefer to go to Indianapolis?"

Emma frowned and mouthed the word "No."

I bent my head down to hear her better, and she whispered, "I want to stay here near Mae and Steve. If I die I want to be near my family. Doctor, I'm too weak to eat, so I can't last long."

With that she appeared to be entirely exhausted, with nothing further to say. She had raised her head ever so slightly as she spoke, but afterward she let it fall back to the pillow.

"Go ahead with the room, Jerry. Let's get her in a more comfortable bed as soon as possible."

Jerome Hayden shrugged his shoulders. "Whatever you say; you're the boss."

Turning to Mae, I advised her, "I'll be here for a while this morning. I want to go over her lab tests, X-rays, and EKG. You go on to the room with her, and I'll see you there in a little while."

Mae looked relieved and nodded as she resumed her place beside Emma. "Okay, Doctor."

❂

I contacted my office to alert them that I would be arriving an estimated ninety minutes late and rapidly completed my rounds before checking with the operator for Emma's room number. The Chest X-ray, EKG, and chemistries were all normal, except for a slightly elevated white blood count of 12,500, against a normal value of 5000–10,000. No sign of pneumonia, and no infection diagnosed from the urinalysis. A nuclear brain scan had been ordered by Dr. Hayden, but it would be hours before it could be completed. In those days we lacked the luxuries of instantaneous results and highly accurate tests with CT scanners or MRIs.

Arriving in Emma's room, I noticed no obvious change in her condition. Her oxygen saturation was only 89%, as measured by finger oximetry, against a normal of 95–100%.

Her blood pressure was 170/85; although elevated, it didn't account for her symptoms.

I sat down with Mae and Steve to go over the history carefully together.

"Start from the beginning, please, and tell me about her illness. She isn't up to a meaningful conversation with me just now."

Steve nodded for Mae to begin: "You two live together; you know her best."

"She's been feeling poorly for about six weeks or so. I noticed her dragging about the house, getting slower and slower, and that just isn't Emma. She ordinarily speeds about her work, getting real impatient with me for being slower than her.

"She just got worse and worse. Yesterday she couldn't keep her eyes open, and today she was slurring her words—said she nearly choked on her food and then wouldn't eat at all. Emma said she was short of breath, but she never smoked or had lung trouble in the past.

"I called Steve to come over, and we had to help her stand up. Her legs were just like jelly, all weak and shaky. I've never seen her like this before. She just seems to be going downhill fast."

Lowering her voice so Emma couldn't hear, Mae asked, "Is she dying, Doctor? I can't bear to lose her."

Mae sat wiping her eyes with a tissue while I turned to Steve to see whether he could shed any light on the situation. But Steve could only confirm, "It's just like Mae said, Doctor.

She isn't running a fever or coughing that I can see. It's a mystery."

"Let me take a better look at her now that I'm finished with rounds for the morning."

I carefully examined Emma from head to foot and could find only extreme weakness, drooping eyelids, slurred and soft speech, and shallow respirations. I began to wrack my brain for possibilities; this didn't look like any stroke I had ever seen.

As I pondered the problem, however, groping for an answer, a scene from my sophomore class in medical school replayed in my head. Suddenly I knew—I had seen this before. It was during the fourth semester, the section dedicated to physical diagnosis, and we were just being introduced to hospital and clinical medicine, with an emphasis of differential diagnosis.

"Good morning, class. Today we have a special guest I'm sure you'll enjoy. Our own Dr. Tether, famous for diagnostic acumen in medical circles, has a patient he wants to demonstrate to you today, a young woman who has volunteered to be here for a part of your education. Without further ado, let me introduce Dr. Tether, famous for his work in neurology."

"Good morning, class. Today I have one of my patients with me. I'll call her Julie. She's a thirty-four-year-old secretary and typist who noticed several years ago that she was having trouble doing her job. Early in the morning she would do fairly well, but by 10:30 she could barely keep her eyes open and her fingers moving on the keyboard. She also felt too tired to walk farther than the elevator just down the hall, while previously she had walked just for exercise up and down two flights to her office.

"By the second week Julie was unable to go to work and stayed home in bed most of the day. Her parents became worried, went to her apartment, and insisted she come home with them till she could see her family doctor. Recognizing that Julie had a neurologic disorder, he referred her to my office for an urgent consultation.

"Julie has had this disease for five years now, and she has graciously consented to stay off her medications for several hours so you can all see the remarkable transformation that will occur shortly—when I administer this medication intravenously."

Julie had difficulty negotiating the single step to the platform where Dr. Tether was lecturing while the class sat in a stadium formation, most of us well above floor level as we watched the amazing demonstration to follow.

Closed-circuit TV monitors provided close-up views of Julie's tired looking face, drooping eyelids, sagging lips, and slow-moving extremities, while the microphone picked up her slurred speech and distorted diction.

"Julie, please tell the class. Is this what was happening to you before we diagnosed and started you on medication?"

In tortured, barely audible speech Julie began, "Yes. This was my life—exactly as you see it now."

Dr. Tether's nurse had drawn up a vial of medication that she now handed to him, along with an alcohol sponge to wipe off the skin for the needle puncture. Meanwhile, she had unobtrusively started an IV line for this purpose while Dr. Tether continued to make remarks about diagnosis and treatment.

What happened next was truly amazing. Dr. Tether quickly injected the medication, and within seconds Julie's eyes opened wide, and she smiled brightly and began moving her extremities with ease. In a normal voice she informed us, "This was my life for a little while until I met Dr. Tether. I'm now living a normal life—as long as I take my medication."

"While we go on with the lecture, the nurse will take Julie out so she can resume her normal medicine by mouth. I don't want her to suffer for the rest of the day. Julie and I gave this demonstration today, class, because neither one of us wants you to forget what you've just witnessed."

◯

"I think I know what's wrong with Emma. We'll know for sure in just a few minutes. I'll be right back." I made my way to the nurses' station, where I had the nursing staff secure for me a vial of Tensilon (generic Edrophonium). I intended to repeat the experiment conducted for my class by Dr. Tether.

The nurses brought a cardiac monitor to attach to Emma, along with an automatic blood pressure cuff and oxygen monitor. Her IV was checked to make certain it was running normally, and we started her on oxygen by mouth. The room became crowded as staff nurses entered to watch the proceeding.

Emma barely opened her eyes to glance up as I asked, "Can you hear me, Emma?"

She barely nodded as I explained, "I think you have a disease in which a chemical is being broken down between the nerve endings and the muscles. The harder you try, the worse this gets, and the muscle fatigues until you're completely exhausted. The voluntary muscles affecting voice, swallowing, speech, and muscular movements of the chest wall and extremities are all involved in your case. If this works, I believe we can help you a great deal. Are you all set?"

A whispered "yes" was all Emma could manage.

"First I'm going to give you a small test dose to be sure you don't have an unfavorable reaction. The staff is going to help me watch the monitors while we wait about forty-five seconds. If everything is favorable, I'll give the rest of the vial rapidly."

Carefully observing to be certain that only two milligrams of Tensilon were drawn up, I turned to Emma: "Here we go. Relax as much as you can."

I injected the first dose as the nurse drew up eight more milligrams. A second nurse was watching the monitors, while a third was timing us.

"Everything's okay so far. Everyone agree? See anything different on the monitors?"

After confirming no untoward reactions, I announced, "Now for the rest."

I rapidly injected the eight milligrams of Tensilon and then turned up the IV to run it in rapidly.

As everyone watched, Emma's eyes fluttered open, she beamed an appreciative smile in my direction, and she began breathing deeply. Next she began moving her arms and legs, reached for my hand, and pronounced clearly and distinctly, "Thank you Doctor, . . . nurses. You're all wonderful."

Mae and Steve, exuberant, had risen to their feet.

"It was like watching a resurrection!" Steve enthused. "Like someone returning from the dead. A miracle. What's the name of the disease, Doc?"

"Emma has myasthenia gravis, a disorder in which a chemical transmitter called acetylcholine is unable to do its work of stimulating the muscle cells to contract. Tensilon is a short-acting anticholinesterase, or chemical, that allows the acetylcholine from the nerve ending to stick around and do its job on the muscle.

"This is a complex disease, mainly caused by autoimmune problems often related to the thymus gland, where immune cells develop. Emma will need to see a specialist at the Indianapolis Medical Center, where she can be tested and stabilized on a regimen of medications.

Right now we're going to get pyridostigmine, sixty milligrams (the brand name is Mestinon), to start Emma on a long-acting dose of medication to be administered every eight hours. What I gave her will soon wear off, but the pyridostigmine will correct that. In the very near future Emma will be able to function—and eat—normally."

With that I made my exit so I could try to catch up in the office. But I wouldn't have missed this for the world. Dr. Tether would have been proud.

THE STRANGE WORLD
OF THE MIND

One cold day in early March a late winter storm had just blanketed the countryside with four inches of powdery snow—and the warm blankets inside my cozy bedroom felt so good at 4:00 a.m. One of our children had been up with a fever and runny nose for much of the night, and I'd had very little sleep, taking turns with my exhausted wife walking the floor and softly crooning lullabies. There's only so much medical science can do for the common cold, despite the expectations of lay people.

I couldn't have been back in bed for longer than thirty minutes when the jangling of the phone interrupted my brief dreams of a soft summer day fishing my favorite pond for the bass lurking beneath the lily pads. Alas, this wasn't soon to be. The hospital operator informed me that I had a patient in the emergency room desperately needing my attention. "One moment for Dr. Hayden, please."

The phone lapsed into silence as moments turned into what seemed like hours as I waited. Was this to be the end of my night's repose, brief as it had been? Just as I started to drift back to sleep, a loud click brought me back to the present. Then came the petulant voice: "Jerome Hayden here."

Reluctantly sighing, I managed, "Hello, Jerry. What's going on so early in the morning?"

"Do you remember Kyle Heath, the seventy-year-old man you admitted two months ago with pancreatitis?"

Despite the early hour and my sleep-fogged mind, I vividly recalled Kyle and his serious alcohol problem. "Sure, Jerry. How could I forget? Is he back? Not drinking again, I hope?"

"Not today anyway, but he apparently has been hitting the bottle again. He's here and needs to be admitted. Early DTs, it looks like. The Glen Falls police brought him in for evaluation."

I barely managed to keep my eyes open as Dr. Hayden droned on and on. No point in interrupting; he would just start over again on his prolonged monologue. When he finally stopped talking, I responded with a curt "Just go ahead and admit him. I'll see him in a little while. Could you just write a few orders until I get there?"

I hung up the phone before he could respond. "What was that all about?" Janet asked sleepily.

"Oh, just another admission," I groaned as I turned over to slumber for a precious few minutes before the alarm buzzer summoned me at 5:30. But this time the usual happened. My mind went into high gear as I envisioned worst-case scenarios.

What had Jerry said about hallucinations, the police, Kyle in legal trouble, and on and on . . . ?

Wide awake now in spite of myself, I muttered, "Might as well get up; I can't go back to sleep."

Janet replied softly, in a voice heavy with exhaustion, "What's wrong, honey? What did you say?"

"Never mind. Go back to sleep; don't worry about breakfast just now. I'll grab something quick. I have to go to the hospital early for an admission."

I dressed rapidly in the darkness, trying not to awaken the rest of the household, and made my way to the kitchen, where the lights nearly blinded me for a few seconds. I grabbed a Danish roll and warmed a cup of leftover coffee to drink in route to the hospital.

Feelings of self-pity swept over me as I made my way to the Ford parked in the drive. The first light of the brand-new day gave voice to a robin, recently returned from a warmer clime, heralding new life from the oak tree in the yard—an optimist and early harbinger of hope, I thought somewhat ruefully.

Hesitating briefly to listen and watch the eastern sky lighten with rose-colored clouds after the snowstorm had swept through overnight, however, I felt myself unexpectedly suffused with peace. I loved the briskness of the south wind caressing my face, teasing me with its still early promise of warmth and better days to come as I momentarily basked in the glow, reflecting on nature's God and His goodness.

During my commute to the hospital the loveliness of the snow-covered fields brought me back to why I had chosen rural practice. I loved the understated beauty of the old red barns, the plowed fields now covered with blowing snow, and the dairy cattle peacefully making their way out to pasture for the day. The men and women who lived here and worked the soil were my kind of people.

The small towns dotting the countryside, with their warm and friendly residents, were so unlike the big cities, where neighbors rarely knew—let alone acknowledged—one another in the high-rise brick and mortar apartments. Here life existed on the more elemental basis of friendship and loyalty. Here one did indeed frequently take on the role of a "brother's keeper."

With such unaccountably pleasant thoughts I arrived at the hospital and made my way to the telephone operator's window. "To which room was Kyle Heath admitted this morning?"

"Good morning, Doc. He's in 207, South Med."

Arriving at the nurses' station, I retrieved the chart and quickly perused the ER notes. Nurse Ruth Mahoney spied me as I did so.

"Dr. Matlock, we're sure glad to see you!"

Something in her voice and the steely glint in her eyes sent a shiver of foreboding down my spine. Ruth, the no-nonsense charge nurse on South Med, was a sixty-year-old, old-school-type RN who brooked no dissent in the running of "her floor."

The sterile notes by Dr. Hayden came alive in my hands as I took stock of his words: "Dressed in pajamas, tall black boots, and short blue jacket when he bought 24 cents of gasoline for his beat-up truck at 3:00 a.m. Couldn't pay for the gas. Argued with station attendant and threatened violence. Arrested by police. Taken to jail. Screaming and disruptive in jail and brought to the ER for medical evaluation. Hands bruised and battered from hitting the bars and walls in jail. Vague about alcohol consumption, and" . . . the list went on.

My throat felt dry as I gazed into the reproachful eyes of Ruth Mahoney.

"It looks like Kyle is really out of it this time," I managed to mutter.

"It certainly looks like something! All I want to know is what you're going to do about it. His screaming and antics have every patient on this hall awake and complaining. I'm not running a jailhouse here, or a sanitarium, and I intend to keep it that way."

My weak and inadequate response: "I'll see what I can do."

"You do that. Dr. Matlock. If you can't calm him down, he can't stay in our hospital."

"I know, Mrs. Mahoney—I know."

With that I retreated down the hallway to Kyle's room, while two of the younger nurses exchanged knowing smiles over my discomfiture, only too happy to avoid bearing the brunt of Nurse Mahoney's righteous indignation.

I thought back briefly to my pleasant reverie of minutes earlier on my way to the hospital.

How could the world so quickly have turned upside down? I had enormous respect for Nurse Mahoney but conceded that she could be difficult. Despite our knowledge that her bark was much worse than her bite, she frequently inspired fear in the medical staff, including even the physicians. She could certainly make life unpleasant, and she had an "in" with the administration. Perhaps not all is joy and sweetness in her world . . .

As I opened the door to Kyle's room I drew back in amazement, staring at the chaotic destruction before me. Never before had I witnessed such a transformation in the sterile, neat appearance of a hospital room. The foul odor emanating from the interior was nearly overpowering, enough to make me feel briefly faint.

Kyle sat in one of the chairs intended for a visitor, TV remote in hand, avidly engaged with a screen with nothing on it but a vertical, rolling blur accompanied by a loud buzzing sound. He had evidently been trying to improve a picture but now seemed to be enjoying the meaningless view on the screen, no doubt a reflection of his inner turmoil.

It would be an understatement to note that he'd had diarrhea, for large, loose, yellow and tan piles covered much of the floor. Not content with that mess, he had taken it upon himself to hand-decorate the cord of the TV remote; in that day the remote was typically connected by a wired cord to the set, and he had smeared his excrement all over the cord, from the remote to the TV, apparently plastering it with his fingers, going on from there to embellish the power cord and wall socket, along with much of the wall, with the abandon of a child finger painting. Apparently, having released his inner artist, he now felt exceedingly pleased with himself.

At least he was quiet now, flashing me a toothless grin of recognition as I stood in the doorway, dumbfounded. "Come in, come on in, Doc. Good to see you. I know you can fix things now. Somethin' went terrible wrong this mornin'. I don' know what got into the cops. I didn' do nothin'."

Stepping with great care, I made my way to the chair on which he sat barefooted in pajama bottoms, his gown carefully rolled up in a pile of filth at his feet and his gray hair flecked with human waste, the vile medium of his artistry.

Kyle glanced down to his left, as though remembering something long forgotten, before reaching down and grabbing a stool-smeared urinal, slopping urine on his feet and pajamas as he tried to hand it to me. I quickly stepped back, forgetting to look behind me and nearly meeting with disaster in the form of another pile of filth.

"No, Kyle. Just set it back down on the floor. The nurses will take care of it later."

Kyle shrugged, spilling about half of the contents on the floor as he obliged, slopping it back down beside him. He pointed to the old-fashioned column radiator that worked on the principle of water heating.

"I tried pourin' it in the water heater, but it wouldn' hold much."

"Kyle, there's no receptacle here to pour anything into—that's a water radiator heater."

Kyle studied the radiator with interest while I looked about the room. The pillow was on the floor, its defiled case wadded up in a corner, and the sheets and blankets from the stripped mattress in wild disarray in another corner. It was then that I noticed the sound of running water.

Stepping gingerly to the bathroom, I opened the door to find his shower going full blast with wadded towels covering the drain and causing water to back up and spill over the low sides.

I nearly fell as I slipped on the floor, which already had the making of a record-setting flood in progress. I managed to grab the faucet handle, quickly turning it off, before glancing in consternation at my formerly shined and polished black shoes, now wet and soiled from the fruits of Kyle's ingenious labors. Grabbing a wet towel, I quickly wiped off the worst of the detritus.

I tracked smeared footprints back into the main hospital room as I exited the bathroom, ruefully recalling my earlier interrupted sleep.

Finally, like a light bulb coming on, Kyle recognized his besmeared situation, smiled broadly, and asked in a pleading falsetto, "Would you clean me up?"

That was it. I'd had enough. I flew through the door with my sopping wet towel, stopped long enough in the hallway to clean off my shoes once again, turned, and threw the towel back into the room, catching sight of Kyle beaming his toothless smile for my edification. Somehow I managed to respond with a cryptic and at least somewhat civil, "No, I won't clean you up."

Turning around to flee back up the hallway to the nurses' station, I found the entire nursing staff, along with my nemesis, Mrs. Mahoney, enjoying my distress. I could feel the redness burning my cheeks as I made my way back to review the chart, equipped as I was with new insights. Once in the nursing station Nurse Mahoney and her staff exploded with uncontrollable laughter while I stood helplessly glaring at them. Finally, I had to laugh as well.

"Mrs. Mahoney, I don't get you. First you yell at me and lay down the law, and then you laugh at my plight. I thought you were really mad and blamed me for the problem."

"Doctor, I am none too happy about the mess, but the look on your face—and those shoes—well, that was priceless! When you've been here longer you'll learn that I only yell at the doctors I like. The rest I ignore. Get it?"

"I guess so. But I agree with you. We can't keep him here. I'll contact the psych floor in Indianapolis and try to make arrangement to transfer him there. He is, to put it mildly, inappropriate for a general medical hospital."

"Dr. Matlock, that will make my day. I don't know what Dr. Hayden was thinking of—admitting him to my floor indeed! He may be worth my yelling at him this afternoon. I think he may be salvageable as a doctor, but many more admissions like this and I'll ignore him but good."

And so began another day of caring for the sick. The staff cleaned and scrubbed Kyle until he shone like a newborn baby. Examining him then, I found him stable for transfer to the kind psychiatrist who had agreed to take him.

Kyle Heath was indeed victim to the ravages of his own alcohol abuse. He was an unforgettable character, someone I would encounter often in his more sober moments—though suffering from liver and pancreatic damage because of his self-destructive lifestyle.

A FORTUITOUS MEDICAL MISTAKE

Thursday, my day off, had ironically become my longest hospital day. At my request Dr. Rob Hendrick, my favorite general surgeon and good friend, scheduled my elective patient surgeries for that day. Between cases I made rounds, visiting my hospital patients and dictating discharge summaries. I never seemed to have time during the rest of the week to keep up with that aspect of my work. It was difficult enough to keep tabs on admissions histories and physical dictations. I always felt too rushed to get to the office to complete the discharges; though I hated to keep people waiting, I hoped my patients believed that about me.

On one typical Thursday morning in mid-summer I was scheduled to assist Dr. Hendrick with a cholecystectomy—a gall bladder removal—as well as a hysterectomy. The cases were deliberately scheduled to give me a one-hour break between the first and second.

After the cholecystectomy, however, I had instead begun making rounds on the medical cases when the operator paged me over the PA system: "Dr. Matlock. Outside call for Dr. Matlock."

I laid down the chart I had been studying and dialed "0" for the hospital operator. "Hello. This is Dr. Matlock."

"Just a second, Doctor. I have a Mrs. Evelyn Sanders on the phone. Will you take the call?"

Mrs. Sanders was the mother of four rambunctious boys ranging in ages from three to sixteen. I wondered as I accepted the call which of them had been injured now. I replied, "Sure, put her through."

"Dr. Matlock, Zach, my ten-year-old, was sick at this stomach and refused breakfast this morning. If Zach won't eat, he must be sick. Now he's having stomach pain as well. Actually, I'm not sure which came first, the pain or the nausea. Could you see him in the ER this morning?"

"Sure, Mrs. Sanders. Bring Zach on in. Have the ER page me when you get here."

"Thanks so much. I always feel better when the boys can see you. I'm really worried about Zach this time. He's usually my healthy one."

"I'll be in surgery again soon, but I'll have the ER go ahead with tests to rule out anything serious when you get here."

After hanging up the phone I dialed ER and spoke with Mrs. Jensen, the charge nurse. "I have a Zach Sanders with nausea and abdominal pain. He's ten years old, and his mom will be bringing him in soon. Could you please get a CBC, Chem 7, chest X-ray, and abdominal series on him? I'll be in surgery for a while, and I'd like to get things started. I promised her I'd see him this morning."

"Sure thing, Doctor. I'll let you know when everything is back."

With arrangements made I resumed my rounds, only to learn that an emergency case had bumped my patient's hysterectomy by two hours. It began to look like another long day in the hospital.

About ninety minutes later the ER paged me. Mrs. Jensen informed me, "Zach is here, and all your lab and X-rays are back. Could you see him soon? He does look quite ill."

Checking my watch and noticing that I had about half an hour before being expected in the OR, I replied, "I'll be right there. Thanks."

I made my way to the ER and had no trouble locating which room Zach was in by the noise being made by two of his siblings. I entered Exam Room 2 and smiled at Zach. His mother stood anxiously at the bedside, conveniently ignoring the pandemonium from the youngest members of her brood. Sixteen-year-old Billy, who wouldn't at any rate have been able to keep the other two quiet, didn't seem to notice. With four active boys, I suppose one would have to learn to ignore a certain amount of noise and hyperactivity.

"Hello, Zach, . . . Mrs. Sanders. I need to ask you a few questions, Zach, and your mom can help you answer if necessary. Okay?"

Zach didn't have much to say. He was paler than usual, his faced pinched, and his red hair clinging damply to his forehead; he was obviously trying to be brave while lying uncharacteristically still.

"When did he first get sick?"

"He said he didn't feel good after supper. He had a little cold, but nothing to be concerned about. The other boys were just getting over colds, and he was the last to get sick. It always happens that way; the rest get sick together, but a lot of the time he never catches their flu bugs."

"Did he eat normally last night?"

"Well, come to think of it, he left most of his mashed potatoes and gravy. That isn't like Zach. He loves his taters."

"What about this morning? Did he have any fever or other symptoms when he first got up?"

"That's another thing, Doc. He said he hadn't slept much. He didn't want anything to eat and complained with a dull ache around his navel."

"Do you still have the pain, Zach?"

Zach looked perfectly miserable, lying very still on the cart. His chart showed a temperature of 100.4, a pulse of 100, respirations of 20, and blood pressure of 90/60. Glancing up at me with a pitiful expression, he nodded in the affirmative.

"Can you point to the pain now? Has it moved at all?"

Zach stifled a groan and pointed first at his navel and then toward his right lower abdomen with his right hand. Placing his left hand over his mouth, he began retching without getting anything up.

"Has he vomited anything up so far?"

"On the way here he vomited twice in a bucket I brought along in case that happened."

"Did he get much up?"

"Only a little. He didn't eat any breakfast to bring up. It looked like some of his supper stayed in his stomach all night, but there wasn't much there."

"Has he had any other symptoms, like a cough or chest congestion?"

"Only a little cough, but like I said he was coming down with a cold."

"Does he have any diarrhea or urinary complaints?"

Mrs. Sanders began with "No diarrhea" before turning to address the patient: "Zach, what about it—does it hurt to pee?"

Zach shook his head and continued to lie stock still on the cart.

I asked, "Zach, does it hurt to move?"

The little boy glanced at his mother, apparently seeking the answer, but I put in, "Your mom can't answer that one for you. Only you know how it feels when you try to move around."

A few tears escaped the boy's eyes as he tried to maintain a stoical bearing. Gingerly moving just a little on the cart, he stopped quickly and nodded in the affirmative. "It hurts real bad when I move."

"Zach, I'm going to carefully examine you. This may hurt a little, but I'll be as careful and gentle as possible. Do you understand?"

Noting his nod, I began, "First I'll check your ears and throat with special lights to see how you're coming with your cold."

I continued to announce my intentions and findings as I proceeded with the exam.

"Your ears are fine. You have just a little runny nose from your cold, and your throat is slightly red."

This little boy was easy to examine as long as I told him what to expect and whether or not he might experience pain.

"Your lungs sound clear, and your heart is beating fine, Zach."

Noticing that slightly bumping the cart was causing him a great deal of distress, I assured him, "You won't have to turn on your side or sit up for me to check the back part of your lungs. I'll just check the chest X-ray for that.

"Now this is the part that will probably hurt some. I'll be as gentle as possible. First I'm going to take a cotton applicator and gently stroke over your abdomen—your tummy—with it. This is an old trick to look for inflammation or infection. You tell me what you feel, okay?"

Starting on his left upper abdomen and stroking to the right, I proceeded down to the umbilicus. He maintained that there was no difference from side to side. However, when I got to the left lower abdomen and gently pulled the cotton applicator over the center line and onto the right lower abdomen, he motioned for me to stop.

"It feels funny, Doc. It burns down there on that side where I hurt so bad."

"Okay, enough of that. Now I'm going to carefully push in on your abdomen to see where it hurts."

Beginning once again in the left upper quadrant, proceeding to the right, and finally working my way down to the right lower quadrant, I gently exerted pressure on the abdominal wall as I palpated for any changes. When I neared McBurney's point, about the center of the right lower quadrant, he experienced severe pain, and I noticed that the abdominal wall remained rigid in that area, with or without deep palpation.

"One more thing, Zach. This may hurt a little more, but it will be very brief. Okay? Ready?"

Zach gamely nodded for me to proceed as I tested for abdominal rebound tenderness. When something is inflamed in the abdomen, especially if there is any peritoneal inflammation, or inflammation of the sac lining the abdominal cavity, pain is reproduced by gently pushing down and then letting go quickly. When the abdominal wall springs back up there is exquisite pain due to the sudden movement. This testing is painful, but there is a more humane way to tell the same thing. Since I had positioned myself on Zach's right side, I placed my left index finger over the mid right lower quadrant and tapped it forcefully with the tip of my right index finger.

For the first time the boy resisted and grabbed for my hands. "Stop! please stop!"

"I'm finished now, Zach. I found out all I needed to know."

"Mrs. Sanders, I'm going to check his X-rays, but I'm quite certain he has appendicitis. That last test indicates peritoneal inflammation. If the appendix is the problem, as I suspect, he'll be one sick young man if it ruptures."

Mrs. Sanders stood a little rigidly but nodded her assent. "What has to be, will be. Do what you think best, Doctor."

I walked the short distance to the Radiology Department to view the X-rays. The radiologist, Dr. Strong, was just reading the morning films from the emergency department.

"A lot of kids in the ER today, Carl. You're looking for the chest and abdominal series on the kid with abdominal pain, I believe."

"Right, Dr. Strong. He's ten and seems to have a pretty classic case of acute appendicitis. His white blood count just came back at 19,000 with a left shift" (a predominance of white blood cells indicating acute infection or inflammation). "Do you see anything on the films? He does have a mild URI."

"No Carl, these are pretty normal films, which as you know may be the case with acute appendicitis."

In those days there were no CT scans for instantaneous diagnosis, and in near certain cases, and even many questionable situations, the safest course of action was to proceed with removing the appendix, since a ruptured organ carries a significant mortality risk. In addition, if the appendix happened to be in an unusual location in the abdomen, the atypical presentation made diagnosis much more difficult

Thanking Dr. Strong for his help, I returned to the ER and placed a call to the OR to speak with Dr. Hendrick. It happened that there had been a further delay with the hysterectomy due to unforeseen minor problems on the surgical floor.

As Rob's voice came over the line, I advised him of our patient in the ER: "He appears to have classic signs and symptoms of acute appendicitis."

Within minutes Rob Hendrick was perusing Zach's cart and gently confirming my findings through his own examination of the patient. Rob Hendrick had large but gentle, reassuring hands and a wonderful bedside manner. He had been known to sing nursery rhymes to small children while he performed minor procedures on them under local anesthesia.

"Mrs. Sanders, I agree with Dr. Matlock's diagnosis. The only safe thing to do is remove the appendix. Dr. Matlock tells me that Dr. Strong, our radiologist, already reviewed the films and didn't find anything else to explain the pain. The only part of the usual examination not done is a rectal exam, but his findings are so typical, and he's having so much pain, that I don't believe it would contribute anything to the diagnosis. With your permission I believe we should go right to surgery. Do you want to call your husband first?"

"Thanks, Doctor Hendrick, but I already have. He has full confidence in Dr. Matlock and has heard good things about you. Please do whatever you have to for our Zachary."

"Carl, go ahead and give him pain medication through the IV the nurse is starting, and we'll put him next as an emergency case. I already told the OR to stand by, and we'll see you in a few minutes. Mrs. Sanders. I don't believe this will take long. If you'll wait in the main waiting room, I hope to see you in about forty-five minutes to an hour, depending on the OR being ready for us."

The case turned out as expected, at least in one way. Zach did indeed have acute appendicitis with early peritoneal inflammation, but no perforation or actual soiling of the peritoneum by bowel or bacterial contents. I expected him to do well post-operatively.

But then, the unexpected often happens in medicine.

Dr. Bill Johnson, the anesthetist who also happens to be a family doctor, asked me a question with unusual gravity in his voice: "Carl, did you listen to this kid's chest? He sounds terrible, and I'm getting up all kinds of yellow sputum by suctioning. In fact, I got a sample for the lab."

Rob and I both stopped and looked at one another.

"I went over the X-ray personally with Dr. Strong. He didn't see anything suspicious at all in the lungs. He did mention that there were a lot of kids in the ER today, though. You don't suppose . . . ?"

". . . that you looked at the wrong films with him," Bill finished. "Stranger things have happened."

Within minutes the three of us stood by the radiology view box in the OR looking at Zach's pre-op films. Without a doubt Zach had right lower lobe pneumonia, heard best from the posterior or back of the thoracic or chest cavity, the only area to which I hadn't listened with my stethoscope because of the boy's pain with any movement and the "clear" X-ray findings.

Dr. Strong, having gotten wind of a possible mix-up in viewing the films, came to look into the OR door, his report in hand. He didn't have on scrubs so remained a few feet away in the doctors' dressing room.

"Sorry, Carl. It looks like we looked at the wrong X-ray earlier. There's no doubt about the pneumonia. I guess the surgery could've been avoided."

At this point Bill Johnson began laughing uproariously and slapped me on the back. "Carl, you're one lucky dog. If you had seen that X-ray that little boy would be on the med-peds floor getting antibiotics for pneumonia while perforating his appendix. It doesn't get any better than this."

Rob Hendrick piped in, "I'm glad I didn't check the X-ray myself. That's my usual practice."

To which Dr. Strong added, "I know. He never trusts our readings."

We shared a good laugh over the fortunate error that had taken place, the nursing staff joining us in relishing the irony of the situation. Although both Dr. Strong and I were embarrassed, I was grateful for the way things had turned out.

Dr. Hendrick and I went to find the family in the waiting room to give them the news about Zach. Rob told them first about the successful surgery and the acutely inflamed appendix, allowing me to finish the narrative. By that time Mr. Sanders had arrived from work, along with his parents, cousins, aunts, uncles, and Mrs. Sanders's extended family.

Reluctantly, I began my postscript: "The good news, folks, is that Zach should make a full recovery. The bad news is that he'll be here several days longer than expected because he also has right lower lobe pneumonia. That will take a while for him to recover from—longer, probably, than any surgical pain."

Everyone started to talk at once, but I held up my hands, palms up, to get their attention.

"I have a confession to make. We just now discovered the pneumonia. I didn't know about it when we took Zach to surgery. There were several children about Zach's age in the ER today, and the radiologist showed me the wrong films, which were normal."

I had noticed Zach splinting his breathing a little but had thought this was due to the acute appendicitis. Every time the diaphragm, the big breathing muscle, moves downward to take a breath it puts pressure on the abdominal organs, including the appendix.

"Much as I hate making any mistake, of course, this happens to be the 'best' one I've ever made in medicine. You only hear about the medical errors for which people suffer and sometimes even die. This medical error may well have saved Zach's life."

Dr. Hendrick stood by, smiling and nodding encouragement, as I continued my explanation: "You see, right lower lobe pneumonia can masquerade as acute appendicitis with a high white blood count, right-sided abdominal pain, and even tenderness when the abdomen is palpated. A chain of fortunate errors occurred here. Radiology mistakenly showed me the wrong films, and I failed to check closer to see that the name printed in fairly small letters on them was that of another patient Zach's age.

"We then proceeded to take out an inflamed appendix nearing the perforation stage, with subsequent peritonitis and profound illness in the offing had it not been removed, not realizing that Zach had two totally separate illnesses. In medicine we're taught, whenever possible, to find one unifying medical problem for a diagnosis. When there are two or more possibilities, the picture can become very clouded.

"So there you have it. I made a mistake. In one way I'm sorry, but in another I rejoice that I was human enough to make a fortunate mistake—one that probably saved Zach's life and resulted in treatment for both of his problems."

With tear-moistened eyes Zach's father, Henry, responded: "You did good, Doc. The good Lord made that happen to save our little boy. I wouldn't have had it any other way. I'm just glad you've been honest and open to telling us all about it. I think more of you now than ever."

Henry began pumping my hand while hugging me at the same time. The entire family was visibly moved. These were people of faith, people who believed that a higher power had intervened to save their child.

I was greatly humbled by this experience as Dr. Hendrick summed up the situation for all of us: "Folks, I believe the good Lord was watching over Zach and all of us today. It's just like Dr. Matlock says: Zach was very fortunate the wrong X-ray guided our hands today. I don't believe it was as much a mistake as it was divine intervention."

Mrs. Sanders smiled through her tears as she added the benediction: "Amen, Dr. Hendrick. Amen!"

NAGGING CHEST PAIN

My mood matched the overcast sky and the drumming of a hard, steady rain on the roof during a lull between patients. It's very difficult to be excited after having been up for most of the night with a 3:00 a.m. OB delivery. A pink, healthy baby girl had entered the world with lusty cries of protest at vacating the dark, warm environment that had been her refuge for the last nine months.

I sat down in the lab for a five-minute break, sipping a cup of strong coffee in an attempt to drive the sleep from my eyes. Despite the caffeine my head sagged, it seemed, almost to my chest, and my eyelids drooped; it was at that moment that a brilliant flash, followed by a nearly instantaneous crash of thunder, startled me bolt upright.

"That was close," Donna exclaimed as she entered the lab, summoning me to see the next patient.

"It sure was. Do you know what it hit?"

Donna peered out the window before responding, "The neighbor's old elm has a large limb split off with a long, smoldering scar on the main trunk. And now the rain is really coming down.

"I just came in to tell you that Clifford Johnson is here. He ran a little late due to the storm, but he's all set. His blood pressure is a little high at 140/90, but his pulse is normal at sixty and regular. He looks apprehensive, but his vital signs are otherwise normal."

"What's his chief complaint?"

"He has a vague, constant, nagging chest pain. You know he's a worrier anyway, and his symptoms are pretty nondescript."

"Did you go ahead and get an EKG?"

Proudly, Donna opened his folder and handed me the just completed EKG, marked at five minutes earlier. "I'm learning your habits pretty well. I knew you'd be asking for this, so I went ahead and ran it."

Having spent months on cardiology services during my training, I had become adept in reading EKGs. In fact, I substituted for the physician who regularly read them at the hospital when he was on vacation or out of town for the day.

"Does it look okay to you? He moved around a little, causing a slight irregularity in the baseline, but this is the best of three attempts."

"Yes, I can see that. But you did good. This is perfectly normal. I'll see him in just a moment, but first I'm going to the restroom to splash cold water in my face. That delivery woke me up at midnight, and I got a forty-five-minute nap after getting home this morning. I ate a quick breakfast and went back to do hospital rounds, so I'm really feeling groggy now. Please tell him I'll be right there. And thanks for getting the EKG already. It helps a lot."

Minutes later I felt refreshed enough to see Mr. Johnson, a fifty-one years old who preferred to be called Cliff. I retrieved his chart from the chart holder beside the door labeled Exam Room 1 and glanced at his problem list and pertinent lab: "Hypertension with borderline cholesterol reading, normal blood sugar but family history of diabetes. Father had a heart attack at age fifty-one. Former smoker who quit three years ago."

With a long list of differential diagnoses racing through my mind, I entered the room to find Mr. Johnson already in a gown, sitting apprehensively on the examination table. I shook hands with him to establish rapport and offer some comfort.

"Good afternoon, Cliff. How are you doing today?"

"I don't know, Doc. I have this funny, nagging pain in my chest. My dad had a heart attack about my age, and I guess I'm just worried. It's probably nothing, but my wife said I should check it out."

With a big grin, he continued, "Especially since I've complained about it for the last twenty-four hours. I guess she got tired of hearing me. But seriously, I've never had anything like this before."

"Can you tell me more about your pain—what if feels like, when it started, whether it's constant—that sort of thing?"

"It's just a dull, nagging pain, just to the left of my breast bone. It's constant, dull like, and doesn't go away, unless it does when I am sleeping. It's there when I go to bed and there when I wake up."

"Heart pain usually doesn't present like that, and your EKG is completely normal, but I need to learn more. I want to be sure of what you're experiencing, and cardiac pain can be very atypical. In men, though, heart pain is usually—but not always—what we would call classical. Women frequently have atypical and unusual symptoms."

"What do you mean by 'classical' pain?"

"Typical angina, or cardiac pain, is usually induced by emotional stress or exertion, lasts a few minutes to a few hours, and is relieved by rest or medical interventions, like nitroglycerin. It's also accompanied by other typical symptoms. It's rarely constant for a whole day or so, but I want to know exactly what it is you're experiencing.

"Do you feel pain anywhere else, like in either arm, your throat, your upper abdomen, or your back?"

"No, it's just right here, just to the left of the breastbone—like, you know, over my heart."

"You say it's constant pain? Can you be more specific? Do you mean it comes and goes or that it never seems to be any better?

"That's it exactly, Doc. It never gets any better. It's just this dull, constant pain. I had trouble doing my work as an electrician today because of it."

"Do you mean that work makes the pain worse?"

"No. No worse. I just worried a lot—couldn't keep my mind on the job. For an electrician, that isn't a safe way to work."

"I should say not. It sounds like we need to get to the bottom of your problem as soon as possible. Do you have any symptoms such as trouble getting your breath, breaking out in a sweat, or being nauseated?"

"I don't have any of that. I just hurt."

"Would you call the pain severe?"

"Not at all—just nagging, like. Dull pain, you know."

"I don't recall you having any history of ulcers or heartburn. Do you have any history of stomach, bowel, or bladder problems that we haven't talked about?"

"No, I have an iron stomach. I can eat anything. I don't know what indigestion is like at all, other than to hear what other people say about it."

"Is there any chance you could have strained a muscle at work? Any heavy lifting?"

"No, I thought about that, but nothing I can think of."

"Is it painful to touch or push on your chest?"

"No, I've been doing plenty of pushing on it too. My wife thinks I caused the pain by massaging my chest all the time when I'm trying to sit and rest. But that isn't the cause. I push on it because it hurts, not the other way around. Unfortunately, massaging the muscles doesn't do anything for the pain. It stays just the same."

"As I recall, you had your gall bladder removed in the past. Is that correct, Cliff?"

"That's right, Doc. But this feels a little like that did when it flared up."

"One more thing before I examine you: Does anything at all help the pain, or does anything give you even a little relief?

"Nope. Nothing helps it or makes it worse. It's just there."

I spent the next few minutes rechecking his blood pressure; listening to his heart and lungs; checking his abdomen; looking for any signs of potential blood clots in his legs; and even checking his ears, nose, and throat.

I have always believed in a hands-on approach to medicine. Sadly, with our state-of-the-art technology today, history and physical examination are becoming of secondary importance. A critical part of the mystery of healing, I'm convinced, is communicated in physical touch by the hands of a caring physician.

With the ongoing stormy weather I knew that a few patients had failed to show up, affording me some extra time. Already weary, I asked Cliff to dress while I prepared some lab and X-ray request forms; then I re-entered the room and sat across from him in a reasonably comfortable straight-backed chair.

"Honestly, Cliff, I'm not sure what's wrong with you. You don't have symptoms typical for a neat diagnosis and treatment regimen. I know you have a special concern because of your family history.

"Your symptoms don't sound at all like heart disease, but I believe the safest approach is to at least check that out. I want you to have a treadmill stress test, a chest X-ray, and a panel of blood tests to look for any special problems, like anemia, liver problems, and so on.

"Donna will be with us in a few minutes. She's on the phone with cardiology testing just now. Meanwhile, do you have any other questions?"

"No, I'm just glad you're checking my heart and lungs. It makes a fella nervous not to know what the trouble is. I appreciate your concern."

Following a brief knock to announce her presence, Donna opened the door and announced, "Good news. They have an opening to do the stress test tomorrow. You can get your blood and X-ray tests done before the stress test."

Shaking Cliff's hand again and excusing myself, I retreated to the lab to think before the last patients were due to come in. Was a stress test necessary? He certainly didn't sound cardiac to me at this point. Cliff was a known worrier, but he did have a positive family history, mild hypertension, and a history of past tobacco abuse.

Following a good night's sleep, I felt a lot better the next morning. I made my way through hospital rounds and headed to the office, glad to see the sun shining again. I had a busy day scheduled and was surprised to see that Clifford Johnson had made an appointment for the last time slot of the day.

Thirty-five patients later I prepared to see Cliff again.

"Donna, could you have Christine call for his results while I visit with him? Hopefully everything is back by now, including his X-ray reading."

"I'll get right on it. While Christine's doing that, I'll start cleaning up the other rooms in preparation for tomorrow."

"Great. Just let me know when you have everything ready."

"One more thing: Mrs. Johnson is with him today. I think he's driving her crazy with his constant complaining. I hope he doesn't have anything serious."

Entering the exam room, I greeted both Mr. and Mrs. Johnson and asked, "Well, Cliff, how did it go today?"

With a quizzical smile he shrugged his shoulders and reported, "They said I did fine. No abnormalities at all on the test. I don't understand."

"That isn't bad news, Cliff; we really hoped your heart would be okay."

Mrs. Johnson interrupted at that point, "It would be good news if he would stop his worrying and rubbing his chest. He's getting on my nerves."

Cliff grinned sheepishly and conceded, "I guess I'm making her nervous too."

Moments later Donna brought in all the reports on Cliff. I glanced over them and reviewed the results aloud: "EKG stress testing completely normal; chest X-ray normal; blood work, including liver function tests, all normal—nothing to indicate the source of the pain."

I don't know who looked the more exasperated, Cliff or his wife, Maggie, who threw up both hands while he gazed sorrowfully at the floor. For a few uncomfortable moments no one spoke. Then Cliff put in, "I'm worried, Doc. What if I have cancer or some other bad disease?"

"What he really means, Doc, is that he's scared stiff about the possibility of heart trouble. He just doesn't want to say it. I know him quite well." Maggie ended her short speech emphatically, folded her arms, and glared at Cliff.

"And you still have the identical pain, Cliff?"

"I sure wish I didn't, but I have to say yes. I guess Maggie's right. This is worrying me to death."

"Cliff, I have a good friend and former teacher who's an expert cardiologist. Would you be willing to see him for another opinion and possible further testing?"

"Well, sure, Doc. Whatever you think. I have confidence in your judgment."

At about that time I was beginning to wonder about it myself but didn't express the thought out loud. In fact, I was even beginning to doubt myself. Whatever his pain was, it wasn't typical of, evidently, anything simple. I had been about to suggest complete GI studies to rule out esophageal or stomach problems when the inspiration to refer to cardiology had popped into my head.

In those days we practiced cardiac stress testing and referral to cardiology for diagnostic workup of chest pain. Sophisticated echo stress testing and nuclear medicine stress testing hadn't yet become available. Cardiologists were doing heart catheterizations and suggesting cardiac bypass surgeries, but our initial workup left a lot to be desired by today's standards.

Within minutes I was on the phone with Alan Hill, cardiologist and associate professor of medicine at the medical school.

"Hello, Alan. I have a puzzling case I'd like for you to see. Clifford Johnson is a fifty-one-year-old male with atypical chest pain, hypertension, borderline cholesterol, positive family history of acute myocardial infarction in his father, and history of previous tobacco abuse. EKG here yesterday and repeat today are both normal. A treadmill stress test was normal yesterday, but he's worrying himself into a state of severe anxiety. He has plenty of risk factors but normal tests, including blood work and chest X-ray."

"I'll be glad to see him, Carl. If he's that anxious, have him here at 8:00 a.m. tomorrow, and I'll work him into my schedule. Have him bring a copy of any tests he's had, and thanks for the referral."

"Thank you, Alan, for your help. I'm sure Clifford will appreciate it."

I felt as much relief as the Johnsons that Cliff would be seen right away by cardiology. He was beginning to make me nervous just watching him continuously rubbing his chest.

✛

I was just getting ready to see patients the next morning at 9:00 when Donna called me to the phone.

"Dr. Hill is on the phone," she announced upon entering the lab where I was preparing my morning coffee.

"Thanks Donna. Could you have Christine transfer him back here, please?"

Within moments I heard the pleasant voice of Alan Hill on the other end of the line.

"Carl, I have news for you. Clifford Johnson is over his pain and feels wonderful this morning."

"Really?"

"Really."

"I guess we wasted your time, then."

"Not at all. You did exactly the right thing. His electrocardiogram today shows an acute inferior myocardial infarction in the lower wall of the heart, . . . but he feels great. Still, I've convinced him to go to the hospital, and EMS is here in the office picking him up."

"I don't understand. Three days of constant chest pain, multiple normal EKGs, a normal exercise stress test, and now he's pain-free with a heart attack?"

"Carl, there's still a lot we don't know in medicine. You did nothing wrong, and I reassured him that no one could have made that diagnosis before the fact with our current technology. He isn't angry with you at all. In fact, he and his wife have been singing your praises for being so thorough despite his having no evidence of heart trouble.

"I'll keep him in the ICU initially, just to be sure he's stable. After the routine monitoring and evaluation, I'll send him back to you. If he doesn't have any problems with the acute phase, I'll just see him once in a while for monitoring and treatment. Your early referral in the face of a negative workup was a great call. Keep up the good work."

I sat down with my coffee for a few minutes' reflection before beginning to see patients. Clifford Johnson hadn't experienced the sweating and shortness of breath typical male victims exhibit with an acute heart attack, but I felt as though I were experiencing these symptoms on my patient's behalf now.

How easy it would have been to miss this diagnosis or pass off the whole situation as the result of an overactive imagination! Without intervention no one could have known how this might have ended. Clifford might have been found dead later on in the week. His case would cause me over the years to listen closely to patients presenting with "nagging chest pain." One could never be completely sure. I mouthed a silent prayer of thanks to the Great Physician for protecting Clifford Johnson—and for helping me prevent a conceivably fatal mistake.

Indeed, there is still a good deal we don't know in medicine. Even now, years later, I'll have to admit that I don't understand how a patient can experience seventy-two hours of continual mild chest pain with all normal tests, including a normal exercise test, only to be relieved after the potential disaster has resulted in a completely blocked artery.

I am grateful to be practicing today in an era of advanced cardiovascular care, with the ready availability of stress echocardiograms, nuclear medicine cardiac imaging, emergency catheterization labs, highly trained cardiologists, and all of the other wonderful advances in modern medicine.

BY THE LIGHT OF THE MOON

One doesn't work in the medical field long before developing a healthy respect for the time of the month whenever there's a full moon. There is nothing quite like sitting on one's deck in the late summer contemplating that mysterious, oversized, yellow-orange orb as it glides above the eastern horizon casting its silvery glow over well-tended fields and barns, while listening to birds settle down in the shrubbery, softly twittering as night steals over the countryside.

On one such night I sat relaxing with my family, enjoying being home as the moon rose majestically, illuminating fields and pastures behind our home. Fireflies blinked their soft yellow lights, while cicadas and tree frogs added their music to nature's growing symphony. I had just started to really relax, hoping that for once there would be an uninterrupted evening of quiet, when the jangling of the telephone shattered my repose. I felt my entire body lurch as the shock of the harsh intrusion penetrated my tired brain.

Throughout the 1970s, of course, all we had were land lines. My home had intentionally been constructed with wall phone jacks in every room, including the bathrooms. We even had a phone jack on the deck.

Sighing with unutterable regret, I vacated my comfortable deck chair and walked to the phone at the far end of the deck beside the kitchen sliding glass doors. From the receiver came the well-known voice of our hospital operator: "Good evening, Dr. Matlock. I have a call from the emergency room for you. Could you hold one moment, please?"

Suppressing a sigh, I answered, "Sure, Peggy. Go ahead and put me through."

"Thank you, Doctor. One moment, please."

As I waited for someone from the ER to come on the line, low clouds began to blanket the sky, blotting out the enchanting illumination and casting the nighttime world into increasing blackness. The atmospheric changes matched my mood precisely.

Moments later the phone began to crackle again. "Hello, Dr. Matlock. It's Nurse Jensen. The emergency doctor is really backed up tonight—typical full moon type rush on business. He's already about two hours behind, and patients are still coming in faster than we can dismiss them. Since you're on back-up call, we would sure appreciate your assistance."

Trying to sound upbeat, I answered, "Sure. I'll be right in. Really bad, is it?"

"It's as bad as it ever gets. No time for anyone to eat dinner tonight, let alone breathe! We're really up against a crush. We sure appreciate your help. See you soon."

Without waiting for my reply, she hung up the phone. Bidding my family a reluctant goodnight, I drove to the hospital in Glen Falls, no longer enjoying the scenery or entertaining pleasant thoughts.

Upon my arrival I noticed that a second emergency doctor had come in early to help but that the two of them were barely making a dent in the census; thirty some charts were still lined up, representing patients not yet brought back to begin the process of evaluation. The sheer volume made the situation look hopeless.

Grabbing the next chart in line, I was making my way to see the patient when I noticed a police officer nearby at a small desk making out a report, a nurse from one of the medical floors standing just outside the room where she could observe the patient.

Turning to her, I asked, "What're the police doing here?"

Mary Adams, a middle-aged nurse, answered, "They're here because this man in Exam Room 7 has been really violent. He's suicidal, and the deputy sheriff had to disarm him prior to transport. We have him in restraints now, but I'm still to keep him under observation. He's tied down hand and foot, but I wouldn't go too close to him if I were you."

"Is that so?"

"Yes, I'm totally serious, Doctor."

Perusing his chart briefly, I read the nursing notes: "Alfred Wayne Carson, 22 years old, suspected substance abuse, suicidal. Loaded 22 caliber revolver taken away from him by the police. Pulse 120, Blood Pressure 155/98, Temperature 99, Respirations of 26."

Taking a deep breath, I entered the room, stethoscope about my neck, and walked up to the cart where Alfred Wayne was tied down on his side, hands restrained behind his back with hospital leather restraints on his wrists. In addition, the wrists had been fastened together, further restricting his movements.

Doing my best to act nonchalant, I began: "Hello Mr. Carson. I'm Dr. Matlock. I was asked to come and check on you. How are you doing?"

He stared up at me through steely blue eyes for what seemed an unduly long time before making a sound. Finally, he replied, "How do you think I'm doing, stupid? You're as dumb and ugly as that cop who brought me in. And I don't have to answer you. Go crawl back in whatever vermin hole you came out of."

I quickly stepped aside as he spat in my direction, just missing me as I dodged. Upset, but doing my best not to show it, I tried again: "Mr. Carson, I'm just trying to help you. Why did you try to spit on me?"

"Because you're there, and I don't have a better target right now. The cop is too far away."

"You know you won't get anywhere with this kind of behavior. Why don't you just calm down and tell me what's going on in your life? Maybe I can help you—I'd like to try."

"Do you want to really help me, Doc?"

"Sure—that's what I'm here for."

"Then get out of this room and leave me alone." With that he unleashed a torrent of profanity in my direction, calling me every epithet in his repertoire.

"Okay. But first I'm going to take a listen to your lungs and heart. From your abnormal vital signs It looks like you took some type of stimulant."

He had apparently decided to give me the silent treatment, for he had nothing else to say and refused to answer any more questions. Making my way behind him as he lay on his side, I listened to his breath sounds through his upper back, trying to stay out of range in case he decided to hurl spit in my direction again. Carefully placing the stethoscope over his side, I listened to his heart as it continued to race. At least there were no murmurs—which, if present, might have indicated an endocarditis or heart valve infection from IV drug abuse. I had already noted the red and brown streaks along the veins in his arms where he had apparently been injecting drugs into his body.

My exam was necessarily brief because he began to thrash his legs about. They were restrained together with leathers, but it looked as though he might decide to kick. I had already had enough of his antics, so I stood in the corner, well away from the cart, and made a few quick notes, ordered lab work and a drug screen, and handed Mary Adams the chart to process the orders.

More than ready for the next patient, I proceeded to the next room, where a worried elderly couple conversed quietly. Barbara Cotton, a pleasant but anxious eighty-eight year old, was accompanied by her ninety-three-year-old husband, Gilbert Cotton, who also looked apprehensive. Mrs. Cotton lay supine on the cart, while Gilbert stood beside her stroking her hand and intermittently trying to check her pulse.

"What seems to be the trouble, folks?"

Mr. Cotton did most of the talking, though it was apparent she was perfectly capable of answering for herself. "It's like this, Doctor," he began. "We were checking her pulse because she felt bad, and all of a sudden I couldn't find it. We talked it over but finally decided to have her checked. We were afraid her heart had stopped."

"That's right, Doctor," she put in. "We were real worried. And I don't like to worry Gilbert at all."

Trying to suppress a smile, I nodded and replied, "I'll check right now. Are you having any chest pain or shortness of breath?"

Gilbert interrupted by reporting, "She doesn't hurt at all. No trouble breathing. She just lost her pulse."

As Mrs. Cotton beamed up at her husband, I nodded my understanding and continued with the examination. I was happy to announce, "Pulse eighty-one and perfectly regular. Heart sounds completely normal. Lungs clear. No sign of congestive heart failure or heart murmurs.

Everything checks out normal, folks."

At that point they both became—unaccountably as far as I was concerned—a little teary eyed, and Gilbert took over again: "You don't know how much we appreciate this. We've been married for seventy years, and I don't know how either of us could ever get along if something happened to the other. Thanks so much for taking your time to examine my sweetheart."

"That's what we're here for, Mr. Cotton—to help people in need of our assistance. By the way, do you have any family here with you tonight?"

I suspected that these two could use assistance in getting back home, as there appeared to be a serious element of dementia involved in this visit.

"Our son is coming to pick us up, Doctor. We came in by ambulance, since she didn't have a pulse for a while."

I tried to explain that she couldn't truly have been pulseless but gave up when I saw the look of disbelief on both their faces. Instead I helped them to the waiting room, where their sixty-seven-year-old son smiled at me and assumed responsibility for their care.

I stood briefly watching them leave, only to hear nurses anxiously calling for assistance behind me. Smoke poured from the room in which Alfred Wayne was a patient. I rushed back to the room, along with several staff members, to determine why it appeared to be on fire. Arriving breathless, my heart pounding and the fire alarm clanging loudly, I was astounded to observe through the haze one of the nurses flailing a wet towel at Alfred Carson's legs and rhythmically beating them over and over again.

"What in the world is going on here?"

"Dr. Matlock, somehow he got his hands worked around to his side pocket and got out a cigarette lighter. He set his pants on fire, so I wet this towel to beat it out."

Seeing that the smoke was beginning to clear, I relaxed a little, responding, "Okay, since he is obviously self-destructive, give him an injection of Valium, ten milligrams, to calm him down. It may take more than that because he's higher than a kite."

Meanwhile, Alfred screamed and shouted at us nonstop. "Take these leathers off. My legs are burned. I'm in extreme pain. I need a shot of morphine. NOW!"

"Just give him the Valium for the time being. When he quiets down, get him undressed so I can completely examine him. It goes without saying we can't keep him here. He'll have to go to an Indianapolis psychiatric hospital. He's totally out of control."

Alfred Wayne continued to spit and curse until the Valium began to mellow his behavior. It took two more five-milligram doses to quiet him down enough to allow me to examine his legs for burns. We were all relieved when the examination disclosed only superficial first-degree burns of less than a two-percent body surface area—tantamount to a localized sunburn of the upper thighs. We were even happier when permission had been given by the on-call psychiatrist to transport him to Indianapolis for ongoing care and treatment. Not surprisingly, his drug tests came back positive for cocaine and amphetamines; his suicidal behavior was likely related to the drug overdose.

It was my duty to apprise his parents of the situation when they showed up, just as the ambulance was pulling out of the hospital drive en route to Indianapolis. I escorted the couple to the chapel just down the hallway, where we could speak in private.

"I'm sorry, Mr. and Mrs. Carson. I believe your son will be okay, but we had to send him on to a psychiatric facility in Indianapolis. The police had to take a gun away from him, and then he set his clothes on fire with a cigarette lighter. He has no serious injuries, but he isn't very rational due to a stimulant drug overdose."

Mr. Carson, his own face flushed and smelling of alcohol, took a deep breath and then began: "I'm sorry for the trouble he caused tonight. Since he started abusing drugs he's a totally different person, not at all like the happy, carefree boy we raised. We've spent a small fortune on him, trying to help him kick the habit, but he always goes right back to the same old friends and behavior. I'm about ready to give up. If he doesn't want help, so be it, I say." With that, he stood up and resolutely stalked out of the chapel.

Mrs. Carson—short, thin, and frail appearing—lingered behind with tears in her eyes. She shyly reached out to shake my hand and in a small, quavering voice offered, "Thank you for helping Alfred Wayne, Doctor. My husband, Charles, just doesn't understand Alfred. We've been married twenty years, after my first husband ran off and left us. He adopted Alfred Wayne, but those two have never gotten along very well. Still, my Charley means well . . ."

Looking abjectly forlorn, she followed her husband out through the exit. As they left I heard them softly arguing about whether or not to make the trip to Indianapolis to see how Alfred was doing. She wanted to, but he preferred to go home and watch television.

We had managed to wade through about sixty per cent of the patient stack when the sherriff's deputies brought in a young man of eighteen for evaluation.

Edward Riley was five feet, six inches tall, clean shaven, and muscular. Soft spoken, diffident, and polite, he sat patiently on the cart, submitting docilely to the nurse's preliminary check of his vital signs. She recorded his chief complaint before handing me the chart; I couldn't help but notice that she was by this time wearing an enigmatic smile and shrugging her shoulders.

The complaint itself was equally mystifying: "Sherriff won't let me preach."

"Hello, Mr. Riley. May I call you Edward?"

"Yes, Doctor. That's fine with me."

"Okay, Edward. I'm Dr. Matlock. What seems to be the problem? I don't quite understand from your complaint to the nurse. This says the sherriff wouldn't let you preach. Can you tell me more about what's going on and why you're here? You seem to be under arrest."

"Yes, sir, I am under arrest. All I wanted to do was to preach."

"Help me understand, Edward. Where were you preaching, and why wouldn't the officers let you preach?"

Sighing and slumping over a little, he began his story: "I was walking along a road in the country when I heard a voice. The voice told me to preach. I'm sure it was the voice of God, so I started to look for a place."

He stopped, as though this explanation should be adequate for me to understand completely why he now found himself under arrest. Somewhat frustrated with this truncated explanation, I tried again. "And where did you find a place to preach?"

"At a house."

"Whose house?"

Sighing more audibly, he started again: "This is the fourth or fifth time I've had to tell this story. People just laugh at me. Do I really have to tell it again? Can't you just talk to the police? They act like they know everything."

"I'm sure they know why they brought you in, but I want to hear your version. I'll be your advocate if you'll let me."

Sadly, and evidently engrossed in the study of his dusty boots, he finally replied, "You can't help me. But I'll try to do what you want. The voice of God told me to 'shout it from the housetops.' Just like the Bible says."

"Shout it from the housetops?"

"That's what I said. So I saw this man who had just finished mowing his lawn. He had a nice two-story house with a tree right near one of the corners. I politely asked if I could get up on his roof to preach."

"And . . . ?"

"And he said no. So I just climbed up anyway to the second story rooftop and preached as loud as I could. I could see he was getting mad, but I kept on preaching while he stood on the ground shaking his fist and threatening to come up after me.

"I guess he changed his mind because he never came up the tree. Instead he went inside while I just kept on preaching. After several minutes this police car pulled up with red light flashing, and two officers got out. They stood down below telling me to come down—that they wouldn't hurt me or anything."

"What did you do then, Edward?"

"I finished my sermon, of course."

"Was there anyone else there listening to you? I mean, preachers usually have an audience to address."

"No, the nearest house was probably two blocks away."

"So why did you do it?"

"Because of the voice, that's why."

"How long did this go on?"

"Well, I climbed up at about 4:00 o'clock and came down about 7:30."

"Did anyone try to come up after you?"

"No, they were afraid I was trying to hurt myself and might jump. So they just talked and talked while I finished my sermon. Very silly, you know . . ."

"It does sound a little silly to me."

Edward, looking offended, sat staring straight ahead for a while before finally observing, "They were the silly ones. I was minding God. I wasn't about to hurt myself or anybody else."

"You seem to be very religious. I don't understand, then, why you would invade someone's property, ignore the police, and continue preaching. Doesn't the Bible teach that we're to obey the laws of the land?"

Turning his head to stare straight at me with evident disdain, he drew a deep breath before concluding his defense: "A lot you know, Doctor. I don't believe you know the Bible very well. Haven't you ever heard that it's better to obey God than man?"

He turned his head away, then, staring fixedly at some invisible spot on the blank wall alongside him. He volunteered no more information as he submitted to my head-to-toes examination, which found him to be an otherwise healthy specimen.

I located officer Jack Donaldson, the sherriff's deputy, in the waiting area. He had remained nearby in case of trouble, as well as to take custody of the young man when we were finished.

"Hello, Jack. Do you know this kid?"

"I sure do, Doc. He comes from a good home, but there's a long history of mental illness in his family. His parents are older and can't always get him to take his medication. He has a diagnosis, I think, of schizophrenia. He's really not a bad kid, but we have to pick him up every so often."

"What are you going to do with him, Jack?"

"Technically, I'm supposed to lock him up and file charges. But the homeowner was a nice guy, and since he saw that Edward didn't appear dangerous—just mixed up and sick—he said he'd just as soon forget it. So if you're finished with him I'll call my partner to come and pick us up. We'll take him home. I'm sure his parents are very worried."

"That's great, Jack. I appreciate your help."

"Glad to be of service. See you later, Doc."

By 11:00 p.m. the pace had slowed down enough that the ER doctor could keep up with the flow of patients. Nurse Jensen was just handing off her report to Ann Kilgore for the night shift, and I had stopped by the desk to see whether they needed any more help when the overhead page, usually silenced at night, blared overhead.

"Dr. Matlock, OB floor stat. Dr. Carl Matlock, OB floor stat."

By now I was totally exhausted, but a period of rest looked exceedingly unlikely. As I dashed to the third floor, not waiting for the elevator, I reviewed the other career pathways I could have chosen, any one of which would've had me home tucked away in bed by this time: radiology, pathology, ophthalmology, . . . and the list went on.

Arriving in time to see one of my patients being wheeled into the delivery room, I was met by a nurse, who handed me a mask, gown, and shoe covers. "No time to change. She came in fully dilated and ready to deliver. We need you in the delivery room right now. Mrs. Martin tells me you've diagnosed twins. She has two other children at home, and this is the third pregnancy. We're doing our best to keep her from pushing, but you'd better hurry."

I barely made the delivery room in time to catch baby Daniel, five pounds four ounces, followed without delay by sister Mary, six pounds one ounce. Reconsidering my vocation as I examined the pair of healthy fraternal twins, I decided that any of those medical professions that kept a man home at night couldn't possibly be as rewarding as the one I was experiencing. Family Practice isn't just my vocation—it's my avocation.

At 3:00 a.m., as I wended my way back home for some brief shut-eye, I noticed the farm fields bathed in soft light and found myself humming, "By the light of the silvery moon . . ."

THE GOOD SHEPHERD

"Richard and Evelyn Corbin are in Exam 3, Doctor Matlock. They brought in little Jason, age six, who appears to be very ill. I've got him ready for you to see."

"Thanks, Donna. I'll be with them as soon as I finish this chart."

Before entering the room I reminisced briefly about the Corbin family. I had known Richard and Evelyn for several years. They frequently attended our church during revivals and other special meetings when their home church met with our congregation. Richard was a manager at a local factory in Glen Falls, and Evelyn worked fulltime as the mother of their three children, two sons and a daughter. Jason was the middle child, and so far as I could remember he had no serious health problems.

I recalled an occasion about two months earlier when Richard had hailed me at the grocery store. He had appeared to be troubled about something and had wanted to know what I knew about iridology doctors. Although we were friends, he didn't continue the conversation for very long after I had voiced my opinion that iridology was more closely akin to witchcraft than to medicine. Sensing his skepticism, I had tried to explain that I wasn't against natural medicine when it was tested and proven; after all, aspirin had come from willow bark and digitalis from foxglove. At that point he simply apologized for bothering me and went on with his shopping.

I had a vague feeling of dis-ease now, a nagging suspicion that I was about to find out why he had been asking my opinion that day. With a sense of foreboding, I knocked and entered the room.

"Hello Richard, Evelyn. And how's my little friend Jason today?"

Richard sat slumped over in his chair, hands tightly clasped together in his lap, staring at the floor. He managed to mumble a soft "Hello" before going completely silent.

Evelyn stood beside the examination table next to Jason. She wore a haunted expression despite her strained, fleeting smile. She held Jason's hand while smoothing his hair and patting his cheeks. Little Jason bravely looked up from the cart on which he was lying on his back. He flashed a wan smile and offered his other hand to me, showing no fear since he was very familiar with me and my family.

"What seems to be the trouble, folks? Can you tell me about it?"

Richard looked up at me for the first time and simply shrugged. After a brief pause he looked over at Evelyn and nodded for her to do the talking.

"Dr. Matlock, I'm afraid we may have made a terrible mistake."

An uncomfortable silence ensued while Evelyn attempted to compose herself enough to continue the narrative. She fought back tears as I offered a tissue. Finally she was able to go on, as Richard was once again staring at the floor: "Jason has been sick for about four months now. A friend of ours told us about her eye doctor, about how wonderful he is in diagnosing and how he uses natural medicine. Only he isn't a real eye doctor. He's an iridologist."

At that point Richard looked up and interjected, "If there was a mistake it was all my doing. I've read a lot about medicines and side effects, and, well, you know . . . "

"It's alright, Richard. A lot of people feel that way. I'm sure you meant the very best for Jason."

Some of the tension visibly lifted from Richard as he exhaled audibly and nodded at me. "Thanks for understanding, Doc."

"Sure. Go on, Evelyn. What can you tell me about Jason's illness?"

"The iridologist looked in Jason's eyes for a long time. That was about four months ago, I think. He told us that Jason had a mild heart condition but that he'll be alright. We were supposed to give him a healthy diet and light exercise until he got well again."

Raising her voice in obvious anguish, she continued, "That was four months ago, and Jason has gotten steadily worse. He's too weak to stay up for more than two or three hours at a time. He doesn't want to play. He isn't eating much at all, and he sometimes seems to have a low-grade fever. He also coughs a little and isn't even interested in his favorite toys."

Her words spilled out in torrents as she went on to describe her helpless feeling as she observed her son's declining health. Richard once again studied the floor as she gave vent to her despair and frustration. Glancing at her husband with a pitying look, she hastened to add, "I don't want you to just blame Richard, Doctor. We were in agreement, and some of our friends kept telling us we were doing the right thing."

"I'm not blaming either of you for anything. In the first place, we don't even have a diagnosis yet. But go on with your story. Anything you can tell me may help with a diagnosis. It's obvious that Jason is quite ill, but we'll do everything possible to help him get well again . . . Isn't that right, Jason? We both know you have a good mama and daddy."

His frail hand once again reached out and held onto my fingers as he smiled trustingly up at me. Evelyn went on for several minutes, describing every symptom she could recall, and I allowed her simply to ventilate. She was going to need all the strength she could muster if Jason was half as sick as I suspected. Richard began to participate, both parents filling me in on every detail as it occurred to them.

When they had exhausted their collective recollections regarding their son's illness, Richard looked sheepishly at me and admitted, "I was afraid you'd be mad at me or think me a bad father."

"I don't think you're a bad father or that your wife is a bad mother. It's important for both of you, as well as for Jason and your other children, that you not get into a blame game. We all need to work together, in harmony, to help Jason get well. Now let me take a look at you, Jason, okay?"

Another brief smile and nod indicated that he was ready. I conducted a head-to-toes examination of the little boy, noting a temperature slightly subnormal, a pulse rate increased to 110, a soft heart murmur, and pallid skin and complexion—but most of all the numerous matted lymph nodes in his neck, axillae, and inguinal areas. I also noted a few small bruises and petechiae—little spots of bleeding in the skin. Upon completing the examination I called for Donna to assist me.

"Could you please take Jason back to our lab area and get a sucker for him (that is, if his parents agree)?"

With Jason safely tucked in Donna's arms and out of the room, I turned to the parents. "Richard, Evelyn, I'm very afraid that Jason has a serious blood disease. He has enlarged lymph nodes and signs of anemia and small areas of bleeding into the skin.

"It's true that he has a heart murmur, but a lot of children have what we call innocent murmurs. They sound something like a violin string vibrating when it's plucked. In addition, anemia can induce a flow murmur as the heart works harder to pump less blood than is normally present. In other words,

I'm not really concerned about his heart, but I'm very concerned about his blood."

"What do you mean, Doc? Could he have a serious disease . . . like leukemia?" asked Richard.

"We won't know until we get the blood tests done. But I'm concerned, for sure."

Evelyn collapsed into a chair beside Richard and fell against his shoulder, weeping, as he hugged her tightly, tears coursing down his own cheeks. No one spoke for a few minutes, as I sat silently with them. There are times when silence and shared sorrow constitute the most important comforts a doctor can offer. My own eyes were moist as I watched these two people about whom I cared sobbing in one another's arms. Finally I offered more tissues, along with the only advice I could think of at that time: "Now remember, we don't have a firm diagnosis yet. Maybe it won't be as bad as what we've discussed, but whatever is wrong Jason will need all our encouragement and help to get better. Don't blame one another or carry around a load of guilt. That won't help Jason. He needs two upbeat parents who love him and one another.

"I would like you to take him to the lab in Glen Falls and have a battery of blood tests done to check his blood count, liver, and other vital organs. Also, they'll have you collect a urine sample, and radiology will get a chest X-ray. Some test results won't be back until tomorrow. However, you can come back after the last appointment this afternoon. I should have a basic idea by then of what we're dealing with regarding the blood work."

After thanking us, the Corbin family left the office. Christine and Donna had been quietly discussing the case and took the opportunity to speak with me in our small lab. Donna began, "You think he has leukemia, don't you?"

"I hope in the worst way I'm wrong. But yes, that's what I think."

Voice quavering, Christine asked, "Is it too late to do anything if he does?"

"Not necessarily. However, the sooner a serious problem is addressed, the better. And yes, people can wait too long for medicine to be able to do anything."

"I sure hope the poor little thing will be alright, Doctor."

"So do I," echoed Donna.

"We all hope and pray for the best."

One of the most difficult challenges with which medical professionals grapple is the seriously ill child. We expect older people to have health problems, to face death, and even to eventually die, but dealing with a patient gravely ill at a tender age is always difficult. I gave the staff, and myself, an extra few minutes to regain composure before continuing with our schedule.

Christine made her way back to the front desk, and Donna started escorting the newly arrived patients to rooms. I stood gazing out the window, watching a lone robin perched on a nearby branch. Even its mood seemed somber on this overcast day.

Donna returned to the lab and announced, "I'm sorry, but it doesn't get any better. Mrs. Brown is here again and wants to talk about her husband, Don. He's getting worse all the time."

"Okay, I might as well get started."

I did indeed find Dotty Brown in a sorrowful state of mind when I sat down to take a history.

"I'm sorry, Mrs. Brown. Donna told me Don isn't doing very well."

"Please, Doctor, just call me Dotty. Mrs. Brown seems way too formal."

"Very well, Dotty. How can I help?"

"You know that we've been married for over fifty-five years now. My Don was always such a strong man, such a hard worker, such a wonderful provider. But now . . . I feel him just slipping away from me."

Dotty paused long enough to dry scalding tears and wipe her nose. I waited patiently before probing, "What's happening to Don now? Is he having more trouble getting around?"

I already knew that Donald Brown was seventy-nine years of age, had Alzheimer's dementia, and was becoming progressively more feeble.

When able to continue, Dotty reported, "This morning he didn't know me for a while, and then he decided he was in the wrong house. It was all I could do to keep him indoors until our son, Elmer, arrived to sit with him. I don't know what to do anymore. Last week I found him out in the middle of the road right in front of our house, and he was totally lost."

"I'm sure you know that we don't have very good solutions yet for Alzheimer's disease. Do you think you could get help—someone to be with him a good part of the day to allow you to get some rest?"

"I don't want to do that until I have to. Don was a good provider, but I'm afraid a private nurse would deplete our funds. And our son, Elmer, has to go to work. He left his job today to help with his dad. Fortunately, he has an understanding boss, but we can't keep asking him to leave work, and we don't have a big family to turn to. Elmer's sons live in Texas.

"Whatever am I to do, Dr. Matlock? It breaks my heart to see him so confused and falling down when he forgets his walker."

"Do you feel it's time to consider a nursing home for chronic care, Dotty?"

Stiffening her back and taking on a determined look, she answered, "That'll be the last resort. The last resort, I tell you. When we got married we promised each other to never let that happen. I still haven't changed my mind about that. I love Don too much to put him in a home."

"Other than getting someone to do private duty, I don't know what else to suggest other than to send a home health nurse to check on him from time to time. That might give you a little relief, but they can only come for brief visits. Perhaps they could give you suggestions regarding Don's care."

"I would like to try that, Doctor. And do you think I could have one more refill of Valium, just the two-milligram dose? I promise not to take it unless I absolutely have to. Sometimes the sadness and stress are just too much."

"Well, just a few. And don't take more than one a day, and then only when absolutely necessary. Sedatives can actually increase depression and grief if they're misused."

○

And so the day droned on . . . and on—a day of frustration, of trying to solve intractable social problems like that faced by Don and Dotty Brown. More than once I found myself offering words of solace while feeling helpless in the face of overwhelming human need and grief.

And then the lab called: "Dr. Matlock, I have a preliminary report on Jason Corbin for you. Dr. Wright, the pathologist wants to discuss it with you. Can you hold for Dr. Wright?"

"Yes, please put him on."

"Hello, Carl, this is Fred Wright. I wanted to discuss this case with you. Jason is one sick little fella, for sure."

"Does he have leukemia, Fred?"

"He does, but I need to do a little more evaluation. It looks like acute myelocytic leukemia, which, as you know, has a poor prognosis if not treated promptly. How long has he been ill?"

"The best I can tell, a little over four months now."

"You mean the parents are just now bringing him in for the first time?"

"Yes—and no. They've been taking him to an iridologist and were told he had mild heart disease. They finally lost faith and brought him to me today."

After uttering several under-the-breath oaths, he finally went on, "Well, they sure waited long enough to get help. He has to be a really sick child from the looks of this blood work. What kind of parents are they, anyway?"

"They're not bad parents—just deceived about the care they thought they were getting. I assure you, they're extremely remorseful now. I just hope it isn't too late to achieve a cure. I'm going to refer them to the Indianapolis Children's Hospital urgently. I know one of the pediatric oncologists there and should be able to get Jason seen right away."

"Whatever you say Carl, but people can sure be stupid sometimes."

I had seen all of my other patients for the day and was only waiting for the Corbins to return as I sat alone in the lab pondering what to say and how to offer comfort. No, Richard and Evelyn weren't stupid people—just good people who'd been taken in by some very bad advice.

Once again I sat staring at the gray landscape as late afternoon rain squalls swept over the fields behind the office. The weather matched my mood perfectly. Hearing the door open behind me, I looked up to see Christine entering the lab.

"Dr. Matlock, do you think I could go on home? Donna told me you were getting bad news from the lab. I don't think I can take any more sadness today. I'm—I'm so sorry. I just feel so terribly bad. I don't want to lose control in front of them. Donna said she would be here. Is it okay?"

"Yes, it's absolutely okay. At a time like this I wish I could just go on home too. Don't worry about it. I'll see you in the morning. Tomorrow will be a better day. Tomorrow is OB day—a happy day for us usually."

"I know, and thank you. I believe they're coming in now. I heard Donna in the waiting room greeting someone."

Several minutes later Donna opened the door and advised me that she had the couple in our consultation room, where my desk and more comfortable office furniture were located.

"They're ready to see you, and I think they're prepared for the worst. They left Jason with Evelyn's parents. He doesn't understand everything, of course, but they didn't want him to hear the discussion."

Steeling myself, I joined the Corbins, sitting opposite them for a frank conversation. The tension in the room was palpable as I cleared my throat to begin: "I'm afraid that I don't have good news for you. Jason does have leukemia. I just spoke with our pathologist, Dr. Wright, who said more tests need to be done, though he's quite sure it is a type of leukemia."

One could have heard a pin drop as Jason's parents sat in stunned silence for a full minute, registering this unwanted information. They exchanged guilty glances, after which Richard sat once again with his head bowed, beginning to sob silently, shoulders heaving, while Evelyn wept softly into her handkerchief. Sensing the need Donna slipped quietly into the room and put her arms around Evelyn. Also knowing the family socially, my nurse shared in the collective grief.

After what I felt was an appropriate time, I began to discuss a course of action: "Richard, Evelyn, as I told you earlier we aren't going to give up hope. I know a pediatric oncologist at Children's Hospital in Indianapolis. With your permission I'll call first thing in the morning and make an urgent referral. They have an excellent staff and can bring all the up-to-date treatment modalities to bear on your son's behalf. It's very important not to give up hope."

Finally Richard found his voice and asked, "Does he have a bad type of leukemia, Doc? I mean, what are his chances?"

"Dr. Wright believes it's acute myelocytic leukemia—and yes, it's a more serious type than the usual childhood acute lymphocytic leukemia. However, treatment is certainly available. I'm not giving up, and neither should you."

After several minutes the couple stood to leave, having cried until there were, at least for the moment, no more tears to shed. Richard took my hand first, saying, "Thanks, Doc. I wish I had listened to what you had to say the first time. We appreciate your help and concern."

Evelyn added, "We certainly do. And thank you, Donna, for staying with us along with Doc. I think I can go home now and put on a smile for Jason. We'll sure do our best, and thank you for everything."

○

I wish I could affix a happy ending to the story, but about six months later we stood at a cold grave site on another windy, overcast day as the minister intoned the words, "Dust to dust and ashes to ashes. We now commend little Jason to the loving care of the heavenly Father he loved with childlike trust."

As I watched the little casket being lowered into the earth, I thought about Jason. He had suffered physically in ways no little child should ever have to experience. Sometimes he cried out in pain, but throughout his ordeal he spoke bravely about Jesus, the Good Shepherd. Silently I said my goodbye, but then, turning to leave, I felt a strange wafting of joy overriding the leaden sorrow. It seemed as though the Good Shepherd was indeed physically present, wrapping his arms around those who grieved, telling all who would listen that Jason was safe and secure at last—home in the arms of Jesus, the Savior of the world.

BUCK FEVER

I t came around every year; I liked to think of it as "buck
fever syndrome." It was highly contagious, often affecting
whole groups of men—and sometimes women as well. I
must admit that during the first year of my medical practice
I missed the diagnosis entirely. The onset coincided precisely
with the day prior to the opening of deer hunting season.

You may have heard about deer ticks, lyme disease, falls
from tree stands, and terrible gunshot injuries affecting those
who have braved the woods on frosty mornings, hoping to
catch sight of that "big one" with the gigantic rack of horns.
But there are subtle variations—more common though
certainly less remarkable—that have evaded the radar.

It was mid-morning at the office with the waiting area
full of those who had fallen victim to the usual colds, coughs,
and sore throats of the fall season when I encountered my
first case. Donna came in with an enigmatic smile, informing
me that Billy Howard was ready to be seen.

Walking down the hall to Exam Room 4, I wondered about that smile. I didn't particularly like the implication that she knew something I didn't regarding this upcoming visit. Still puzzled as I entered the room, I opened with, "Good morning, Billy. What seems to be the trouble today?"

Billy was seated in one of our chairs, bent over, holding his abdomen and intermittently groaning in a most pitiful manner. He finally regained his composure and answered in a weak voice, "I don' know, Doc. I woke up at 3:00 a.m. with terrible cramps, and now I'm havin' diarrhea like you never seen before."

"Are you nauseated, Billy?"

With that he grabbed his mouth and jumped up, mumbling about needing to go the bathroom. I opened the door for him, and he clattered down the hall, entered the bathroom, slammed the door, and proceeded to heave loudly enough for the front office to hear.

While I waited on him to return, I began making notes about his symptoms—but paused when I heard Donna pass by in the hallway, snickering. I hated to admit it, but I was becoming somewhat peeved by her lighthearted manner. I happened to know that Billy was one of her admirers, but she felt him to be a hopeless bumpkin. Still, she had no cause to laugh at him when he was this sick.

Billy re-entered the room about five minutes later, the front of his shirt damp with what I assumed to be moisture from having heaved in the commode. He continued to hold his abdomen but looked a little better. I could hear Donna in the bathroom down the hallway, humming as she cleaned, and I'm afraid I was focusing more on that than on Billy's symptoms. She was just too blasé about this unfortunate young man's dilemma. I never paused to consider that the behavior was out of character for her, that something had to be amiss in my thinking. My preoccupation led to my first missed diagnosis of buck fever syndrome.

Like an automaton, I completed a thorough examination of Billy, who groaned as I palpated the abdomen, but his bowel sounds were normal. In fact, the entire examination was unrevealing. We had already discussed the possibly tainted food he had consumed the night before. It seemed to be an open and closed case: gastrointestinal food poisoning with vomiting, diarrhea, and weakness.

"Do you think you can keep anything down, Billy?"

"I think so, Doc," he managed between moans.

"If you aren't able to keep down liquids, I'll have to admit you to the hospital for IV fluids, Billy."

He managed to sit back up on the examination table and in a stronger voice answered, "Won't be necessary, Doc. You just give me some of that vomitin' medicine, and I'll be okay."

I finished writing out his prescriptions and was preparing to exit the room when Billy exclaimed, as though in afterthought, "Doc, I need a note for work."

Like many of the men in the community, Billy did some small-time farming, but he also worked at a Chrysler plant in nearby Glen Falls.

"Oh, sure, Billy. Just a moment."

Retrieving my pen, I started to write, when Billy interrupted me once again.

"It has to be for at least three days or I won't get paid. I'm most awful weak, Doc. I believe it'll take at least that long. Don't you think so too?"

The first red light should have gone off in my head, but I'm ashamed to admit that the implications eluded me. As a physician I try to believe people, at least until they give me reason to do otherwise.

"Sounds reasonable—yes, it will take a while to regain your strength."

Billy beamed and thanked me profusely as he made his way to the front office to pay his bill. He seemed to be feeling better already. I gave little thought to his situation as Donna swept by me in an uncharacteristically carefree manner, still humming softly. And that's how easy it can be for the uninitiated to miss the serious diagnosis of buck fever syndrome, a seasonal malady striking with amazing predictability each fall.

If that makes you think I might have been a little naïve, just accompany me to the next examining room, where Donna had placed a chart in the rack on the door with the words "Acute Back and Neck Pain."

Ron Trueblood sat rigidly on the side of the examining table, looking straight ahead as though turning, even to acknowledge my entrance, would have caused him great pain. Ron was a little more polished than Billy in his manner of speech and decorum, but few men, regardless of their degree of education or finesse, are resistant to the ravages of buck fever. Ron, I know, clerked in the local hardware store.

"Hello, Ron. What's happened to you?"

"I did a lot of sweeping last night at the hardware, but I really hurt my back helping my dad in the barn last night. I moved a lot of hay bales so he could have the space for another horse stall, and I guess I overdid it."

"Have you ever had back and neck trouble in the past?"

"Oh, once in a while, but nothing serious. Old Doc Langley always gives me a few pain pills and muscle relaxers, but he's out today. So I thought I'd try you. You see my wife and kids anyway, and Doc Langley is gettin' old."

"Sure, I'll be glad to try and help. Do you think you can lie back on the exam table?"

With a grimace Ron managed to lower himself to a supine position. "I made it, but it sure hurts."

"Do you have any pain shooting down your legs—any numbness or tingling?"

After careful thought, Ron responded, "No, just pain in my back and neck."

"How many bales did you move, Ron?"

"Oh, about fifty or sixty."

"That many?"

"Yeah, I should've known better. That always did hurt my back, but Dad needed to put up a new stall. I felt like I should try to help, you know."

As he talked I examined him, checking off normal reflexes in the legs, negative straight leg raising tests, and confirmation of no sciatic component of the pain. Normal abdominal examination ruled out serious internal pathology.

"Could you possibly roll over onto your abdomen, face down?"

"I think so, Doc. Just be patient with me, please."

Slowly, Ron rolled over so I could check his back.

"Thanks, Ron. Now let me know if I touch any particularly tender spots."

Methodically, I palpated from lower back to posterior neck muscles. Although he twitched a lot during the exam, I found no trigger areas for the pain.

"Take your time, please, but you can get up off the table. Do you need me to help you?"

"I think I can make it. Just give me a minute."

Slowly he extended his legs over the side of the table, slid to the floor, and stood for several moments gripping the table, back and neck ramrod straight. Turning around to face me, Ron grinned and commented, "Made it, but it sure hurts."

As I filled out a prescription for a few Tylenol #3 and a muscle relaxant to cover seven days, he stood stiffly at attention. I glanced quizzically at him as he explained, "Hurts too bad to sit down right now . . . Oh, and, Doc, could you give me a note for work, please? It usually takes me about three days to recover when my back and neck are this bad."

"Three days sounds about right. Okay, Ron."

Ron walked stiffly down the hallway, and I thought little more about his case as I continued to see patients with flu-like symptoms until noon. We had a one-hour break for lunch that day, as the schedule was lighter than normal. I found Donna and Christine with box lunches of fried chicken, tomatoes, slaw, fresh butter, and rolls making their way to the lab area for lunch.

Christine spoke up: "Since we had a break coming, Donna got us the special at House's pharmacy and general store. You were busy, and Donna thought you might want to go pick out your own lunch. They have a lot of business today—guys loading up on deer slugs for their guns and buying hunting jackets and camouflage clothing."

Somehow I felt as though I were being set up, but for what, I had no idea. Both ladies wore beatific smiles, but I didn't like the way Christine seemed to wink at Donna.

"Yeah, sure. That would be a relaxing change of pace. I always like their burgers the most."

I exited through the front door since the waiting room was empty at the noon hour. Just before it closed shut, however, I thought I detected laughter coming from the lab.

✛

As I entered Barry House's combined pharmacy, soda fountain, fast food bar, and general farm and dry goods store, I saw the usual crowd lined up at the lunch bar. Four older men occupied one of the booths for those preferring more comfortable seating, and the other was empty.

I sat down in the unoccupied booth and began to peruse the menu. I did find it relaxing to listen to the local banter as the men in the next booth joked and discussed current events. I had just about decided on the special when Barry House approached.

"Mind if I join you?"

"Of course not, Barry. Have a seat. What do you recommend?"

"You can't go wrong with our special. That's what I'm having. Busy day, Doc?"

"Busy enough. There are a lot of flu and upper respiratory illnesses around."

"I know. I've been filling your prescriptions. You helped save our business by coming to town. I was beginning to wonder if a rural pharmacy was a good idea."

"I wouldn't think you'd have a problem. A farmer, a homemaker, or just about anyone else can find everything here—other than major farm implements, anyway."

"Just about, but all the same I'm glad you set up practice here."

"Don't you get a lot of prescriptions from Dr. Langley?"

"A little, but he's really old school. Dispenses about all his prescriptions, except for narcotics and a few others, right from the office. Buys them real cheap too, judging by the ones patients have shown me—all generics, of course—a lot of it just over the counter medicines they could buy here just as cheap."

"I know all about it, Barry. A lot of his patients think I'm expensive because I insist on seeing them if they need an antibiotic. His nurses just give them three days of intramuscular penicillin without him ever seeing them. It's hard to compete with that kind of practice."

While we waited for our food to arrive, one of the older men from the next booth approached to exchange pleasantries.

"Hello, Barry, Doc. Nice fall day."

Smiling, I answered, "It sure is, John."

Barry put in, "Sounds like you two know each other."

"Yes, John Holt was one of my patients my first week of practice. We're well acquainted." (Patient privacy was hardly an issue in those days; besides, everyone in town knew just about everyone else and everything about them.)

"That's right, Barry. Me and Doc go way back to his startup days. He's taken real good care of me. There is one thing I'd like to know, Doc."

"What's that, John?"

"I didn't know Levi Trueblood has horses now."

"I don't understand, John. I don't believe I know Levi Trueblood."

"Sure you do, Doc."

"I don't understand, John."

"Levi is Ron Trueblood's old man."

"I'm sorry, but I still don't follow."

I noticed the hint of a smirk on Barry's face at the same time I heard the loud guffaws from the other old geezers in John's booth.

"Well, it's like this, Doc. Levi was injured by a horse that threw him when he was a kid. He's a cattleman. Has no use for horses—hates 'em, in fact."

By this point a little alarm bell was going off in my head, and my face was beginning to feel hot. Enjoying himself immensely, John rocked back on his boots and tucked his thumbs behind the suspenders on his bib overalls. He bobbed his head up and down as he continued, "Yes sir, Doc. Billy Howard and Ron Trueblood were just in here a few minutes ago. Bought up most of the deer slugs in the place. Told us how you gave 'em each three days off. Right thoughty of you, Doc. Yes sir, right thoughty . . . Now, if I was still a young feller and wanted time off to hunt, would you oblige me as well?"

By now the old codgers in the next booth were coming over to join in the fun. The laughter was so uproarious that shoppers in the back of the spacious storeroom turned around to stare. As the exiting diners shuffled for the door, one of them turned back to me and exclaimed, "Better bar your doors, Doc. When word gets out there'll be standin' room only. Yes sir, you'll have the biggest practice in the county."

Barry House had difficulty refraining from laughter but managed a sympathetic half-smile as he advised me, "Don't pay any attention to those old loafers. They have nothing better to do than lounge around town and gossip."

As the door slammed shut John shouted over his shoulder, "Buck fever, Doc. It's buck fever. Most of the local boys get it."

○

Arriving back at the office I suffered through the greetings of my office staff. Donna and Christine led me to the lab, where they had cut the photo of a deer from one of our magazines and hung it on the wall, labeled "Buck Fever. See Doc Matlock for cure. Three days off work to hunt."

"Okay, you two've had your fun, and I suppose I deserve it. You should've heard the laughter during lunch. With the local gossip line I'm sure to be the butt of jokes for the next week or so. By the way, how did you two know I was being set up?"

"It wasn't difficult. Those two came in together this morning in Billy's Ford pick-up, the one with the loud muffler and guns in the rack. They jumped out laughing and joking, obviously not realizing Christine had spotted them.

"She waved me over to the window, and we watched them talking for a few minutes. Then Billy came in first, holding his stomach and making faces, while Ron stood outside talking to another patient and smoking a cigarette. A little while later Ron stomped out his cigarette and started a slow walk to the door, holding his body rigid for the first time."

Christine chimed in, "We were careful not to let Billy see us watching Ron during the dramatic entrance. I guess he was practicing for you."

"Well, I certainly wish you'd filled me in on what you observed."

Donna piped up, "And if we had, what would you've done? Called them liars?"

Christine added, "We really didn't know what to do. We thought you might catch on without help, but we didn't know how they'd react if you did. What if they got really angry and threatening?"

"So your excuse is that you were concerned for my safety?"

"That's about the size of it."

By this point I had somewhat recovered my sense of humor and began to chuckle. I retreated to the lab to keep from being glimpsed at the moment by the afternoon patients who were just beginning to filter in. Seated by the window gazing out over the changing fall landscape, I finally gave vent to muffled laughter.

I was amazed at the audacity of those two slackers who had bragged about their exploits in town, apparently not caring whether I heard about it—or even considering that possibility. I marveled at their resourcefulness even as I entertained uncharitable thoughts about their deeds.

Midway through the next morning the office once again filled with patients complaining of respiratory illnesses. I had just finished seeing John Holt, still smiling about buck fever syndrome despite his own head congestion. He shook my hand as I ushered him into the hallway and told me, "Don't worry about it, Doc. They're seeing you because Doc Langley finally caught on to their antics. They're really harmless—just never quite grew up."

He started to say something else but didn't finish because of sudden loud pandemonium in the waiting room.

"Excuse me, John. I'd better check on that racket."

I rushed down the hall to the waiting room, where an excited crowd had gathered, filling the room to overflowing. Everyone was talking at once, some incoherently, until those immediately in front of me separated to allow four men through. The resourceful group hefted a thick, stretcher-sized piece of plywood on which a different Billy was stretched out, moaning—Billy Jackson of the "ulcer" fame. The entire Jackson clan, including, no doubt, some extended family members, were talking at once, all trying to tell me what had happened.

I held up my hands to restrain the crowd while Donna and Christine quickly cleared the room John Holt had just vacated, after which she beckoned, "You men with Billy, follow me."

Billy had on camouflage clothing, but his right ankle was twisted in a grotesque position, and he groaned and whimpered as they carried him down the hall.

Placing the board on the examination table with Billy still on it, they stood about the now crowded room to observe the proceedings. Seeing Billy's father, I pulled him aside and motioned to Donna, who managed to get everyone else headed back to the waiting room. I could hear the grumbling as she herded them back down the hallway: "Shucks. I wanted to see how he would fix that bum ankle. Sure looks bad."

Her voice fading with distance, I heard her reply: "Dr. Matlock needs room to work, so hurry along."

Within seconds she was back in the room checking vital signs while Mr. Jackson related what he knew of the injury.

"Billy went deer hunting this morning, Doc. Fell out of the tree stand when he saw a big buck right beneath 'im. Didn't even get a shot off."

Donna already had Demerol ready to inject for pain as she related his vital signs to me.

"Go ahead and give him one hundred milligrams intramuscular now. Then we'll have to get the boot off that foot to see the damage."

Mr. Jackson stood nervously beside the table until I asked him whether he wouldn't like to go back to the waiting area and have a seat. I could see that he was pale and sweating.

"Yeah, sure, Doc."

Mr. Jackson headed straight for the exam door and the waiting room, muttering about how hot it was in there. Donna followed him down the hall to make sure he made it without fainting. He didn't stop until he was outside in the cool air, trembling and fumbling to light a cigarette.

When the medicine had relieved some of his pain, Billy nodded that he was ready for us to try whatever needed to be done.

"I have to get the boot off, and we're going to cut the pants leg to expose your ankle and leg."

I'll give this to Billy—he was game. He gritted his teeth and gripped the rough edges of the plyboard as we removed the boot, cutting the side to get his foot out safely. After cutting off his sock, the gross deformity and pale discoloration of arterial compromise became obvious.

"Fracture dislocation of the ankle, Billy. I'll have to straighten it out quickly."

He nodded once and clinched the board more tightly. Grasping his big toe, I pulled straight upward, holding my breath and praying that everything would fall back into place. Sure enough: the break had been extensive, but everything was loose and fell back into place with upward traction on the great toe, and hence the ankle.

I supported the leg at about a thirty degree elevation by continuing to hold traction on the toe, while Donna brought a metal short-leg brace we had reserved for just such an emergency. With relief I watched the color return as Donna checked the dorsal pedis pulse of the foot.

"Good pulse, Doctor. Shall I begin to wrap the splint in place with Ace bandages?"

After making the foot and ankle secure, leaving the toes out so we could check circulation, I finally relaxed a little. By then I noticed Christine watching from the doorway. When she confirmed that the situation was under control from our side, she told me, "I think you'd better come out and calm his family down. His mother is hyperventilating, and one of his sisters is pacing the floor like a caged animal."

Having examined him thoroughly for further injuries and finding nothing immediately obvious, I followed her to the waiting room.

"Would someone get Mr. Jackson back inside so I can talk to everyone at once, please?"

With everyone, including non-family members, crowded into the reception area, I began, "I believe Billy will be okay. He had a fracture dislocation of his left ankle. Donna helped me reduce it back in place and splint it. He'll need an orthopedic surgeon for an open repair, but I believe he'll be alright."

With that his mother fainted and had to be taken back to another room to be placed on an examination table. The rooms were all empty by now anyway, their occupants having joined us in the outer office to enjoy the ruckus.

Christine contacted Art McKay at the mortuary to bring his ambulance to the office for transportation. When he arrived, he and the other EMTs wheeled their cart back and moved Billy onto it for transportation. The unfortunate hunter, already feeling a lot better, shook my hand as he was wheeled out to the ambulance. "You saved me again, Doc. First ulcers, and now a broken ankle. But I sure feel bad about that big buck."

As the EMTs did a final check on the cart straps, I asked, "You didn't say how this happened, Billy. What caused you to fall out of the tree stand?"

Mournfully, Billy shook his head. "Doc, I forgot to fasten my safety belt. When I saw this big buck right below me I got excited, grabbed for my gun, accidentally shot it straight up in the air, and fell nigh onto the deer's back. I guess I never seen a deer so scared in all my born days. He took off like his tail was on fire."

It took an extra two hours to clear the office after the delay, and some patients wanted to reschedule for the next day. That was just as well—the morning had been exhausting enough. At least we would have a little time for a quick lunch before the afternoon rush.

The rest of the day proceeded uneventfully, and the hospital called with the information that Billy Jackson would have surgery the following day and was otherwise uninjured. As we locked up for the evening and the ladies were headed to their cars, I commented dryly, "You know what was wrong with Billy, don't you?"

"No—what, Doctor?" asked Christine, surprised.

"Buck fever syndrome, of course. It has many manifestations."

"I won't forget," Donna replied.

Christine laughed: "Neither will I. Working for you is sure exciting. I wouldn't miss it. And I wonder what the town gossip will be tonight. With Art McKay and his ambulance crew here, they probably already have somebody dead and buried."

Chuckling, I replied, "I wouldn't be surprised. See you tomorrow."

○

One year later, on the day before deer season, Billy Howard was back in the office. I don't know whether he recognized my skepticism as he related his tale of woe—once again of nausea and diarrhea.

"Is Ron Trueblood with you today?"

"No, Doc. Why do you ask?"

"Oh, never mind. How long have you been sick this time?"

"Since I ate supper last night, Doc, like I said."

He looked at me somewhat quizzically as I waited for him to recount the story for the third time.

"Okay, Billy. I'll give you some Phenergan for nausea, just in case. I don't think you'll need anything for diarrhea. I believe you'll soon be over the symptoms."

I handed him a prescription for twenty-five milligram tablets of Phenergan with instructions to take them every four hours, as needed for nausea, and then turned on my heel to exit the room.

"Doc, just a minute. Can I have a note for work, please?"

"You mean for today?"

"No Doc. I told you before, it has to be for three days or I don't get paid. I'll probably be sick that long anyway. It always takes me a while to recover."

I was standing there for a moment, reflecting, when inspiration hit me. I quickly scribbled out a note: "Billy

Howard will be unable to work for three days due to acute malingering."

He squinted at it for a moment and asked, "What does that last word mean, Doc?"

"It describes your condition, Billy."

"Oh—okay, Doc. Thanks."

It was on the fourth day that Billy returned to the office briefly, asking to speak with me. I was anxious to hear what he had to say. Donna led him back to the lab, where I was studying test results. Billy stood nervously for a few minutes while I finished the stack I had before me. As I walked over to where he stood waiting, head down, nervously fidgeting, he looked up and stated, "Hello, Doc. I just wanted to tell you that the last diagnosis you wrote down for my absence made things a little tough for me. My boss didn't like that word, "mal . . . ?" How do you say it?"

"You mean the 'acute malingering'?"

"Yeah, that's it. I just wanted to let you know not to use it again. I almost lost my job. They aren't going to pay me for those days off." He looked down again before continuing, "I just thought you ought to know."

"I'm just trying to be honest, Billy."

"Yeah, I know, Doc. Sorry. See you later."

That was the last time I had to deal with buck fever syndrome. Ron Trueblood didn't appear at all that fall. It could be the two had found a new doctor, one as yet uninitiated in the finer points concerning buck fever.

NEIGHBORS TO THE SOUTH

From a window seat I stared out on the darkened landscape below as the Delta Airlines jet winged its way south from Indianapolis at 9:00 p.m. Eastern Standard Time. I was excited for several reasons. First, because I had never before flown on a jet plane. I had been fortunate to be a passenger on a small prop plane several years earlier, when flights were still permitted down into the Grand Canyon on sightseeing tours. That experience had been unforgettable.

I had never before flown, however, nearly seven miles high at the speed of five hundred miles per hour. My destination was Miami—then on to Honduras, Central America, by a slower prop plane early the next morning. The flying would take several hours, but I had no desire to rest. The night sky was clear, and the only sounds punctuating the stillness were the dull roar of the engines, hissing from the air vents, and the occasional small voice of a child as passengers settled down to nap.

I hated to leave my family behind, but the primitive villages of Honduras, tucked into the mountains and jungle areas, would have been no place for small children and my lovely wife. This was no vacation, anyway. I had volunteered to travel with a group of doctors, nurses, dentists, and hospital and clinic workers to examine patients in Honduras with the Christian Medical and Dental Society.

We brought along medicines, first aid kits, bottled water, snacks, and whatever else we could cram into our suitcases for the trip. The group converged on Miami from all over the United States and Canada for the flight to San Pedro Sula, Honduras. I had with me my malaria prophylaxis pills, as recommended at the time, since we would be flying into Anopheles mosquito territory, and the risk was considered moderate.

My only other departure from U.S. territory had been on family vacations to Canada, so I was excited about the opportunity to serve in a foreign country where the need was great. We would be working in primitive villages with very limited access to medical care.

I enjoyed the flight over the blue, rolling waves of the Gulf of Mexico, noticing that I couldn't distinguish on the horizon where the sky ended and the water began. Finally, Central America's varied tropical shades of green came into view on our left as we approached our destination; as though tinged by the color saturation, even the ocean waves took on a greenish hue.

After landing, our medical group was expedited through customs based on our being on a humanitarian mission. We were soon loaded into vans and headed for our destination, El Progresso, Honduras, a medium-sized town from which roads led into the interior of the country. Exiting the airport, we encountered a wall of stifling heat, high humidity, and mingling masses of humanity hawking all kinds of services.

I knew just enough Spanish to get myself into trouble speaking with native Hondurans and soon decided that my most optimal plan would be to rely on our interpreters. A simple greeting of "Buenos dias" was enough to release a rapid-fire torrent of Spanish I couldn't begin to follow.

Our group was stationed in a church school dormitory in El Progresso, and each of us began sorting supplies, readying ourselves for the next day. We would be on our way to a remote village in the interior by 7:30 a.m.

I spent a fitful night trying to sleep. The men were situated in a large room with twenty "beds" that were little more than coarse straw fibers woven between two wooden rails for a frame, elevated two feet off the floor on stout wooden posts. Blankets were spread over the "mattresses" to make them more conducive to sleep, but I realized to my consternation that I had entered a different world.

It seemed as though everyone in town owned a flock of chickens—and that the roosters couldn't tell time. From 3:00 a.m. on a rooster owned by the school crowed loudly, until he had every chicken within the radius of a few miles awake and returning his greeting. After fifteen minutes or so the bird "conversation" would die down, only to resume with equal gusto twenty or thirty minutes later. It became readily apparent that alarm clocks would not be required.

We slept with all of the windows open because of the stifling heat but noticed a remarkable chill in the early morning hours just before sunrise. Awakening very early, I realized why extra blankets had been piled at the foot of my bed.

Arising at 6:00 a.m., I soon experienced my next cultural shock upon entering the shower: no hot water. I shivered through a very brief shower, reminding myself not to get any water in my mouth. There was running water, but it came from a local river of dubious quality.

Using my toothpaste, I rinsed my mouth with a tiny amount of water. We had been warned not to drink any of the water in the facility that hadn't gone through special filters, but I felt as though I had to do something to rinse the foul taste from my mouth and didn't have any bottled water on hand. After a breakfast of soft tacos, eggs, chicken, salsa, and rice, we once again boarded our bus, this time for our trip into the countryside.

Traffic signs were few and far between. No speed limits were posted, and our driver relied on his horn and quick reflexes to maneuver in traffic. I found it best not to watch most of the time and sat hunched over in the seat awaiting the inevitable crash and trying not to think about it too much.

After we had cleared town the automobile traffic on the rural roads was sparse, and I began to relax a little. Our bus was soon engulfed by large crowds of people, however—men, women, and children—most walking in the same direction. There were also a few on bicycles or horseback. By 8:00 a.m. it was already very hot. Clouds of dust were being kicked up by the crowds and the passage of the bus. Curious, I asked our driver, "Where are all these people going?"

Smiling, he glanced my way before replying, "To see you, Senor."

We were all stunned, for there appeared to be thousands of people swarming the highway, headed our way, to visit our three family doctors, one medical student, two nurses, one pharmacist, one dentist, three translators, and half a dozen helpers (the surgeons had stayed behind to work in the small hospital in El Progresso, and several of our doctors had remained with them to help with special surgeries and procedures not usually available to these people). The task we faced appeared to be gargantuan.

Honduras was a very poor country with a low per capita standard of living, and large areas of the rural population lacked such basics taken for granted by North Americans as electricity, indoor plumbing, air conditioning, automobiles, shopping malls, and access to health care.

Once we had finally arrived in the village and quickly set up our clinic, we prepared to do our best to accommodate the crowds. Alberto Hernandez, a seventy-year-old volunteer from Arizona, interpreted for me as a long line of people formed outside the small schoolhouse in which we were to see patients.

"Just like in the New Testament, Doctor—teeming crowds to see the physician, No?"

"You're right about that, Alberto. Unfortunately for them, the doctors today are very human and will have difficulty doing justice to this mass of humanity."

Outside the doorway people were lined up three to five abreast, in an ever growing queue. They seemed to have a far different concept of personal space than do North Americans, as they crowded together in compact masses, talking, laughing, and visiting while awaiting their chance to see the doctor.

They also cared little for privacy—and made no pretense about the issue; every window was lined with spectators: mostly children, but adults too, watching as their friends and neighbors visited with the doctors, nurses, pharmacist, and dentist. The atmosphere was that of a holiday celebration.

Our task was facilitated somewhat in that only the littlest children were undressed for an examination. Also, we quickly decided to limit our consultations to one chief complaint per adult. In my own practice people often wanted to discuss several issues, but we had no time for that as we confronted far more than we could ever hope to accommodate.

It took a while for me to adjust to the sea of faces visible through every window and doorway, all eyes watching my every move and all ears attuned to every word as Alberto translated for me. Only a few of the adults were embarrassed enough to whisper their complaints; most seemed not to notice their curious neighbors.

As I was examining a sick infant, our pharmacist, Jim Farley, approached. Pausing in my examination, I asked, "Can I help you, Jim?"

"Doc, I have an idea. There must be three or four hundred children here under the age of ten. Their schoolteacher speaks excellent English, and she told me a lot of the mothers have brought them in to be treated for parasitic worms. What if I had her form these kids into a line with their mothers and have one of the volunteers weigh each one so we could go ahead and treat them with the appropriate dose for the usual parasites here?"

Glancing around at the ever-lengthening lines, I enthused, "Sounds like a great idea to me. We'll never be able to see this many people with the small group we have here. Anything to expedite the process is a wonderful plan."

Soon enough the teacher had set up a long line of children, after which she approached our table diffidently, speaking first to Alberto in Spanish. It was only when he nodded yes that she looked up at me.

"Doctor, most of the mothers would appreciate it if they could be treated for parasites as well. Do you think there would be enough medicine for them also? I mean, would you care?"

"If there's one thing we have enough of, it's medicine for parasites. I have no objection as long as it's okay with Jim Farley, our pharmacist."

Thus we commenced treatment for the many children and mothers who were otherwise healthy, or at least not acutely ill. I found it interesting that so many wanted to be treated, so I had Alberto arrange for one of our routine questions to cover the possibility of parasite infestations.

Juan, an elderly Honduran, appeared next in the line. Alberto began with our usual line of questioning, Juan listening to him carefully before answering, "I have arthritis in my hands and back. Do you have any medicine for arthritis?"

"Alberto, ask him if he's still working and, if so, what he does for a living."

Following an animated discussion Alberto turned back to me and reported, "He says he works bent over with a machete for several hours a day. He cuts lawns for people who can afford it. He makes the equivalent of two to three dollars per day. It's his only source of income, Doctor." Pausing to swallow the lump in his throat, Alberto continued, "Doc, we don't realize how good we have it in the good old USA. I don't know how these people manage to survive."

Sadly, all we had to offer Juan was a package of acetaminophen, with instructions for how to take them. There was another challenge: Juan couldn't read. He did have a twelve-year-old grandson with him who could, however, and we went over the instructions with him. (In the 1970s the illiteracy rate in Honduras was fifty-five percent of the population over the age of fifteen. Dedicated educators were making slow inroads toward bettering this challenging situation.) Juan and his grandson thanked us profusely as they walked slowly to the next station we had set up. They both wanted vitamins, another commodity we had in plenty.

At about mid-morning a disturbance broke out in the line. We looked around to see two young men coming our way, half carrying and half dragging an ancient-appearing lady who appeared to be of Indian descent. Alberto jumped up to assist them, as I was holding a one-year old on my lap and listening to his heart while he, in turn, studied me intently. Handing the child back to his mother, I hurried over to assist with the elderly patient. We laid her on a table and found an old jacket to roll up under her head.

Despite her naturally dark pigmentation, her face appeared pallid. Beads of sweat wreathed her forehead as her eyes fluttered open. In a weak voice she attempted to thank us. Alberto explained that Maria had been standing in line without shade for more than three hours, following a one-hour walk to the village, and that she had apparently fainted. "These are her great-grandsons, doctor. They want to know if you can help her."

I don't recall ever having felt so helpless, with no laboratory for rapid diagnosis; no equipment other than a thermometer, blood pressure cuff, and stethoscope; and no good lighting. Attempting to hide my self-doubt, I smiled at Maria and nodded that I would do my best. Noticing a portable blackboard on wheels, I had some of the men roll it over to shield the old woman from the stares of curious onlookers and began an examination as Alberto stood at my side assisting with communication. Maria smiled wanly as she explained her problem: "Doctor, I have a bad pain in my stomach, and a big swelling. Sometimes I cannot eat because of severe pains. I hoped you could help me."

"Are you nauseated, Maria?"

Through Alberto, she answered, "Not now, Doctor."

"Alberto, have one of her grandsons go to the pharmacy for some bottled water. Her blood pressure is only 88/54, and she appears dehydrated. We need to get some fluids into her—that's all we have with us, I'm afraid."

I noticed Alberto standing with his head bowed, silently moving his lips, and knew he was praying. When he opened his eyes and looked up, I encouraged, "Thanks Alberto. I hope you said a prayer for me too. I'm not certain what else to do yet."

"I prayed for all of us, Doctor. God is with us and will help us."

I felt buoyed by his words of encouragement and childlike faith in God. I noted that Maria had pale conjunctiva and a soft systolic heart murmur but clear breath sounds. Then, as I came to the abdominal portion of the examination, I found a herniated intestinal mass that I hoped was benign. With gentle pressure over the mass I carefully reduced it back into the abdomen through the abdominal wall's muscle defect.

The schoolteacher had found an old sheet to cover Maria's legs and pelvic area to her lower abdomen, affording her a little privacy during my examination. We had left her faded, patched blouse in place, simply lifting it slightly to position the stethoscope during the exam. Still, it appeared as though from everywhere hundreds of eyes were following my every move. More importantly, however, following Alberto's prayer I felt the eyes of my heavenly Father on me, helping me to care for and treat the poorest of the poor. Maria finally stabilized with a blood pressure of 125/88, and I felt a great burden lifted from my shoulders.

When the old woman finally managed to sit upright on the side of the table, one of the village leaders came to determine how the situation was progressing. Pedro spoke fair English, so I was able to communicate directly with him. Following introductions I began, "Pedro, is it possible to have Maria sent to El Progresso to the hospital where some of our surgeons are operating? They promised to assist with any serious surgical cases that might come up."

"I think so, Doctor—that is if the old truck, he will start. Sometimes he doesn't start so good, I think. I will check and be right back."

Within a couple of minutes we heard the grinding of ancient gears and the screech of worn brakes as Pedro pulled up to the side of the building, the crowd giving way. Pedro left the truck idling as he entered the building, all smiles. "He start okay today, I think. Much good luck, Doctor, but I no trust to turn him off. We start right away if okay with you, Doctor."

"That's wonderful, Pedro. You are a great help and an answer to prayer."

Beaming with pleasure, Pedro helped Maria's great-grandsons get her into the cab with him, after which they climbed into the open truck bed for the ride into town. As the truck chugged down the dirt road, the crowd broke into spontaneous applause. Pedro waved cheerfully out the window, and the boys in the back also waved with gusto from their privileged perch.

After we had seen several more patients Alberto said something in Spanish to the crowd and turned to me. "Doctor, I don't know about you," he exclaimed, "but I'm starving. The ladies have prepared tacos and a special treat for us over the outdoor ovens. I told the people to take a lunch break— maybe even a short siesta—while we have lunch."

With a sigh of appreciation I stood and stretched my legs briefly. "Interesting but tiring day, Alberto," I commented. "I appreciate your help and thoughtfulness."

"That's okay, Doc. My stomach told me it was high time for a break. Let's go see what the special treat with the tacos is all about."

Arriving beneath the shade of palm trees, we joined the others in an area in which crude chairs and benches had been set up for us. With gratitude I accepted a large soft taco filled with meat, vegetables, and sauces. The food had been carried by volunteers from the school where we were staying, so I had no concern about the vegetables.

Alberto approached with a mischievous look on his face. "The ladies of the village are very proud of their surprise, Doctor. They are bringing it over now. Have a look."

Suddenly I lost my appetite, as the head of what had been a large, ugly goat was presented to us for our culinary enjoyment. It had been fully cooked and was apparently safe to eat, but try as I might I couldn't bear to indulge with those in our group who were brave enough to give it a try. As graciously as I could, I asked Alberto to express my deep thanks for the wonderful tacos they had prepared, conveying that I was too full to eat anything else. That was, in any case, the truth: my hunger pangs had entirely disappeared.

○

Before resuming work Alberto and I took a brief walk down to the river that flowed alongside the town. This was a peaceful site with trees growing along the banks and wild flowers in profusion. We stopped, however, upon hearing voices and decided to go no further; I received sudden insight into the sanitation problem when we encountered ladies returning from the river loaded down with freshly laundered clothes.

Upstream, two men were bathing in water nearly to their necks, while a young boy stood relieving himself in the water nearby. Alberto smiled and shrugged: "Everything happens in the river, Doc. People bathe, relieve themselves, wash their clothes, . . . everything. That's why disease is so rampant in some of these small villages. The teacher tries to educate, but a lot of them believe the old ways are best. In spite of its name, there isn't a lot of progress in and around El Progresso."

Sadly and thoughtfully I returned to examine many more patients. A heavy sense of futility filled my mind as we resumed our work. Are we really doing any good here? How little I have to offer these people, yet they express their thanks with such graciousness. At that point I thought back to Maria and her family. Well, maybe I had at least helped one . . .

Just then a teenaged mother brought her little ones to me for examination. The youngest, an eighteen-month-old girl with expressive brown eyes, smiled shyly at me, and once again I became the family physician, loving my work and doing my best to spread cheer and goodwill as I performed it.

It proved to be an unexpected relief that there were no phones anywhere—not in the village, the school, or anywhere nearby. Thus unaccustomed form of silence was much appreciated.

The afternoon wore on as I encountered laughter and sorrow: laughter with happy little children peeking from behind their mother's skirts, and sorrow when encountering seemingly hopeless cases. A boy who had been working with a machete in a mountain village a few days earlier had traveled several miles to have his injured leg looked at.

"How did you do that, son?" Alberto asked.

"I slipped on some rocks and dropped the machete on my leg. It is very sharp. I have much pain now, Senor."

Alberto relayed the response to me in English as I examined the wound. The young man was very stoical, but even so he flinched when I touched the inflamed skin near the long laceration.

"Alberto, tell him I'm very sorry about his wound. It's deep and seriously infected with what we call acute cellulitis. I'm sending him to the pharmacist station. The nurse there will give him an injection of penicillin, and he'll have to wait several minutes to be sure he has no reaction to it. Then we'll give him a packet of Keflex capsules to take at home for ten days. He must go to the clinic in El Progresso in two or three days to make sure the wound is healing. Can you explain all of that to him so he understands how important it is to follow up with therapy? That wound could become life threatening if it doesn't respond to treatment."

"Sure, Doc. No problem. I will scare him really good with lurid tales of horrible death or loss of a leg if he doesn't take care of this."

Alberto launched into his fluent Spanish with many a gesture, frown, and looks of anxiety and even horror as he lectured. Following the diatribe the young man walked meekly to get his injection and medication, a worried look on his face as he left our area.

"Alberto, I thought you were kidding. It looks as though you scared him half to death."

Smiling, Alberto replied, "Doctor, you have to understand these kids. They fancy themselves to be very tough. And you know how the young are, never expecting anything bad to happen to them. I just told him all you said and asked how I could notify his mother if he didn't do as he was told and was found dead along the trails."

"I see, Alberto. How many children did you say you've raised?"

"I didn't say, Doctor, but I have eleven—five sons and six daughters—and they're all good and obedient kids to this day."

Just then we were interrupted by the schoolteacher, Mrs. Blanco: "Excuse me, Doctor, Alberto, but could you see this baby next? He is only two months old, and his mother walked two hours to get here. She stood in line all day, hungry and weak, too proud to ask for food or even water. I'm having some of the ladies fix her a little meal now, but her baby does look very ill."

The young mother wore a dress that at one time had probably been pink and white but was faded from wear and dusty from the long walk on the road; at least a size too large for her, it hung loosely from her shoulders.

She apparently had a lot of Spanish blood, as she was very light complexioned; in appropriate attire and surroundings, it occurred to me, she would have looked like a classic European fairytale princess. However, her drawn face appeared prematurely aged from worry and care. She looked as though she might faint from exhaustion, and we both stood quickly to assist her. Alberto helped her sit in his chair as I took the baby in my arms. One of our nurses came to assist, while Alberto hurried over to get some cold water from one of our coolers to revive the mother.

She spoke quietly to Alberto as he handed her some cool water, and he looked up and alerted us, "She says to be very careful of his back. He has an open sore and is paralyzed from the legs down."

The nurse sat down beside the mother and took the baby from me, carefully turning him over so we could look at his back. A large meningomyelocele that had never been treated opened from his lower spine. Sadly, the meninges, the membrane over the nervous system defect, was slowly leaking spinal fluid. Flies were already trying to settle onto the wound and had to be fanned away by the nurse. His little legs appeared withered and useless and little Rodrigo himself very listless, showing little interest in the proceedings, the bottle of formula, or the nurse holding him. His axillary temperature was 100, and his anterior fontanelle was sunken from dehydration.

The nurse discarded the dirty rag that functioned as his diaper, replacing it with a clean one from our supplies after carefully cleansing his little bottom. She proceeded to gently wash his emaciated body with a moistened cloth before wrapping him in a clean blue baby blanket from our supply. His mother, who didn't offer her name, gazed at me in profound sorrow and asked in English, "He's going to die, isn't he?"

I silently studied the frail, tiny frame before me, thinking about my own family, how fortunate we all were to have been born in the United States, and how pitiful this little family was in comparison. The nearest neurosurgeon was miles away, no pediatric ICU was available, and there was no possibility of administering IV antibiotics or other life-saving treatments.

Mrs. Blanco stood behind the girl, who appeared to be no more than fifteen or sixteen years of age, and nodded at me, encouraging me to answer her. It took me a few moments to work the lump out of my throat as I noticed Alberto's moist eyes and heard the sniffles of the nurse as she gently rocked little Rodrigo.

"Yes, young lady, I'm afraid he's going to die. But I can see that you've done everything you could for him. This isn't your fault."

I watched as a solitary tear zigzagged its way down her right cheek before going on: "He's very sick now and experiencing a form of shock. I doubt if it will help, but I think we should at least try some penicillin for him."

I knew I was grasping at straws in the wind but felt compelled to do something for this stricken young life that seemed to be ebbing away before my eyes.

"Will it make him well again?" she asked, a flicker of hope in her previously dulled eyes.

"No, I'm afraid not. He has a serious infection, probably a form of spinal meningitis from the open wound, and that is likely to be fatal."

"I thank you for your truthfulness with me, Doctor, but I prefer to just keep Rodrigo comfortable until he dies."

With that she reached for the infant, whom our nurse surrendered willingly into her arms. Mrs. Blanco assured me softly, "It's okay, Doctor. This is one of my former students. Her parents are deceased, and she will be welcomed into my home for as long as she wants to stay. We will care for little Rodrigo there."

I felt a leaden sadness settling over me but had nothing else to offer. As Mrs. Blanco led them away, her arm around the girl's thin shoulders, I was grateful that at least there was someone to help this mother—little more than a child herself and in such dire circumstances—and her little one, so ill.

That night as we rode back through the countryside in our bus after darkness had fallen, the only illumination came from the faint lights of oil lamps and candles in the tiny huts and shacks, clustered into small villages along the roadside, and the brighter light of the moon and stars overhead. I had never seen so many stars before; there were no electric lights to obscure them here.

That day had changed me forever. I had seen stark grief and hopelessness in the face of a young girl who should have been enjoying the benefits and joys of late childhood. Alberto had explained to me that she had been abandoned by the man who had fathered her child when he had first seen the deformity. He had for whatever reasons felt shamed and had opted to leave her to her own resources to deal with the affliction.

As we loaded into the bus to return to our home base, Mrs. Blanco had stood in the gathering darkness, thanking us for coming and pleading with us to return as often as possible. Even if I entertained self-doubts, she at least believed that we had done untold good for her village. She was a highly educated woman, willing to sacrifice her own comfort in order to live alongside her people in their squalor and privation.

✛

We finished out our week and boarded the flight for home at the airport in San Pedro Sula. I watched as the beauty of the landscape receded into the distance, obliterating the suffering and sorrow indicative of a third world country.

Perhaps I hadn't accomplished much, but I would return two more times in the years to follow to do whatever I could in the scenic, sad country of Honduras. One of the essential duties of a physician is to "comfort always," even when little else can be accomplished.

THE MAKING OF A NURSE

One of the joys of my life has been to see all three of my children involved in the medical field. My oldest, Cynthia Sue, whom we called Cindy, from an early age demonstrated a love and concern for people. She enjoyed visiting my office when she was old enough to understand what my profession was all about. On one particular day I had been seeing the usual volume of patients with colds, sore throats, ulcers, chest pain, trouble breathing, and so on, when a tentative knock sounded at the side door.

Donna answered, thinking that perhaps a delivery man was bringing us some supplies, but to her surprise she found my curly-headed strawberry blond clutching one of her favorite dolls. My wife was right behind her, of course; they had been out shopping and wanted to stop by and say hello. The twins were at home with their grandmother, and Cindy wanted to see me. I was delighted by this unexpected visit and, happening to have an empty exam room available, ushered them in to have a seat while I visited my next patient. When I had finished consulting with the elderly couple in the next room and handed their charts to Donna to complete their orders for blood work, she smilingly observed, "I think you'd better return to see your daughter. She wants you to check something."

"Okay, I'll do that right now."

Entering the examination room, I found Janet sitting while Cindy stood beside her doll—fully undressed and ready for evaluation on the examination table.

"What have we here, Cindy? Is your dolly sick?"

"Yes, Daddy. She's sick. Needs to see you."

I got out my stethoscope and made a great pretense at listening to the baby's heart and lungs, while Cindy watched in fascination. As I turned the doll over to check her back, the doll responded with a mechanical "Ma-Ma. Ma-Ma" followed by "Hug me tight."

"I believe I know what's wrong, Cindy."

She looked up at me with her most serious expression and asked, "What, Daddy?"

"Your baby has a cold and wants you to comfort her. Take her home and give her a bottle. You just need to feed her and hold her very tight."

Cindy beamed with pleasure, since this particular baby could indeed take a bottle.

"'kay, Daddy. I'll give her a bottle. Thank you."

With that the future RN rewarded me with a hug and a kiss. Cindy and Janet had made my afternoon. As they were leaving Donna offered Cindy a sucker—"for the baby," of course. With great solemnity she accepted the gift, after which she rewarded my nurse with a smile and hug. Cindy took caring for her babies very seriously.

When we had first brought home our twins, David and Diane, from the hospital, it had been necessary for us to watch little Cindy closely due to her overzealously caring nature. She wanted to push them around in her baby buggy, and when that didn't work out she was allowed to sit by her mother and hold one of her siblings on her lap while Janet cared for the other. Cindy served as a second little mother to her brother and sister, and the three remain very close to this day.

When Cindy was about six years old she accompanied me to the grocery one Saturday. While shopping I received the inevitable call that one of my OB patients had arrived and was imminently expected to deliver her third child. With regret I left a cartful of groceries with a hurried explanation to the clerk. Grabbing Cindy's hand, I directed, "Come on, Cindy. I have to go deliver a baby right now. We'll finish shopping later."

Cindy, beyond excited at the prospect of going with me to the hospital, asked, "Will it be a boy or a girl, Daddy?"

"I won't know until it's born, dear. Please hurry."

"Yes, Daddy."

Fortunately, the grocery store in Glen Falls was only one-half mile from the hospital. Unfortunately, however, labor and delivery was located on the third floor, and the elevator was notoriously slow. Arriving in record time, I started to run up the stairway, only to stop and look behind me. Cindy was resolutely following, as instructed; I had nowhere else to leave her.

"Hurry, honey. We don't want to be late."

The pattern continued: I would run up four or five steps and then pause to make sure she was following. I needn't have worried: she had no intention of staying very far behind and was proceeding as fast as her little legs would carry her.

Upon our arrival on the OB floor, one of the nurses found Cindy some ice cream and a book while I hurried to the delivery room just down the hallway. That afternoon my little girl was posted as sentinel just a few feet from the delivery room door, as there was no other place to safely keep her.

I didn't make it a practice to take my children on hospital rounds, but this was an emergency—and Cindy loved every minute of it. I don't know whether she "read" much in the book, but she did hear the lusty cries of a healthy newborn right after she had entered the world. On another occasion she was with me when I had to rush to the ICU to assist with a critical patient. She was duly impressed both by the monitors and by the frenetic activity on the part of the nursing staff. I don't know whether or to what degree either experience encouraged her to make a career of nursing, but she graduated from high school at the age of sixteen and entered nursing school a month and a half prior to her seventeenth birthday.

I still remember her trying to keep up as she followed me up the stairway that day I had to leave the groceries behind. I like to think that she is still following in my footsteps as she cares for her patients and sometimes helps in OB when she is working as evening supervisor.

I often wondered whether my children would be burned out with all things medical based on their experience with the long, tiring hours I had to spend working. My duties kept me away sometimes during birthday parties, Christmas celebrations, and other holidays. It seemed as though I invariably had to deliver a baby on any given special family occasion. During holidays I tried to be there for my family, and in the summer we took wonderful vacation trips together, visiting most of the lower forty-eight states by automobile and seeing firsthand the varied beauty of these United States.

My wonderful wife and companion, Janet, never failed to support me and shared my interest in medicine, consistently encouraging our children to be the best they could be in whatever vocation they might choose. I attribute their caring and gentle dispositions to her guidance and nurture.

Initially David, observing my often frenzied lifestyle, manifested no interest in medicine, but he became fascinated by science and pursued medicine in college. He, like me early on in my career, has chosen to become a family doctor in a small town. For a few years, in fact, I was privileged to work alongside him and help my son build his practice.

Our daughter Diane attended business college and has spent her working career in hospitals as well, serving as a certified nursing assistant, medical transcriptionist, and registration clerk. She also enjoys caring for people and meeting their needs.

I suppose I didn't need to worry about the possibility of inadvertently discouraging my children from entering the field of medicine. When they were small I would often regale them with funny stories about situations that had happened at work. They were used to my discussing operations and medical stories that the average person probably wouldn't consider appropriate dinner table talk. To this day my wife puts up with medical stories at the dinner table during family gatherings; actually, she enjoys them as much as we do.

Service to others, I would contend, is one of the greatest responsibilities any of us has in life; I personally know of nothing any more satisfying than helping someone in need. It was precisely this that my wife and I endeavored to instill within our children from a young age.

MEDICINE THEN AND NOW

The practice of medicine in the 1970s occurred in a much different world than the one we know today. Some facets are better now, while other aspects most definitely are not. Communication, for example, has changed for the better. When I began practice I had to totally depend on land lines for direct information. After several months I saw that something more would be necessary in order for me to stay in touch. I purchased my first pager, but it too had significant limitations. A buzzer would be activated, informing me that the hospital operator had a message to convey, but that solution was less than ideal, requiring me as it did to search for a payphone whenever I happened to be driving. I quickly discovered that payphones were few and far between in a rural practice. Later on, pagers that conveyed a short digital message became available—that is, if one happened to be within range. The situation was improving, but I still couldn't communicate without a phone.

Office records were much different as well. I began my practice seeing twenty patients on my initial day in practice— still the approximate daily flow for many clinicians today. Records constituted only brief accounts of patient history and any positive findings. The government hadn't yet intervened in the realm of medical records.

I had the luxury early on of spending ten to fifteen uninterrupted minutes with a patient, simply listening to them talk and conducting the pertinent examination. After several months I knew most of my patients fairly well. They also knew me and realized that the amount of time spent would be relative to the presenting complaint.

A complicated visit might require a half hour or even longer, but the record itself was succinct and to the point. Within two years I was typically seeing thirty-five to fifty-five patients per day, and sometimes more; I regularly worked from 7:00 a.m. to 6:00 p.m., hastily downing my lunch at noon, often while standing in the lab studying the next chart or fielding calls from the hospital.

Another major difference was that everyone paid the same amount for parallel care. In 1973 I charged $7.50 for a routine office visit, $15.00 for a physical, and $300.00 for prenatal care and delivery. High-volume practices were possible because medical records were short—not counting those for hospital admissions, of course; these we dictated to be transcribed by the medical records department. Although these reports did take more time to complete, only minimal writing was required.

Significant changes have progressively eroded that way of practicing. Within a relatively short time the federal government became more involved in setting standards, and physicians were obliged to document social history, family history, past medical history, and whatever else might be required in order to receive payment for services rendered. For a family practitioner who knows most of his patients well, this step has too often constituted a complete waste of time. The new methodology isn't only more time consuming but is also costlier, with increased time spent documenting, increased need for paper charting, a slower turnover in terms of the number of patients seen, and less quality time spent with the very people we are trying to help.

Increased documentation was sold to doctors as the only way of getting paid for the work they performed. More complicated patients who require more time should, so the system dictates, have to pay more. The catch comes in with the increased time needed to document, document, document . . .

The real destroyer of physician efficiency, however, came with the eventual advent of electronic medical records. While I'm the first to admit that they're easier to read, they unfortunately don't prevent all errors. In fact, physician fatigue plays an increasing role of which few patients are aware; long after the last patient has been dismissed and the staff has gone home to their families, the doctor faces the exhausting necessity of finishing dictations or typing out twenty or thirty charts. All of this is being done under the headings of "patient safety" and "improved care." Never mind that the doctor can see only one-third to one-half of the patients he previously managed per day. Nor does the situation take into account that he needs the equivalent of a small army to oversee the electronic record, backup data, and electronic generation of bills, as well as deal with the inevitable system crashes and other technical complications.

We now need the services of nurse practitioners, physicians' assistants, and increased numbers of medical assistants to accomplish the same amount of work. And woe to the clinician who accidentally charges at a level above or below what has been charted. I understand, of course, why it is illegal to overcharge a patient, but I have never become reconciled to the concept that it is equally illegal to undercharge a needy patient. I have been advised that such discrimination is unfair to those who are able to pay more and could even result in a felony charge for unfair practice. Hence, we also need an army of coders to go over what we have done and correct erroneous charges before invoices can be sent out.

Sadly, today in the United States a physician can do everything that is asked and still lose money in private practice. Insurance company reimbursements and government medical payments are frequently less than sufficient to pay the staff for their services. In addition, the cost of electronic records with start-up and maintenance fees is becoming prohibitive for the solo practitioner. I see more and more doctors joining physician and hospital groups in order to afford the cost of medical practice. Solo practice has all but disappeared, relegated of necessity to the land of the dinosaurs.

Physicians are increasingly subjected to "group think," as records are perused by people we pay to come up behind us to verify that we have crossed every T and dotted every I. One can do everything correctly in terms of patient involvement, but if fatigue intervenes and the work isn't properly documented, it is considered not to have been accomplished at all. Inadvertent oversights in record keeping afford an easy way for an insurer to deny payment.

A major concern of modern medicine has to do with the security of the medical record. In the past a thief would have had to break into my office and somehow locate a given record in order to steal it. The other major security threat to paper charts, of course, was destruction by fire, flood, or some other form of natural disaster. I never experienced any of those problems with my charts, but today I have a new and very legitimate concern: hackers—and they are ubiquitous online. I believe that our medical records today are much more compromised and less secure than they have ever been before. Regardless of firewalls, hackers seem able to intermittently break through and steal whatever they want.

On the other side of the coin, there have been amazing breakthroughs since the seventies in the practice of medicine. Patients with cancers once considered incurable are now routinely achieving remission and even cure. Unconscious patients can be rapidly diagnosed with CT scanners and MRIs. We no longer have to stand by monitoring them to see whether they will wake up. We obtain quick and reliable information in a matter of minutes, greatly assisting in prognosis and treatment.

Robotic and laparoscopic surgeries have allowed patients to recover much more quickly from what used to amount to major procedures. The length of hospital stays has been greatly reduced, patients are ambulated and able to function much more quickly, and outpatient surgery has transformed much of medical care. Cardiac patients with unstable angina and even acute myocardial infarctions (heart attacks) have been given a new lease on life with clot-busting drugs, stents, and bypass surgeries.

Remote visits via closed-circuit monitors can be accomplished with specialists hundreds of miles away, and paramedics in the field can transmit EKGs from the scene to assist in resuscitation and rapid triage to a hospital with a twenty-four-hour cardiac catheterization lab. In addition, there are exciting new treatments in the pipeline to improve the lives of Alzheimer's patients; drugs that can reverse the brain damage in that terrible disease are even now being developed. Technology truly is transforming medicine.

I remember that when I first began practicing medicine ulcer patients were common, as were a host of terrible complications accompanying their disorder: gastrointestinal bleeding, gastric and duodenal obstructions, perforation with peritonitis or pancreatitis, and intractable pain. After Tagamet was released, however, ulcer management was revolutionized. Today we have even more potent alternatives, and hospital admissions for ulcers and their subsequent complications are uncommon.

When I graduated from Indiana University Medical School in 1971, I remember being told that we would have to read, study, and remain informed, at the risk of being out of date within five short years. Although a difficult concept to grasp at the time, I have found this to be very much the case. My old medical textbooks are not only dated but almost entirely out of date. My medical library has been replaced several times over to keep up with the many mind-boggling advances in medicine, and I devote many hours each year to CME: continuing medical education.

When all is said and done, I can state unequivocally that I would not have chosen any other profession in the world. It has been both exciting and rewarding for me to meet literally thousands of people, make many friends for life, and enjoy the wonderful experience of having many people I have known and respect honor me by calling me their doctor.

If you as a patient experience being seated in the examination room across from a doctor struggling on a computer, studying the screen while seeming to ignore you, be as gracious as you can. Understand that the physician doesn't like this any better than you do, and that the ubiquitous electronic medical record isn't what attracted him or her to the field of medicine. It's a necessary evil that we can't do without—but too often the tool used to evaluate a physician's accomplishments.

I'm pleased to report, however, that there is hope on the horizon for even that complication. Voice recognition programs are starting to make my life easier as I dictate my charts to the computer. I spend valuable minutes correcting errors when the computer doesn't understand me, but the technology is improving all the time.

For any aspiring physicians I have one word of advice: be sure that you love people and are a "people person." Everything in medicine seems ephemeral. Nothing stays the same for long—with one exception: those people we call patients.

They are still the same fascinating individuals that make the practice of medicine worthwhile. The child's smile, the old man's rambling stories, the anxious mother's concerns, the young man's insecurity, the hypochondriac's fear of cancer, . . . and the list is endless—each one of these individuals is a wonderful human being fashioned in the very image of the Creator.

ACKNOWLEDGMENTS

I want to thank Credo House Publishers for making this work possible: Publisher Tim Beals for his guidance and support throughout the project; Donna Huisjen, who made valuable contributions as the editor; and my dear wife, Janet Matlock, who labored through the early iterations, telling me what was working and what wasn't.

Made in the USA
San Bernardino, CA
24 August 2019